Searching for the Roanoke Colonies

Fig. 1. *The Baptism of Virginia Dare*, by Sidney Newbold, occupies a place of prominence in the Virginia Dare Room in the Alumni House at the University of North Carolina at Greensboro. (Photo by Dan Smith, courtesy of the University of North Carolina – Greensboro Alumni Association.)

Searching for the Roanoke Colonies
An Interdisciplinary Collection

Edited by E. Thomson Shields Jr. and Charles R. Ewen

Office of Archives and History
North Carolina Department of Cultural Resources
Raleigh

*This collection is dedicated to the memory of
David Beers Quinn (1909-2002),
the dean of Roanoke colonization studies.*

Table of Contents

Introduction

Folklore and Literature

History

List of Illustrations

Foreword

This volume results directly from a commitment to coastal research by East Carolina University (ECU) in partnership with many other academic and governmental institutions both within and outside North Carolina. It is based upon a rare and wonderful gathering of scholars from many fields and institutions for the purpose of examining an issue from multiple viewpoints. The mystery surrounding the establishment, struggle, and disappearance of the English colonies on Roanoke Island in the 1580s is especially well suited to multidisciplinary inquiry. Even though the central question remains, this volume proves that a broad-based approach yields both a deeper understanding of the problem and many different kinds of explanations.

The September 1998 Roanoke colonization conference on Roanoke Island, North Carolina, was not the only conclave of scholars to examine the mystery of the "Lost Colony." The symposium titled "Roanoke Decoded," organized by lebame houston and BeBe Woody and held at the same place in 1993, was one of the first major gatherings of scholars from a variety of disciplines to address the topic of Roanoke colonization. Several of the papers from that earlier conference appear in the present volume, including those of Joyce Youings, William S. Powell, Thomas Davidson, and the dean of Roanoke colonization studies, David Beers Quinn. That initial meeting also helped establish at ECU the Roanoke Colonies Research Office (RCRO), which is housed in and sponsored by the university's College of Arts and Sciences and directed by Tom Shields, who also edits the *Roanoke Colonies Research Newsletter* and maintains the RCRO Web site, *www.ecu.edu/rcro/*. The RCRO is a worldwide clearinghouse for information on all aspects of the Roanoke colonization experience and a useful resource for Contact Period researchers and lay people alike.

In December 1993, shortly after its establishment, the RCRO helped organize and underwrite a small conference with a big agenda: to examine shoreline erosion on the north end of Roanoke Island and the implications of that erosion for archaeological research at the Fort Raleigh National Historic Site. That conference helped the National Park Service and the archaeologists working at the site realize how much erosion had occurred in just the preceding twenty to twenty-five years. Several material findings brought to light at the 1993 conference appear in the present volume as well.

In a rare, hurricane-free September in 1998, the most recent (and I hope not the last) conference to consider the Roanoke colonization process took place once again on Roanoke Island, where it all originally happened (even if we don't yet know the exact spot). An actress portraying Queen Elizabeth I (on loan from the production team at *Elizabeth R* and Company) welcomed this assemblage of scholars from many disciplines. The meeting was cosponsored by the RCRO and the Southern Coastal Heritage Program (SCHP), a consortium of academics with related research interests from ECU, North Carolina State University, the University of North Carolina at Wilmington, the North Carolina Division (now Office) of Archives and History, and the North Carolina Sea Grant Program. The SCHP is located at ECU and is directed by Charles Ewen.

True to its promise, the 1998 program did examine the colonial experience on and around Roanoke Island from multiple perspectives. Absorbing, dynamic, and provocative, the presentations drew from established studies and works in progress. The mix of archaeological, historical, literary, and folkloric viewpoints enlivened the proceedings, provided fresh insights into old problems, and elicited enthusiastic questions and comments from the audience.

The importance of these 1998 conference proceedings and parts of the 1993 conclave mandates their preservation and dissemination; it is appropriate that ECU, the chief sponsor of the 1998 gathering and an important contributor to the initial conference in 1993, is collaborating with the North Carolina Office of Archives and History to publish the collected presentations. The book's format follows that of the 1998 conference and captures the lively interchange that characterized its predecessor. While these provocative yet authoritative essays will set the standard for future research by Roanoke scholars, the volume will nonetheless appeal to any reader interested in the events surrounding England's first attempts to settle the North American continent. This book will inspire many to seek answers to the questions it raises.

W. Keats Sparrow, *Dean*
Harriot College of Arts and Sciences
East Carolina University

Acknowledgments

The support of the Southern Coastal Heritage Program is gratefully acknowledged for all its assistance—from the symposium that inspired this book to its help with the production of the final volume. Carleton Wood, director of the Elizabethan Gardens in Manteo, was very helpful in the selection of the cover art and in securing permission for its use. It is provided courtesy of the Elizabethan Gardens. Mike Booher photographed this image of the Virginia Dare statue located there. Finally, we would like to thank Dr. W. Keats Sparrow, dean of the Harriot College of Arts and Sciences at East Carolina University, for his unflagging support of the Roanoke Colonies Research Office and the Southern Coastal Heritage Program.

E. Thomson Shields Jr.
Charles R. Ewen

Editorial Method

In the following essays will be found minor variations in the spelling and treatment of certain words and phrases by various contributing authors. Examples include "Raleigh" and "Ralegh"; "Hariot" and "Harriot"; "Cittie of Ralegh" (or "Raleigh") and "City of Ralegh"/"Raleigh"; "*Tiger*" and "*Tyger*"; "Fernandez" and "Fernandes"; "Algonkian" and "Algonquian"; "Roanoacs" (Native Americans) and "Roanokes"; and "Jamestown," "Jamestowne," and "James Towne." The editors have chosen to allow each author to employ his or her preferred way of expressing the words or phrases in question.

A Matter of Perspective: The Present State of Roanoke Colonization-Related Studies

E. Thomson Shields Jr.

One summer while I was in graduate school, my family gathered at a cottage in South Nags Head, where we had frequently vacationed when I was growing up. During those vacations we would at least once take the turn at Whalebone Junction and go to Fort Raleigh National Historic Site on Roanoke Island to see the "Lost Colony" fort. And during those vacations we would usually go to see Paul Green's symphonic drama *The Lost Colony*. But that summer during graduate school, things were a bit different. First, because I was now studying early American literature, I went to Fort Raleigh by myself to see what a scholar—as opposed to a teenaged tourist—might find there. Second, the National Park Service had created a new area since I had visited as a kid—the Thomas Hariot Nature Trail.

Being a good junior academic, I had picked up a facsimile edition of Hariot's 1584 *Briefe and True Report* along with some other books at the shop in the visitor center. As it turned out, the Hariot Nature Trail was lined with interpretive signs connecting plants and trees in the forest with passages from Hariot's book. Always the prepared scholar, I pulled out a pencil and started writing notes in my recent purchase. One of the more striking connections that the interpretative signs made was between the spoonleaf yucca, with fibrous curls coming off its leaves, and Hariot's "plant of silk." Standing in front of the plant that had most likely inspired Hariot's words gave me an entirely new perspective on early American exploration writings. Rather than seeing words in isolation—or at best, as connected only to other words in other books—I now saw them as blending very real experiences with the imagination. Out of those notes grew an article I am still proud of: on how early American writers used their desires—such as the coveting of Oriental goods like silk—to describe their real-world experiences.[1]

It is that same sense of new perspective gained by looking through new eyes at a familiar subject—the late-sixteenth-century English expeditions to Roanoke Island—that this collection hopes to provide. The essays presented here explore new discoveries as well as new ways to look at already known materials. The articles come from work presented over the past few years, starting with selected papers read at a 1993 symposium titled "Roanoke Decoded" and continuing with selected papers delivered at the 1998 Roanoke Colonization Conference, along with a few items that were submitted especially for consideration to be included in this volume.[2]

All of this work, whether by seasoned experts long recognized for their Roanoke-related research or by new scholars making their first forays into the subject, comes in the wake of culminating studies done for the mid-1980s celebrations of the four hundredth anniversary of the Roanoke voyages. At that time, histories such as David Beers Quinn's *Set Fair for Roanoke*, Karen Kupperman's *Roanoke: The Abandoned Colony*, and David Stick's *Roanoke Island: The Beginnings of English America* gave a very complete overview of what scholars had discovered to that point about those sixteenth-century English expeditions. Additionally, a series of publications from the Division (now Office) of Archives and History, North Carolina Department of Cultural Resources, brought out on the occasion showed other possible directions for study—from Paul Hoffman's treatment of the connection between the Spanish in America and the Roanoke voyages to Robert Arner's discussion of the "Lost Colony" in literature to Quinn's own idea of what happened to the "Lost Colonists."[3] Not all the new perspectives suggested by these publications have been taken up here, but several have, in addition to other perspectives not even considered at the time.

For example, the first group of essays begins by examining the place of the Roanoke voyages as a part of culture—from the literary and artistic culture of the sixteenth century to the literary culture of late-nineteenth- and early-twentieth-century America to the continuing folk culture of eastern North Carolina. Humans need a good story, factual or not. The Roanoke expeditions and the "Lost Colony" have provided great material for factual and nonfactual stories. Research exploring how society has attached itself to stories based on the Roanoke voyages has its roots in works such as *Paradise Preserved*, William Powell's history of the Roanoke Island Historical Association, and Arner's *The Lost Colony in Literature*.[4] For this volume, Kelley Griffith more fully explores one aspect of Arner's work by focusing on the literature of the late nineteenth and early twentieth centuries that used Virginia Dare as a figure of romance. Karen Baldwin, moving in a different direction, investigates through folklore how the idea of lost people and places, epitomized by the "Lost Colony," is a running theme of eastern North Carolina culture. Whether in literary "high culture" or popular folk culture, the Roanoke voyages have provided Americans with stories through which to develop their own perspectives on what the world should or could be.

Two of the essays explore an area of research just beginning to open up— examining how the writings from the Roanoke voyages relate to sixteenth-century artistic traditions by exploring how the stories were first written. The tools of literary criticism, in particular close reading and character analysis, underlie Lorraine Robinson's examination of John White's self-portrayal as the hero of his narratives about the 1587 expedition and the 1590 attempts to return and find the "Lost Colonists" he had reluctantly left behind. My own essay discusses how the language often cited to depict Ralph Lane as an unrepentant blowhard unwilling to accept blame for the failure of the colonization effort he led in 1585-1586 was, in fact, nothing more than the expected rhetorical language of the day—was Lane truly the boaster we have called him? All of these essays about the place of Roanoke colonization in culture—sixteenth-century or later—suggest new ways to look at the original documents of the voyages.

The second group of essays treats the history of the Roanoke voyages. Some extend earlier ideas with the perspective of new research. William Powell published his article, "Roanoke Colonists and Explorers: An Attempt at Identification" in 1957 and revised it as "Who Were the Roanoke Colonists?" in 1987, but with his subsequent research—explained particularly well in his piece on Ananias Dare—in two of this volume's essays (both originally delivered at the 1993 symposium "Roanoke Decoded"), he updates what we know about who the colonists of the 1580s Roanoke voyages were.

Two other essays in the history section take figures familiar to students of the Roanoke expeditions and ask us to see them anew. Olivia Isil depicts the Portuguese pilot Simon Fernandez favorably, countering his frequently villainous portrayal in histories and, even more often, literary works about Roanoke colonization. Michael Leroy Oberg, using the methodology of ethnohistory, asks us to read the available documents concerning the Native Americans most closely associated with the Roanoke voyages, Manteo and Wanchese, through a Native American perspective— what must it have been like for a Native American encountering the arriving English in what is now eastern North Carolina, and what must it have been like for these two Native Americans to travel to England, as they did?

The two final historical essays, one by Quinn and one by Thomas Davidson, explore subjects about which we have limited information by taking a new perspective on the information we do have. Quinn examines a possible relationship between the English financiers of the Roanoke voyages and the travelers to the New World, especially the 1587 "Lost Colony," and proposes some new and surprising ideas. Davidson compares Jamestown to the Roanoke voyages in order to suggest the supplies with which the Roanoke expeditions might have been outfitted. Almost all of the historical essays demonstrate how looking at familiar material from a new angle helps us more fully understand events surrounding Roanoke Island in the late sixteenth century.

The final group of essays investigates what anthropology and archaeology can tell us about what happened on Roanoke Island and throughout the region when the English arrived and interacted with the area's native people. First, in order to provide the necessary historical perspective, Bennie Keel reviews archaeological activities over the past century at the north end of Roanoke Island, the location of Fort Raleigh National Historic Site. Two other essays examine the interaction of the English colonizers with non-English societies. John Mintz and Thomas Beaman explore an interesting question of material culture—how the olive jar, an item associated with the Spanish world, arrived at an English colonial site while England and Spain were at odds. Seth Mallios anthropologically explores how differently the Algonquian people of present-day eastern North Carolina and Virginia and the Europeans who first encountered them understood trade and gift giving and how those differing perceptions led to violence between the two cultures. In simultaneously examining both material culture and the documents of the Roanoke voyages, a new perspective on the interactions among the English, Spanish, and Native Americans emerges.

A final perspective needed is an idea of what to explore next. Fred Willard and Barbara Midgett suggest where new archaeological work on the Outer Banks might find further traces of the English expeditions. Dennis Blanton not only talks about the weather but suggests that researchers do something about it—examine its role in the outcomes of the Roanoke voyages. Blanton, who recently studied the effects of drought on the Roanoke and Jamestown colonizing expeditions,[5] reveals that the "Lost Colony" arrived during one of the worst droughts of the past millennium. He suggests, however, that we also need to examine other climatological occurrences of the period, such as the frequent hurricane-like storms noted in the narratives of the Roanoke voyages.

All these essays enlighten us on the Roanoke voyages and their place in American society. But just as valuable is the perspective gained by looking at these differing approaches to studying the Roanoke expeditions in relation to one another. Recognizing how John White and Ralph Lane used language to portray their roles in the expeditions can help explain why Simon Fernandez's role in them may have been misunderstood. Knowing how well or poorly the backers of these undertakings supplied the colonists can help explain why the settlers may have surreptitiously traded with Spanish colonists in the Caribbean, thereby bringing Spanish olive jars to an English colony. Methods of literary and rhetorical study can help enlighten historical study. Historical study can help enlighten archaeological study. And the intertwining of perspectives can go on and on until, perhaps, we can better grasp what my coeditor, Charles Ewen, calls in the collection's concluding essay "the questions that count" concerning the first English attempts to colonize North America.

Current research on Roanoke colonization, thus, is highly interdisciplinary. It is a rich field of study for folklore, anthropology, history, literature, archaeology, art, ethnology, and other disciplines not even represented in this volume. My postmodern leanings make me want to write that current research into the Roanoke voyages provides a good story, whether that story is true or not. But instead I will write that research into the Roanoke voyages and the "Lost Colony" provides a variety of stories, each giving an important glimpse at the truth of what happened during these voyages and how they still matter to us, but a truth seen in each story from its own perspective.

NOTES

1. See my "East Makes West: Images of the Orient in Early Spanish and English Literature of North America," *Medievalia et Humanistica* [new series] 19 (1992): 97-116.

2. Special thanks are due lebame houston of *Elizabeth R* and Company in Manteo, North Carolina, who made all of the local arrangements for the 1998 Roanoke Colonization Conference—from the free use of the Pioneer Theater to the appearance of Barbara Hird as Queen Elizabeth. *Elizabeth R* and Company (P.O. Box 486, Manteo, NC 27954) produces the play *Elizabeth R* every summer in Manteo, as well as other productions with connections to the Roanoke colonization efforts of the 1580s.

3. Many of these books are still available. See the Historical Publications Section page at the North Carolina Office of Archives and History's Web site at *www.ncpublications.com.*

4. Arner's *The Lost Colony in Literature* (Raleigh: America's Four Hundredth Anniversary Committee, North Carolina Department of Cultural Resources, 1985) is a revision of his essay, "The Romance of Roanoke: Virginia Dare and the Lost Colony in American Literature," *Southern Literary Journal* 10 (spring 1978): 5-45.

5. See David W. Stahle et al., "The Lost Colony and Jamestown Droughts," *Science* 280 (April 24, 1998): 564-567.

Remembrance and Renewal: Modern Belief and Legend in the Region of the "Lost Colony"

Karen Baldwin

Folklife in contemporary coastal North Carolina demonstrates direct and indirect cultural connection with the earliest period of attempted English colonization and contact with Native Americans. Foodways, healing belief systems, supernatural and historical belief narratives, and festival customs with English and Irish antecedents survive, if not thrive, among communities of kin, settled for nearly four hundred years in the sounds region of the state.

Outsiders are surprised to learn of the longevity of Anglo-identified cultural traits; insiders take it in stride. There is, after all, a popularly accepted explanation. I heard it again one fall day in 1992, offered by a New Jersey native, now owner of a Cape Hatteras campground. People in Rodanthe celebrate what is called "old Christmas" on the Saturday closest to January 5 because, as she avidly offered, they are descendants of the "Lost Colony." Her explanation is founded in a core belief well known in these parts, unfamiliar to outsiders, that a small band of English settlers, lost to history, survived from the sixteenth century in undiscovered isolation somewhere in the eastern reaches of the state, unaware of the Julian-Gregorian calendar shift or unwilling to give up the old for "new" Christmas.[1]

Indeed, "old Christmas" at Rodanthe is quite a reliquary of Anglo-Irish midwinter custom, a factor contributing to its place in this consideration of metaphoric context for modern legend. It is an all-day party, increasingly boisterous and drunken as night gathers the largest crowd inside the old schoolhouse turned community center. Following an oyster roast and a chicken pastry supper, the band strikes up early rock 'n' roll tunes, and the floor fills with slow-dance huggers and jitterbuggers. Fights break out occasionally in the boozy hubbub, and the dancers scatter till the fighters are separated and banished to the side rooms or out into the night. The highlight of the evening, the reason many come, even though they dislike the drinking and the fisticuffs, is the annual appearance of Old Buck, a masquerade bull that bursts into the room for a brief rampage sometime between 10:00 P.M. and midnight, scattering the giggling, screaming dancers to the walls. Old Buck is a North Carolina Outer Banks ritual animal disguise figure—akin to the hobbyhorses, bulls, and sheep described for British Isles festivities from the fourteenth to the twentieth century and among Christmas mummers in the outposts of Newfoundland.[2]

Celebrating the "Lost Colony" and continuing efforts to solve its mystery are significant to contemporary eastern North Carolina folklife in several ways. Legend extends and reinterprets what is known and still mysterious about the fate of the 1587 colonists—compensating for the unsatisfactory lacks and gaps in historical knowledge. Primacy is one of the concerns still driving interest in discovering what happened to

Virginia Dare, her family, and fellow adventurers. Because the lineage from the firstborn English child and other offspring of those 1587 folks was broken, because the colonists were "lost" to Anglo-European conventions of reckoning history, they also "lost" rightful recognition as the original English colony, the primacy claimed later by Jamestown settlers. Emphasis on primacy, of course, is (dare I say?) a primary feature of Anglo-European world views.

Contemporary belief statements link the earliest known white settlers in locations throughout the region to the colonists who disappeared from historical records in the sixteenth century. Reportedly, the oral traditions of the Lumbee Indians conclude that their migration inland from their coastal origins represented a transplanting of descendants of the "Lost Colony" English, assimilated by coastal Algonkians. Virginia Dare, "lost" to history, becomes a regional symbol of primacy, independence, and virtue and an icon of innocence, transforming the colonists' destructive invasion of Algonkians' land, lives, and culture. Contemporary eastern North Carolina references to what I call the " 'Lost Colony' belief complex" can be offered as explanations for the age or oddity of a regional custom such as Rodanthe's old Christmas. Fully developed narratives out of the "Lost Colony" complex are not as easily found in oral performance as are such kernel references, but Melvin Robinson's "Carteret County solution" to what he called "The Riddle of the Lost Colony" draws from and reinforces belief in purported descent held among families through the region. Robinson proposes that the word "CROATOAN," which John White found in his 1590 search for the colonists he had left on Roanoke Island three years before, referred to Portsmouth Island, and when the colonists moved "50 miles into the maine," they traveled into Downeast. "The markings on the trees," Robinson suggests, "were very probably carved casually by Lane's men, when they made Roanoke Island their temporary headquarters (in 1586)." White feigned joy at seeing the "fayre Capitall letters" in order to cover up the terrible mistake he'd made in landing the 1590 voyagers at the wrong island.[3]

Robinson's solution derives from environmental factors as well. According to Robinson, northeast gale winds, characteristic for short periods in midsummer, blew the 1587 colonists off their original course and landed them at Portsmouth instead of Roanoke. Naturally occurring inlets along the Outer Banks shift and shoal and can appear or disappear during a single violent storm. Returning to the same inlet and island three years later might have been virtually impossible. Robinson claims that Cedar Island was where the settlers "seated" on the mainland. According to Robinson, the Willises, Taylors, and Smiths Downeast are likely descendants of colonists who resettled in the "maine." White, he asserts, was the one lost.[4]

Descendants of families noted to have surnames of the "lost" colonists are found in locales throughout eastern North Carolina, according to F. Roy Johnson's 1983 book, *The Lost Colony in Fact and Legend*, written with Thomas C. Parramore.[5] Johnson, a prolific publisher of local history and folklore titles from his small press, compiled legendary accounts locating the "lost" colonists in every corner of eastern North Carolina. "Lost" colonists found their way to Gates and other northeastern counties and crossed cultures and bloodlines with Chowanoke Algonkians. They moved south and inland to Crusoe Island in the Green Swamp. They joined Pasquotank Indians and lived on Kite's Ridge in the Great Dismal Swamp on the Camden-Currituck county line. Anglo-Americans who believe in their own or their neighbors' descent from the "Lost Colonists" are reported widely in eastern counties.

From the core "Lost Colony" legend develop tangential narratives incorporating supernatural motifs in examining the fate of the iconic Virginia Dare and annexing other accounts of mysterious disappearance and lamentable loss. Virginia Dare lore well illustrates how the "Lost Colony" mystery is fertile ground for popular literary and cultural treatments. A story of a white doe, ostensibly based in Indian narrative, incorporating historically familiar Wanchese and Manteo and introducing new Indian characters, chiefly the sexual male counterparts to the virginal Dare, first appeared in 1861 as a short novel by Mary Ann Mason, serialized in the *Semi-Weekly Raleigh Register*.[6] Folklorist Richard Walser used Mason's "The White Doe Chase: A Legend of Olden Times"[7] as the basis for his 1980 print version, "Virginia Dare the White Doe."[8] Mason, by her own note, heard the legend " 'At her mother's knee in early childhood . . . though with the Legend, was imparted no explanation; that has been supplied by the imagination of the writer.' "[9] A long narrative poetic treatment of the story, also based on Mason, appeared in 1901 as *The White Doe: The Fate of Virginia Dare: An Indian Legend*, Sallie Southall Cotten's fund-raiser project for the North Carolina Federation of Women's Clubs.[10] Cotten proposed "The White Doe" as "probably the oldest and possibly the least known of all the legends which relate the history of the United States . . . a genuine American legend."[11] F. Roy Johnson and Thomas C. Parramore drew from several sources, including Walser and Cotten, for the Virginia Dare tale in their *The Lost Colony in Fact and Legend*. In their version, Virginia has grown to a sexually desirable beauty and is pursued by a youthful and worthy Indian suitor, Okisko, and by Chico, a "wrinkled and cunning old witch doctor." Because Virginia spurns his attentions, Chico "use[s] his magic to change her into a snow white fawn, thus preventing his rival from winning her."[12]

International tale motifs link the white doe tale to oral narratives of transformation,[13] and a healthy context for supernatural belief tales exists in the region's Anglo- and African-based cultural traditions, transmigrated into the region from the Jamestown area and co-mingled since the mid-seventeenth century.

White-tailed deer are favored quarry, and oral narrative stocks of hunters include tales of ghost deer, albino deer, gigantic deer, deer incapable of being hit, and deer that disappear once hit. One version of the white doe legend continues in eastern North Carolina as a family hunting tale, told by a young man whose great uncle is the tale's main actor:

My grandmother used to tell us these stories. . . . We'd go over . . . on the weekend, an', to keep us from gettin' into trouble, or, right fore dinner, she'd tell us a story. An' this was a story . . . she'd swear was true, an', my grandfather swears it's true. It was . . . my *great* . . . *uncle* would go hunting, every afternoon, an' he go to the same spot to still hunt. An' every afternoon he'd see this deer come up to him, was kinda white, er, not really white, but lighter than most of the other deer. An' he said he'd wait for it to get in range of his gun . . . back then it was musket-loadin', he didn't have but one shot. He'd shoot, an' he'd swear the deer would fall down. But he'd go run to where he thought the deer was, an' it was gone, never a trace of the deer, an' he'd come home and he'd say, "I just *knew* I shot that deer." So the next day, he'd go back, an' this went on for about a week, an' he shot and he could never kill this deer. An' so . . . a man said he was jinxed; that was a witch. He said the way to break the curse was to get you some silver and make you a silver ball . . . to put in your gun. So he did. He melted down some dimes, silver dimes, an' made into a (musket) ball. And he went out and the deer came out and . . . he waited . . . waited, and this time he waited as close as he could possibly hit. . . . He shot and the deer fell. He said, this time he saw the deer fall. So he *ran* over to the place where the deer was, an' it was gone again. But there were, there was blood there. So he *knew* he hit it. So he searched and searched and searched until that evenin', an' he finally gave up, an' went back home, an' told people he was sure he shot the deer. When he got in, his wife told him that a woman in the community was gone to the hospital, that she had broken her hip. An' he got to thinkin', that's where he had shot the deer . . . in the hip. An' supposedly, I can't remember whether this is true, but . . . when the doctors were settin' her hip, they found traces of silver . . . in her hip. The deer never showed up again . . . after that . . . at that place. The lady, she ended up in bed for the rest of her life . . . she ended up dyin' *of* that broken hip.[14]

Core elements of the "Lost Colony" belief complex concern the mysterious history of John White's misplaced or missing colonists. In a metaphoric realm of the "Lost Colony" complex exist legends and oral history about other community disappearances, more recent losses that re-sound the "Lost Colony" theme and resemble its perplexity. Missing-community legends are metaphors for the region's changing land forms, shifting watercourses, transforming wind and weather, and the effects of human exploitation of the region's land and water resources. Diamond City on Shackleford Banks and Dymond City in Martin County are both discussed here, and these are only two among a number of other former communities whose disappearances are symbolically reinterpreted and celebrated through legend and custom, foodways and festival-folklife expressions concerning loss, displacement, and disappearance.

Diamond City on Shackleford Banks was one of several settlements of shore whalers and sound fishers, villages of fewer than one hundred people separated from each other along the barrier island. Diamond City, closest to the lighthouse at Cape Lookout, takes its name from the distinguishing pattern painted on the tower. Markets for whale products had perilously diminished by the turn of the twentieth century, and the Bankers suffered a rapid series of devastating coastal storms, culminating in 1899 with two monster hurricanes—one in August, which hit directly on Cape Lookout and Diamond City, and another in October. This was the end for the Ca'e (or Core) Bankers, who packed up and floated their small houses over the sound on skiffs to resettle in villages along mainland Core Sound. Some moved into the waterfront district of Morehead City called The Promised Land. Three and four generations removed from the original Ca'e Bankers, many still hold a sense of displacement and loss and rehearse family historical accounts of the simpler, nobler lives of their Banker forebears. The emblem of this celebrated loss is the Cape Lookout Light, still a beacon out to sea, but more importantly a monument to lost cultural and property inheritance.

Today the diamond-patterned Cape Lookout tower is both a center for customary social activities and a visual symbol of regional/historical relevance. Former Diamond City folks used to sail the sound between Harkers Island or Beaufort and Shackleford Banks in skiffs and sharpies of local construction. Their descendants motor across in fishing work boats or skiffs, still locally made, to camp near the lighthouse, have moonlight picnics, fish the surf line. The lighthouse as emblem of folk cultural meaning appears as a scaled-down replica in mainland yard ornamentation and in grave decoration; on individually hand-decorated sweatshirts made by a Harkers Island woman whose family owned one of the remaining houses on Shackleford; in murals painted on the outside wall of a retail fish market in Beaufort owned and supplied by a Harkers Island fishing family and on one wall inside the Harkers Island Elementary School cafeteria. Former Diamond City folks on Harkers Island were still close enough to see Cape Lookout Light, even on cloudy days. A significant custom among descendants of Ca'e Bankers on Harkers Island is to drive down to the end of the main road at Shell Point at least once each day to look out over the water to Cape Lookout Light. Regional identification with the lighthouse marks community among families in this area of Downeast, where folklife forms may signify both native residency and recognition of difference from "outsiders," "dingbatters," people "from off."

Within the cultural geography of ideas in the sound region, even mainlanders use the phrase "from off" as in "people from off" to refer to outsiders newly resident. The insular image is literal for both coastal islanders and those mainlanders who still live in "islands" of high or drained land, separated by pocosins, swamps, morass grounds, forests, or vast corporate farms.

Those who live near Dymond City, a vanished community in Martin County, retell the history of the place as a matter of insiders' knowledge. A young woman native of nearby Jamesville comments on how "movers in" have erroneous perceptions of the area: "Some people new to the area take for granted that Weyerhaeuser developed the logging business here, but the pulp mill is comparatively recent. One of the earliest logging operations is the one at Dymond City, a town that once existed on the J&W Tram, which is only a memory and a railroad bed. Where once the logging town thrived, now stands wild timberland and swamp with a maze of 200 miles of roads."[15] Indeed, Dymond City was one of many lumber-mill towns that sprang up through the area in the 1880s and disappeared as quickly, once the old-growth timber was extracted.[16] Shortly after the Civil War, English investors organized the Jamesville & Washington Railroad and Lumber Company to log 30,000 acres of forest in Martin and Beaufort Counties.[17] Although one folk etymology claims that this Dymond City's name derives from the locale's numerous eastern diamondback rattlesnakes, some with "as high as 15, 16 rattles o[n] 'em," history records the town was named for one J&W investor.[18]

Dymond City grew up near the head of Deep Run Swamp, midway between Jamesville and Washington.[19] The railroad carried logs, wood shingles, and turpentine up to the Roanoke to be transported by steamer across Albemarle Sound and through the Dismal Swamp Canal to Norfolk's port, or down to the Pamlico River to be shipped out of Pamlico Sound and down along the Atlantic coast. Some of the workers were transplants from Pennsylvania, England, and Ireland, family and friends who moved in to work with Abraham Fisher, the company manager. African Americans, former slaves who lived in nearby Jacktown, walked to Dymond City each day to work. Shad Griffin, born in 1893, lived in Jacktown as a young man, and in 1985 he was the last living link to the lost town: "[I was a] teenager, in my early teens. I worked up there making bricks, making turpentine. [They] farm what they called Jacktown now, but at that time they did not. Most of the industries was burning tar, hauling logs, things of that kind."[20]

Dymond City buzzed with activity from the 1880s to 1900, when the accessible timber had been logged out and what had been "a veritable city in the woods" began to disappear. Sixty thousand acres of timberland between Washington, Jamesville, and Pinetown comprise the former Dymond City area. The forest has regained its ground. Besides the J&W Tram Road, only a building foundation remains, submerged in swamp water, and a lone tombstone in the woods marks the grave of

> William J.
> Son of Abraham Fisher
> Born 1859
> Died 1885
> At rest.

Dymond City is now considered a dangerous, scary place. Completely isolated, it is home to a variety of wild animals. People fear getting lost in the labyrinth of unmarked, unpaved roads through 60,000 acres of wilderness. Even back when Dymond City was thriving, many feared getting lost, but those who whispered in church and talked loudly in cemeteries had a way of dealing with that fear. Mrs. Annie Mae Williams remembers how loudly the people who came from Dymond City talked: "Early in the morning, when some of them . . . went to work, they'd holler . . . to see who was . . . going in and which route they were taking. And they said the reason so many people . . .

talked so loud then, is because they'd talk to one another a mile apart, woods in between. And they'd be hollering at one another to see what they'd done or what they were gonna do during the day. And they said that's why the people back there got to talking so loud to one another. It won't because they were deaf, it was because they were so far apart."[21]

Annie Mae Williams's father worked for another company as a logging foreman in the Dymond City area, and she remembers that "they had lots of big times up in there": "They run moonshine back in there as well as logged and cut timber and had these great big parties. . . . The roads were so bad at times they'd keep changing the paths to go through because when they cut these logs sometimes it was rainy and wet. The log wagons would mire down so deep in the mud and mire that they'd change their routes. They kept it hard to find out exactly how you were going into Dymond City. Some loggers stayed in Dymond City in houses they'd built and didn't get out to visit their families or friends in six or seven months."[22]

Shad Griffin, who lived near one entrance to Dymond City, knew of many people running from the law who hid out in the vast timberlands. For many years, young men on a dare camped in Dymond City to be "tough." At present, Dymond City is braved only by hunters, ATV "mudders," rowdy underage party drinkers, and curious ghost-light-legend trippers.

Throughout several surrounding counties, Dymond City is notorious for appearances of unexplained lights, and stories about Dymond City's mysterious lights illuminate the history of the place and the folklife of its people, then and now. Accounts of sightings of lights at Dymond City share common features. One or more unaccountable lights, round and white like car headlights, hover in the distance down a road or appear in the tops of trees. Visible for only a few seconds, the lights then disappear. People who drive into the Dymond City wilderness at night report that lights follow their cars. Others say they have seen the lights "go through" oncoming cars. Typically, encounters with the Dymond City lights are frighteningly sudden. "We were riding out there one night just messing around," one resident recalled. "We were on the Tram, and we saw a light at the other end and we noticed we weren't ever getting any closer to it. So we started running fast . . . 65 or something, and we never could catch it. We were going along and it just went out. And we turned around at one of the crossroads and the light was right on top of us. I ain't lying. . . . I know we were running at least 80 to 85. That was when they kept the Tram in real good condition. And we could not leave that light . . . and all of a sudden, it just went out. And you know if it had been a car behind you with all that dust, it would have stopped. It couldn't have followed you."[23]

Another resident of Barbertown, very near Dymond City, told of experiences with lights in the local Dismal Swamp: "The lights me and (my friend) saw weren't no car lights. . . . These here were one single light, and they were tree high sitting over to the side of the Tram. They ain't no car lights, that's for sure. Not up in no tree!"[24]

Variously, the light is said to be a lantern carried by the conductor of the old train looking for something he lost, the headlight of the old train, or Abraham Fisher. Many of the sightings occur along the J&W Tram Road, the old railroad bed. There, the lights are visible at great distance because the J&W Tram is so straight. The original surveyor, the Englishman Francis Lightfoot, laid six miles of road straight out from Jamesville through dense forests and swamp lands, sighting on a dark night to a torch held by a man high in a pine tree. Some say Abraham Fisher was the man who climbed with a torch into what was called the "six mile pine" at the edge of Dymond City.

Stories of looking for and occasionally seeing mysterious lights at Dymond City are woven through the after-dark socializing among area teens for whom Dymond City is a "lover's lane"; telling scary stories about Dymond City is a customary part of "making out" there. Sighting tales also help initiate new members of the social cohort. Once the stories are told and the group has driven into the dark forest, new members are dared to get out of the car. If an initiate takes the dare, the rest of the group drives away, stranding the poor sucker in the woods.[25]

Excursions along the ghost-lit former railroads of eastern North Carolina take legend-testing teens out to Earleys Station, between Ahoskie in Hertford County and Aulander in Bertie County, or to Poortown, likewise in Bertie County; to Chocowinity in Beaufort County south of the Pamlico River and to Bunyan, on the north shore, also in Beaufort County; near Plymouth at the mouth of the Roanoke River in Washington County; in the vicinity of Cove City in Craven County; and between Pactolus and Stokes, farming communities in eastern Pitt County. Reports of sightings at those locations reach well back to times when youthful light hunters traveled by horse and wagon. All of those ghost lights, like Dymond City's, appear along the routes of former railways that up to the first half of the twentieth century crisscrossed through the eastern counties to carry in supplies and carry out extracted materials. But the Dymond City light also symbolizes a vanished community.

Consciousness of the so-called "Lost Colony" of Roanoke Island is an eastern North Carolina phenomenon, directly influencing some folklife traditions and popular cultural forms, providing contextually resonant meaning for others. Expressed belief about descent from those left behind in 1587 and legends bearing witness to the peregrinations and possible fate of the first colonists are still part of both family and local narrative stories. Popular cultural permutations of the "Lost Colony" and the iconic Virginia Dare continue to be promulgated for touristic, commercial, and patriotic purposes. Less directly, yet powerfully and pervasively, the "Lost Colony" of Roanoke Island resonates with commemorated experiences of vanished and displaced communities throughout the region. Dymond City represents just one of many losses, resulting from storms and changing shorelines, depletion of natural resources, and other elements of the natural and cultural history of coastal North Carolina. This pervasive experience of lost community, consciously or unself-consciously sustained, must be recognized in reexamining the meaning of the "Lost Colony." Beyond issues of primacy and historical lineage, the dramatic power and poignancy of this "original" loss is a metaphoric foundation upon which folk belief and legend reconstruct subsequent disjunctions and losses.

NOTES

1. In his article "Old Christmas at Rodanthe" (*North Carolina Folklore Journal* 10 [July 1962]: 22), folklorist Richard Walser sets the calendar shift in a local, regional perspective: "Present-day folk in Dare County account for Old Christmas in this way: When in 1582 the Gregorian Calendar was substituted for the Julian Calendar in many Catholic countries, resistance in other areas such as Protestant England delayed its adoption until much later. Finally, in 1752 the English officially began using the new calendar, and in that year dropped eleven September days to bring themselves into line. [M]ore tradition-minded folk would have none of it. They insisted that the actual occasion was still December 24, which by counting forward eleven days thereby came on January 5. Even this mathematical reasoning was not immediately translated into action. For years the old Julian Calendar was followed in isolated areas—such as on the North Carolina sandbanks, for instance—and even after the Gregorian came into general use for secular purposes, the January 5 date was stubbornly retained for Christmas. The new Christmas day was said to be man-made."

2. See Herbert Halpert and G. M. Story, eds., *Christmas Mumming in Newfoundland: Essays in Anthropology, Folklore, and History* (Toronto: University of Toronto Press, [1969]), and E. C. Cawte, *Ritual Animal Disguise: A Historical and Geographical Study of Animal Disguise in the British Isles* (Cambridge, U.K.: D. S. Brewer, 1978).

3. Melvin Robinson, *The Riddle of the Lost Colony* (New Bern: Owen G. Dunn, [1946]), 35.

4. Robinson, *Riddle of the Lost Colony*, 27-31, 52.

5. F. Roy Johnson and Thomas C. Parramore, *The Lost Colony in Fact and Legend* (Murfreesboro, N.C.: Johnson Publishing, 1983).

6. Robert D. Arner's *The Lost Colony in Literature* (Raleigh: America's Four Hundredth Anniversary Committee, North Carolina Department of Cultural Resources, 1985) psychologically critiques a sequence of works published from the seventeenth century to the twentieth, including several of those discussed here.

7. Mrs. M. M., "The White Doe Chase: A Legend of Olden Times," *Our Living and Our Dead* 3 (December 1875): 753-771.

8. Richard Walser, "Virginia Dare the White Doe," *North Carolina Legends* (Raleigh: Division of Archives and History, North Carolina Department of Cultural Resources, 1980), 8-9.

9. Walser, *North Carolina Legends*, 8-9, 69.

10. Richard Walser, assisted by E. T. Malone Jr., *Literary North Carolina: A Historical Survey, Revised and Enlarged* (Raleigh: Division of Archives and History, North Carolina Department of Cultural Resources, 1986), 30.

11. Sallie Southall Cotten, *The White Doe: The Fate of Virginia Dare: An Indian Legend* (Philadelphia: Lippincott, 1901), 6.

12. Johnson and Parramore, *Lost Colony*, 76.

13. The tale motifs from Stith Thompson's *Motif-Index of Folk Literature* are [D114.1.1.1 girl to deer—Ireland] and [D114.1.1.2 woman to doe—India]. Stith Thompson, *Motif-Index of Folk Literature: A Classification of Narrative Elements in Folktales, Ballads, Myths, Fables, Mediaeval Romances,*

Exempla, Fabliaux, Jest-Books, and Local Legends, 6 vols. (Bloomington: Indiana University Press, 1955-58), 2:16.

14. Michael A. Waters, "The White Deer Legend," transcribed by Karen Baldwin (unpublished manuscript, East Carolina University Folklore Archive, Greenville, 1991).

15. Kathy D. Williams, "Dymond City: Where's That?" (unpublished manuscript, East Carolina University Folklore Archive, Greenville, 1991).

16. David Cecelski, "In the Great Alligator Swamp," *Coastwatch* (May-June 1997): 19-21.

17. Wendell Peele, "Ghost Town," in "Martin," in *A New Geography of North Carolina,* 4 vols., ed. Bill Sharpe (Raleigh: Sharpe Publishing, 1954-1965), 4:1949-1950. See also Frances M. Manning and W. H. Booker, *Martin County History,* 2 vols. to date (Williamston, N.C.: Enterprise Publishing, 1977—), and Shelby Jean Nelson Hughes, ed., *Martin County Heritage* (Williamston, N.C.: Martin County Historical Society, 1980).

18. Williams, "Dymond City."

19. William S. Powell, *The North Carolina Gazetteer* (Chapel Hill: University of North Carolina Press, [1968]), 153.

20. Williams, "Dymond City."

21. Williams, "Dymond City."

22. Williams, "Dymond City."

23. Christina Cratt, "The Mysterious Lights at Dymond City" (unpublished manuscript, East Carolina University Folklore Archive, Greenville, 1990).

24. Cratt, "Mysterious Lights."

25. Cratt, "Mysterious Lights."

John White's Moste Excellente Adventure:
A Colonial "Rule, Britannia"

Lorraine Hale Robinson

For many years, scholars of Roanoke and other colonization efforts have examined the journals kept by colonizers. The principal foci of this scholarly study have been the historical and the social/cultural aspects of what the documents reveal. But journals and related primary texts of the period may serve another equally illuminating function: they can be read as literature, created consciously or perhaps subconsciously to do more than merely transmit factual information.

Accounts of the first English settlements in the New World were written to accomplish varied purposes: to disseminate information in order to kindle public interest in the ventures; to record England's rise to international hegemony (especially the struggle with Spain); and to extend knowledge in a world in transition from the Middle Ages, a period during which (with the exception of the Crusades) local and regional—rather than global—concerns predominated. But John White's narratives of his voyages to Roanoke Island in 1587 and 1590 accomplish these purposes and more, transcending the usual roles of such reportage and affirming that White is, indeed, both the hero of his own story and a specific, individual personification of the expanding English hegemony of the time.

White's texts cross traditional boundaries, functioning as formulaic hero/adventure tales, a literary genre in which suspense and action predominate. The writer reveals himself to be bold, wily, and opportunistic—a hero who experiences fantastic phenomena and overcomes incredible antagonists and obstacles in his explorations. And White's writing—as literature—affirms to himself, to the English nation, and to the world the hegemony of the English *man* and of English *men*.

Specifically, the narratives of the 1587 and 1590 voyages present a larger-than-life White, the "very model" of the consummate English hero of the age: active (even when faced with the colony's disappearance), vital, decisive, assured, chosen. But these qualities are subtly conveyed: for example, rather than baldly stating that he is energetic or decisive or assured, the narrative repeatedly reports White in situations requiring those desirable traits—and on each occasion, he rises to meet the situation's challenges.

An especially interesting aspect of the text is the shape and proportion of the narrative—how much writing is devoted to specific time periods or activities. These accounts by John White, vigorous "man of action," follow a chronological order but vary as to how much detail the writer chooses to insert at different points in the story. Where White hurtles the audience along with detail absent or at most sketchy, the reader encounters a charged and energized leader possessing the personal qualities of decision and speed. Where the narrative is dense with copious detail, the audience encounters a leader of deliberation, thoroughness, judgment, and balance and an adversary (or adversaries) intentionally and expansively "demonized." Sometimes the adversary is an individual, such as Simon Ferdinando; at other times the adversary is collective, such as the Spanish.[1] In both cases, the worse his antagonist, the better and more heroic White appears, confirming his "moste excellente" qualities and increasing the impact of his triumphs on his audience.

In that way, John White microcosmically represents the whole of the English nation, an Every-English-man. White's personal battles with his 1587 antagonist, Simon Ferdinando, are the Anglo-Iberian power struggle in miniature. For the English audience of the period, reading White's narrative (a cultural *and* literary creation) validated their spirited and, to them, absolutely justifiable English nationalism.

Action Hero

"John White's Narrative of His Voyage, the fourth voyage made to Virginia, with three shippes, in the yeere, 1587. Wherein was transported the second Colonie" is the author's account of the period from April to November of that year; he evidently compiled it from his journal.[2] White portrays himself as a decisive and visionary leader who impels himself and his companions toward adventure and destiny, focusing most heavily on the details that support his specific literary as well as broader cultural purposes.

The driving narrative jump-starts the action adventure, its energy felt from the opening passages, which sweep the reader swiftly aboard ship and move quickly from Portsmouth to the Isle of Wight to Plymouth, and then on to Virginia:

Aprill
Our Fleete being in number three saile, viz. The Admirall, a shippe of one hundred and twentie tunnes: a Flie boate, and a Pinnesse, departed the sixe and twentieth of Aprill from Portesmouth, and the same day came to anker at the Cowes, in the Isle of Wight, where wee staied eight dais.

Maye
The 5. of Maye, at nine of the clocke at night, we came to Plymmouth, where we remained the space of two daies. The 8. We waied anker at Plymmouth, and departed thence for Virginia.[3]

In less than a fortnight, the English expedition under John White's vigorous direction is off. White the Bold has described the assembled fleet, weighed anchor at Portsmouth, called at the Isle of Wight and at Plymouth, and set sail for Virginia. The brief passage—three short sentences—expends not one syllable on preparations and planning in England but moves directly to the activities of the departure. Thus, the account shifts the focus onto what is important to White and his English audience: the actions leading to the triumph of an Englishman over his adversary.

In Spite of Simon Ferdinando and Other Trials

John White's long series of disputes with Simon Ferdinando is a kind of classical debate in which the disputants engage in repeated, almost stylized thrusts, each of which reaffirms the heroic nature of John White, protagonist. At this point in the narrative, White's vehicle for establishing himself as hero is his extensive description of the Sisyphean struggles against Ferdinando, master of the *Lion*, who is carefully "set up" as the antagonist.

White as governor is the leader of the expeditionary force, but Ferdinando, as master of the ship (a critically important position), will, according to White, repeatedly endanger the entire undertaking. White alternately implies or avers that the ship's master is incompetent or not a good English "team player." The power struggle intensifies as the narrative progresses. In no fewer than ten instances, Ferdinando's deficiencies are presented in "purple" detail. Only eight days into the voyage, Ferdinando "lewdly forsooke [the] Flie boate, leaving her distressed in the Baye of Portingall"[4]; then he provided faulty information: "it was iudged, that this Island was inhabited with Sauages, though Fernando had tolde vs for certaine, the contrarie."[5] White offers empirical evidence of Ferdinando's misinformation when he reports that the company actually sighted "eleven Sauages, and divers houses halfe a mile distant from the steepe, on toppe of the hill where they staied."[6]

The persistent damning of Simon Ferdinando (or Fernando; White is not consistent in the spelling) runs throughout the 1587 account. And the worse Ferdinando is made to appear, the better and more excellent Governor White appears, having had to contend not only with the obvious and usual challenges of such a voyage but also with the carefully chronicled deception, self-indulgence, incompetence, and general slackness of the ship's master.

For example, Ferdinando promises salt at Rosse Bay, but shortly afterward backpedals, saying that "he knewe not well, whether the same were the place or not."[7] On the following day, while at anchor at Boqueron Bay, White describes how Ferdinando denies the expedition promised access to gathering plants that were intended to be transported to Virginia. And on the very day following, Ferdinando bypasses entirely, and without White's authorization, the island of Hispaniola, a planned port of call. It is clear from White's catalog of events that the expedition will have to succeed *in spite of* Simon Ferdinando.

But White's writing is more than just a catalogue of Ferdinando's deficiencies. White also manipulates the tone of the narrative to his own advantage. Anti-Ferdinando irony is pervasive. On the sixth of July, the hardworking expedition "came to the Islande Caycos, wherein Fernando saide were two salt pondes, assuring vs if they were drie, wee might finde salt to shift with, vntill the next supplie, but it prooued as true as the finding of sheepe at Beake."[8]

No sheep at Beake, no salt at Caycos

White's irony, however, is not reserved for Ferdinando's professional "deficiencies" only. White reports: "[I]n this Island, whilest Ferdinando solaced himself a shoare, with one of the company, in part of the Island, others spent the latter part of that day"[9] in hunting, seeking salt, and engaging in activities that contributed to the success of the expedition. In this biting assessment, Ferdinando is presented as the self-indulgent noncontributor.

According to White, the incompetent Ferdinando can't even find Croatoan, riding at anchor "two or three dais" before deciding that he was "deceaued." The same paragraph lays out more of Ferdinando's professional deficiencies for the audience: "[H]ad not Captaine Stafforde bene more carefull in looking out, then *our* Simon Fernando, wee had beene all cast away upon the breache, called the Cape of Feare."[10] From the context, White's "our" is clearly ironic.

In typical hero/adventure-tale style, while on the 1587 voyage John White not only struggles against Ferdinando but also encounters the fantastic: animals of almost mythic size. White describes a day in June when he and his party contend with tortoises so large that sixteen men carrying just one tortoise were exhausted from the effort.[11]

Another "adversarial life-form" that White and his expedition encounter is "savages."[12] In the narrative, White orchestrates and manipulates a cultural bias against these people that in turn becomes part of the fabric of his evidence of the admirable, heroic, and superhuman nature of the English members of the expedition—in contrast to the devious and barbaric nature of the native population. As White writes, "These Sauages beeing secretly hidden among the high reedes, . . . espied our man [George Howe] wading in the water alone, almost naked, without any weapon, saue onely a smal forked sticke."[13] The entire "Sauage" band could kill the lone, virtually unarmed, fiercely brave, noble, and larger-than-life Englishman only with great difficulty: the savages "shotte at him in the water, where they gaue him sixteene wounds with their arrowes; and after they had slaine him with their woodden swordes, beat his head in peeces."[14]

But White carefully avoids some of the credibility problems that can arise from wholesale stereotyping of the native population. In sharp contrast with White's wholly critical depiction of Simon Ferdinando, the "Sauage" Manteo in particular comes in for the highest praise that White can give: those who are so wise as to befriend the expedition, serving as guides and so on, are adjudged to have behaved toward White and his party "as . . . most faithfull English[men]."[15]

Personal Experience as Microcosm

John White's personal struggles in the 1587 voyage are also a miniature of the larger global struggle between England and Spain. Spanish hegemony would be seriously damaged by Francis Drake's 1588 defeat of the Armada, but Spain's sea power was by no means immediately eliminated nor English dominance assured. In a kind of hit-and-run guerrilla warfare at sea, Spanish treasure vessels become targets for the enterprising White and his party.

"The fift voyage of *Master* Iohn White into the West Indies and parts of America called Virginia, in the yeere 1590" follows the same brisk pattern established in his earlier account. In five short sentences, White moves the reader from Plymouth to the Barbary Coast to the Isle of Mogador to the Santa Cruz road:

> The 20 of March the three shippes the Hopewell, the Iohn Euangelist, and the little Iohn, put to sea from Plymmouth with two small Shallops.

> The 25 at midnight both our Shallops were sunke being towed at the ships stearnes by the Boatswaines negligence.

> On 30 we saw a head vs that part of the coast of Barbary, lying East of Cape Cantyn, and the Bay of Asaphi.

> The next day we came to the Isle of Mogador, where rode, at our passing by, a Pinnesse of London called Moonshine.

> Aprill
> On the first of Aprill we ankored in Santa Cruz rode. . . .[16]

The same energized action that characterized the 1587 expedition is evident in the constant busyness of the 1590 adventurers: White and his party seek salt, forage for food, take soundings, and, most especially, engage treasure-laden Spanish vessels returning to Europe. For the first five months of this expedition, White and his company of adventurers seize every feasible opportunity to "grab the money and run."

Details of these sea raids occupy much of the 1590 narrative. White's expedition gives chase to and captures treasure ships, pillages settlements, and takes prisoners. In this account, the Spanish as a whole now serve the same literary function—unremitting Sisyphean antagonist—that Simon Ferdinando served in the story of the earlier voyage. Echoing the 1587 pro-English account of George Howe's slaughter at the hands of a band of "savages," White reiterates the "natural superiority" of the English forces: only one of the English was killed and two wounded, but "of theirs [the Spanish] 4 slaine and 6 hurt."[17]

Additional evidence of the English "superiority" can be observed in White's description of his competent and heroic 1590 companions. Captains Edward Spicer and Abraham Cooke (or Cocke) both display great nautical skill, and the courageous and self-sacrificing Cooke contrasts sharply with the "lewd" Simon Ferdinando.[18] After one of the smaller boats is overturned, "foure that could swimme a litle kept themselves in deeper water and were saued by Captaine Cookes meanes. . . ."[19]

As in the 1587 account's tale of giant tortoises, the 1590 text focuses on treasures "fantastic" as well as financial. Once again, the voyagers encounter the New World's unbelievable bounty: on May 4, in just three hours, the expedition killed "an incredible number of foules"[20] and in August "caught great store of fish in the shallow water."[21] White presents this New World as an almost limitless land of Cockaigne: only fritter trees are not found. (More contemporarily minded readers might use the Big Rock Candy Mountain as an Edenic point of reference.)

Gothic Thriller Author-Hero

Besides presenting himself and his fellow Englishmen as courageous action-heroes swashbuckling across the land- and seascape, John White incorporates characteristics of yet another literary genre, the gothic thriller. The final section of the 1590 text is devoted to the discovery of what was *not* there—the "lost" colony. In a miniature gothic thriller set within the larger framework, White builds suspense with his descriptions of darkness, portents, and silence. He heightens the tension and sense of mystery through his detailed account of the repeated delays in landing near the settlement: "it was so exceeding darke, that we ouershot the place a quarter of a mile: . . . and called to them friendly; but we had no answere, . . . [and found at daybreak] in the sand the print of the Saluages feet of 2 or 3 sorts troaden yt at night, and as we entred vp the sandy banke vpon a tree, in the very browe thereof were curiously carued these faire Romaine letters CRO . . . but we found no . . . signe of distresse."[22] For White, his companions, and his readers, the unexplainable remains ineffably and tantalizingly mysterious.

Among the few remnants reported discovered at the settlement site is a handful of White's personal possessions: books, framed pictures and maps, armor—all accouterments of a cultivated Englishman of status. Even in his account of his departure from the mysteriously abandoned settlement, White ratifies his own superiority. After a "stormie and foule" night at anchor, "it was agreed by the Captaine and my selfe [White], with the Master and the others, to wey anchor, and go for the place at Croatoan. . . ."[23] This is a fortunate decision since, as he writes, the expedition "chanced . . . into a channell of deeper water . . . [and] could never have gone clear of the poynte. . . ."[24] The captain and White are the principals in this decision; "the Master and the others," secondary—almost an afterthought—another ratification of White's confidence in his own hierarchical superiority to someone in the position of sailing master.

Anointed Man of Destiny

White's sense of his hierarchical superiority reinforces for the audience the idea that White himself is "chosen." For White, "Man of Destiny," even seemingly unfortunate occurrences such as the particularly bad weather following the Croatoan departure are cast in a positive light: when he and his companions are forced to return to England, they learn of several rich treasure ships that, after a fierce battle, the English have taken. White devotes a lengthy passage to the battle, detailing its casualties and the vessels' treasure load.[25] Once again White has used the shape and proportion of the narrative to aggrandize himself as Proto-Englishman.

The May, June, and July segments of the 1590 voyage likewise present particular "evidence" of White's anointed status. The English are depicted as both skillful and lucky, repeatedly being "in the right place at the right time." White writes: "we were forced to diuide ourselves, . . . but then by reason of darkenesse we lost sight of each other, yet in the end the Admirall and the Moonelight happened to be together the same night" to successfully engage the Spanish fleet.[26] Further testimony to his "chosen state" appears in White's description of the sea journey northward from Kindricker's Mountes (north of contemporary Rodanthe) to Roanoke. After a dangerous sea breaks over the boat, "by the *will of God* and careful styrage of Captaine Cooke [they] came safe ashore."[27] Together, God's will and English skill triumph.

Ready to return home, White concludes this section of the narrative exuberantly, rejoicing over his "good fortune": first, in hearing the news that more Spanish treasure has been taken, then in his reunion with other vessels from England. Even the winds blow so that the expedition's destination must perforce be home to England: "seeing the winde hang so Northerly, that wee could not atteine the Iland of S. George, we gaue ouer our purpose to water there, and the next day framed our due course for England."[28]

A principal component of the narratives of both the 1587 and the 1590 voyages is the larger-than-life quality that White, the hero, achieves through his struggles with his various adversaries. The audience encounters repeated descriptions of White's luck, all contributing to the concept of White as "chosen." Particularly strong evidence occurs in the passages that detail God's "siding" with the English and punishing White's enemies.[29] White implies that Ferdinando is deliberately evil: "Fernando grieued greatly at their safe comming: for he purposely left them in the Baye of Portingall . . . but God disappointed his wicked pretenses."[30] As in the incident at Kindricker's Mountes, God and Englishmen again roundly defeat the antagonist: "Fernando the Master with all his company were not onely come home without any purchase, but also in such weakness by sickness, and death of the cheefest of their men, that they were scarse able to bring their ships into the harbour."[31] In yet another not-so-subtle "poke" at Ferdinando, the "cheefest of their men" die, but the base Ferdinando survives.

Conclusions

John White's accounts of his voyages, taken together as *literary* creations, give one man's view of what happened but reveal more than the simple linearity of events or even their own kinship with adventure/hero tales. For White, writing his adventures becomes a self-validation of them, a certification of an English man's quest for his culture's external evidences of success: wealth, prestige, stature, and power. As England of the sixteenth century develops into a dominant world power, this English audience's literary and political expectations are fulfilled, first in White's personal struggle with Simon

Ferdinando for individual hegemony and second in the nation's global struggle with Spain for international hegemony. The inference is clear: adversaries are vanquished; the English, justified.

Through skill, judgment, decisiveness, good fortune, and providential aid, John White, author-hero, triumphs. In both the 1587 and 1590 narratives, having bravely vanquished his opponents, having courageously encountered the "fantastic," and having resourcefully seized New World and Spanish treasure, John White endows himself with the near-mythic qualities that the increasing English hegemony required of its hero-explorers in the age of discovery and exploration. White's vivid narratives record events but also, importantly, reveal the tenor of an age and the portrait of an individual for both of whom peripatetic heroic adventure is a real possibility.

NOTES

1. Though most often referred to in modern histories by the mixed English and Portuguese/Spanish version of his name, Simon Fernandez, John White's anglicized version of the name is used for this analysis. The very un-Englishness of the name also creates "adversarial distance" for White's audience—which was very possibly unaware of or uninterested in what, for them, might be negligible cultural differences between Portuguese and Spanish persons or names.

2. The full citation for this work is: David Beers Quinn, ed., *The Roanoke Voyages, 1584-1590: Documents to Illustrate the English Voyages to North America Under the Patent Granted to Walter Raleigh in 1584*, 2 vols. Hakluyt Society Second Series, No. 104 (London: Hakluyt Society, 1955; reprint, New York: Dover, 1991).

3. Quinn, *Roanoke Voyages*, 2:516-517.

4. Quinn, *Roanoke Voyages*, 2:517.

5. Quinn, *Roanoke Voyages*, 2:518.

6. Quinn, *Roanoke Voyages*, 2:519.

7. Quinn, *Roanoke Voyages*, 2:520.

8. Quinn, *Roanoke Voyages*, 2:522. *Beake* is the English spelling for Vieques, Puerto Rico.

9. Quinn, *Roanoke Voyages*, 2:522.

10. Quinn, *Roanoke Voyages*, 2:522. Emphasis on *our* added.

11. Quinn, *Roanoke Voyages*, 2:518.

12. Quinn, *Roanoke Voyages*, 2:525.

13. Quinn, *Roanoke Voyages*, 2:525.

14. Quinn, *Roanoke Voyages*, 2:526.

15. Quinn, *Roanoke Voyages*, 2:530. In contrast to his depiction of Native Americans, White is relatively unconcerned with presenting a balanced picture of England's Iberian enemies—not surprising, given English public sentiment of the period.

16. Quinn, *Roanoke Voyages*, 2:599.

17. Quinn, *Roanoke Voyages*, 2:605.

18. Quinn, *Roanoke Voyages*, 2:517.

19. Quinn, *Roanoke Voyages*, 2:612.

20. Quinn, *Roanoke Voyages*, 2:601.

21. Quinn, *Roanoke Voyages*, 2:609.

22. Quinn, *Roanoke Voyages*, 2:613-614.

23. Quinn, *Roanoke Voyages*, 2:617.

24. Quinn, *Roanoke Voyages*, 2:617.

25. Quinn, *Roanoke Voyages*, 2:619-620.

26. Quinn, *Roanoke Voyages*, 2:605.

27. Quinn, *Roanoke Voyages*, 2:611, emphasis added.

28. Quinn, *Roanoke Voyages*, 2:622.

29. A popular theme in England of the period, an especially vivid expression of the notion that the English and God are "on the same side" can also be found in William Shakespeare's *Henry V*, in which, after the battle with the French, Henry states to Fluellen, "God fought for us" (*H5* 4.8.120).

30. Quinn, *Roanoke Voyages*, 2:525.

31. Quinn, *Roanoke Voyages*, 2:538.

Ralph Lane and the Rhetoric of Identity Creation

E. Thomson Shields Jr.

If there is a favorite villain in the fictional versions telling the story of England's attempts to colonize Roanoke Island—at least after Simon Fernandez, the Portuguese pilot portrayed by turns as incompetent and evil—it might be the governor of the 1585-1586 colony, Ralph Lane. In her 1948 historical novel *Roanoke Hundred*, Inglis Fletcher gives what has become a typical portrayal of Ralph Lane through a scene reminiscent of that in Disney's *Pocahontas*, in which Governor Ratcliffe sends the youngest colonist, Thomas, off alone to find John Smith, who has slipped off into the woods to meet Pocahontas. In Fletcher's novel, as the troubles between the English settlers and the native people of the Albemarle and Pamlico region grow worse and worse, Lane sends Colin Grenville out alone to scout the local Native American villages; the only reason Fletcher's Lane sends the young man out on such a dangerous mission is that Colin is a ward of Sir Richard Grenville, admiral of the fleet that brought Lane's colony to Roanoke Island and a man with whom Lane has feuded. As Fletcher describes the scene, Lane speaks to Colin:

"I have decided to send you to Wococon. From there you will take journeys along the rivers and to the great lake. I want a report on the activities of Indians in all the towns thereabout."

Colin bowed.

"Can't you speak?" Lane said sharply.

"Is it necessary? The governor has given an order."

Lane flushed. "You will go tonight at moonrise. You will take a canoe. I want you to go alone."

Colin waited silently.

"I said *alone*!" The governor's voice rose. The men in the room stopped talking.

Colin thought, He wants me to make objection. He wants to prove that I am afraid. Well, he will never prove that. He turned to leave.

"I don't want you to take anyone from Wococon, either. Do you understand?"

"Sir, I understand. I am to take a canoe at moonrise tonight, to go to Wococon, from there to visit Indian towns on the islands, rivers and the great lake."

"Yes, by God! And I want a complete report. If I find you have disobeyed and taken men with you, I'll have you in the stocks."

Colin smiled slightly. "Sir, I will leave at moonrise. Have you further orders?"

"No, by God, no, nor do I want insolence from you, Master Greenvile! . . ."[1]

There was silence in the room as he walked out and closed the door quietly.

Cavendish said, "God, Lane, you put a burden on that boy! Do you want him to be killed?"

"Churchman went alone among the Indians. He was not killed. . . ."

"Churchman went as an evangelist, a man of God. You are sending this lad out to spy. Won't the Indians know the difference?"

Lane hit the table with his fist. "The Indians? They are little above beasts. Do you think they reason as a white man reasons? . . ."

Lane turned to the clerks. One at a time the others left. The governor did not appear to notice. The last to go was Provost-Marshal Gorges. He said, "There is time for me to catch Grenville before he leaves, if you decide to change your order. It is an hour before moonrise."

"I won't change my order, Gorges." Lane's voice rose again. "I'll take the responsibility."

Gorges shrugged. "As you wish, sir. But if anything happens, there'll be a row from here to the Throne." He walked out. The door slammed.

Lane lifted the tankard. The clerks picked up their papers and slipped out noiselessly. The governor sat alone.[2]

Fletcher's version of Lane has all the elements of the villainous charges sometimes laid against him in fiction, legend, and history. He is vindictive, arrogant, and violent. He understands little of human nature, Native American or English. In every way, Fletcher portrays Lane as the epitome of a bad leader.

Similar pictures of Lane are given in other sources. For example, though Lane plays only a small, nonspeaking role in Paul Green's 1937 symphonic drama *The Lost Colony*, the drama's narrator, the Historian, describes Lane by saying that the fort and town built by the 1585-1586 expedition, the "Citie of Raleigh," were "firmly established and would likely have survived but for Lane's harsh treatment of the Indians."[3]

Modern historians tend to give a more complex picture of Lane than do writers of fictionalized accounts who need more clear-cut "good guys" and "bad guys." Still, David Beers Quinn, while seeing Lane as a good leader, has less confidence in Lane's personality. In his 1985 work, *Set Fair for Roanoke*, Quinn assesses him thus: "Lane was hot-tempered and did not deal easily with opposition; he was also, as we know from his letters, vain and boastful. As a professional soldier he tended to fall back on the use of force rather readily, instead of wasting time on diplomacy, and this may have helped to sour relations with his Indian neighbors."[4] Quinn does finish with the statement, "At the same time, it is clear that he was an effective leader in that he kept his men in good health if not always in good spirits."[5] Still, such a qualified definition of good leadership does little to save Lane's reputation. Quinn's words come dangerously close to damning with faint praise.[6]

Yet the same documents that Quinn uses to describe Lane as "vain and boastful," Lane's own writings, deserve to be reexamined. When compared to writings by other sixteenth- and seventeenth-century explorers and colonizers of North America, of both English and other European nationalities, what appears to modern readers as "vain and boastful" emerges instead as a standard rhetorical stance used by leaders of expeditions to explain what always seems to need explanation—why the expedition or colony was not more successful than it was. Almost no job, however well done, gains universal praise. A person can simply look at the letters to the editor in the *Virginian-Pilot* to see that no matter how hard crews from the power companies in the Hampton Roads region worked to restore power after 1998's Hurricane Bonnie, voices were still clamoring that the job done was inadequate. Lane's situation—and that of leaders from other expeditions—was no easier. Consider that leaders of exploration parties and colonizing efforts, such as Lane, had to answer to their European backers, who often saw little or no initial return on their investment, and the need for a rhetorical strategy that explains why such a venture was a success despite apparent failure becomes evident.

One of the works most responsible for Lane's reputation is his own version of the events on Roanoke Island in 1585-1586, his "An account of the particularities of the imployments of the English men left in Virginia by Sir Richard Greeneuill vnder the charge of Master Ralfe Lane," first printed in the 1589 edition of Richard Hakluyt's *Principall Navigations*.[7] Returning to England without having waited for Grenville's return with new colonists and fresh supplies, Lane finds that he must defend his decision to abandon his colonization attempt while still portraying himself as a good leader and successful man. Lane accomplishes both by embedding a narrative of an imagined perfect expedition within the story of the expedition's failed attempts to find the riches desired by European backers—an imagined story of what could have been done if the proper conditions had been available.

For example, describing what he would have done to reach a bay filled with pearls that Menatonon, the Native American king of Choanoke,[8] had told him about, Lane writes: "I woulde haue sent a small Barke with two Pinnesses about by Sea to the Northward to haue found out the Bay he spake of . . . while I with all the small boats I could make, and with two hundreth men would have gone to the head of the River of Choanoak, with the guides that Menatonon would have given, which I would haue been assured should haue bene of his best men. . . ."[9] Lane continues on for another two paragraphs or so describing this idealized perfect expedition, a narrative filled with *woulds* and *shoulds*. To preface this narrative, however, Lane tells why this perfect expedition was not accomplished. "If your supplie had come before the end of April," Lane writes, addressing Sir Walter Raleigh, "and . . . you had sent any store of boats, or men, to haue had them made in any reasonable time, with a sufficient number of men, and victuals to have found us untill the new corne were come in. . . ."[10] By the end of the story of the failed attempt to find either the pearls or a rich copper mine another group of Native Americans had told him about, Lane has his apologetics perfected. He notes that he could have found both the pearls and the copper "if the lorde had bene pleased" that sufficient supplies had been left at the start of the stay on Roanoke Island, or if God "had not in his eternall prouidence now at the last set some other course in these things, then the wisdome of man coulde looke into" and sunk a ship filled with supplies given to them by Sir Francis Drake's passing fleet.[11] Lane embeds within his narrative of rich lands the tale of how his chance at success had been thwarted. Lane's embedded story of the perfect expedition saves both his own reputation and that of the lands he explored.

Lane's rhetorical use of narrative, particularly his ability to develop himself as a heroic character in his own story, is a form of what Stephen Greenblatt called in the title of his 1980 book *Renaissance Self-Fashioning*.[12] Paraphrasing Greenblatt, in the sixteenth century many writers began to use the fictional characters in their works to define themselves as important parts of society. Because they blurred the line between the fictional characters and themselves, these writers were able to fashion their public personae as if they were literary characters—figures who submit to the absolute power outside themselves that controls their destiny and use what is given to them by that power greater than themselves to fight against the chaos or evil of the world.[13] What Greenblatt calls "self-fashioning" might equally well be called the rhetoric of identity-creation. Lane and others like him are not just defining themselves but convincing others to accept the identity defined.

Modern readers are generally disinclined to accept Lane's rhetorical stance. Lane seems to be a self-serving whiner, a man who refuses to accept responsibility for the shortcomings of the colonization attempt he led. His narrative is filled with unfulfilled intentions. The most famous of these is his plan to find and colonize what is now assumed to be the Chesapeake Bay region. Lane writes:

> My meaning was further at the head of the Riuer in the place of my descent where I would haue left my boates to haue raysed a sconse with a small trench, and a pallisado vpon the top of it, in the which, and in the garde of my boates I would haue left fiue and twentie, or thirtie men, with the rest would I haue marched with as much victuall as euery man could haue carried, with their mattocks, spades, and axes, two dayes iourney. In the ende of my marche vpon some conuenient plot would I haue raised another sconse according to the former, where I would haue left 15. or 20. And if it would haue fallen out conueniently, in the way I woulde haue raised my sayd sconse vpon some corne fielde, that my companie might haue liued vpon it.
>
> And so I would haue holden this course of insconsing euery two dayes march, vntil I had bene arriued at the Bay or Porte he [Menatonon] spake of: which finding to be worth the possession, I would there haue raised a mayne forte, both for the defence of the harboroughs, and our shipping also. . . .[14]

What strikes the modern reader is what Lane did *not* do—set up his series of forts between the Albemarle and Chesapeake regions. Yet for many readers in Lane's day, what he intended to do mattered more than what he accomplished in determining what sort of person Lane was. Outside forces could always prevent the achievement of a desired goal. Fate—in this instance, a storm that blows away the supplies and ship that Drake has left to help tide Lane and his colony over until Grenville's return—is the force to which anyone, even the leader of a colonizing expedition, must bow.

Two different sorts of works can help modern readers recognize that what they see as Lane's self-serving apology was not taken as vain boasting in the face of a failure for which he was responsible. First, at least one work that could easily have either denigrated Lane or, perhaps worse, ignored him altogether was Thomas Hariot's mainly descriptive text, *A Briefe and True Report of the New Found Land of Virginia*.[15] Published in 1588 and reprinted as part of Hakluyt's 1589 edition of the *Principall Navigations*, both the separate publication and the Hakluyt edition begin with a note from Lane and Hariot's impassioned defense of both the lands explored and the explorers. Before he begins any of his observations about Roanoke Island's riches, Hariot writes:

There haue bin diuers and variable reportes with some slaunderous and shameful speeches bruited abroad by many that returned from thence [i.e., Roanoke Island]. Especially of that discouery which was made by the Colony transported by Sir Richard Greinuile in the yeare 1585, being of all the others the most principal and as yet of most effect, the time of their abode in the countrey beeing a whole yeare, when as in the other voyage before they staied but six weekes; and the others after were onelie for supply and transportation, nothing more being discouered then had been before. Which reports haue not done a litle wrong to many that otherwise would haue also fauoured & aduentured in the action, to the honour and benefite of our nation, besides the particular profite and credite which would redound to themselues the dealers therein; as I by the sequele of euents to the shame of those that haue auouched the contrary shal be manifest. . . .[16]

Hariot then goes on to speak about members of the 1585-1586 expedition who have spoken out against the lands of Virginia: "Of our companie that returned some for their misdemenour and ill dealing in the countrey, haue beene there worthily punished; who by reason of their badde natures, haue maliciously not onlie spoken ill of their Gouernours; but for their sakes slaundered the countrie itselfe."[17] Hariot, in addition to defending Virginia, also defends Ralph Lane. Add to this Lane's opening remarks prefacing Hariot's *Briefe and True Report*: "Thus much vpon my credit I am to affirme: that things vniuersally are so truely set downe in this treatise by the author therof, an Actor in the Colony & a man no lesse for his honesty then learning commendable: as I dare boldely auoch it may well passe with the credit of truth euen amongst the most true relations of this age."[18] Though done with a sense of modesty, Lane vouches for his own goodness as a leader who helped explore a rich and potentially profitable land, no matter what slanders some have laid against it, by vouching for Hariot's credibility. That Hariot places this defense of Lane at the start of his work and that Hakluyt repeats it indicate the acceptance of Lane's self-fashioned identity by his contemporaries and the success of Lane's identity-creation rhetoric.

The second class of works modern readers might examine to understand the acceptance of Lane's rhetoric consists of the first-person narratives of leaders of similar expeditions—for example, Capt. John Smith's story of the Jamestown colony. In Smith's 1624 version, *The Generall Historie of Virginia, New-England, and the Summer*

Isles,[19] he, much like Lane, tells the "if only" story of what Jamestown could have been. Unlike Lane, however, Smith portrays how much worse the expedition could have been, rather than how it might have been improved. First, he reminds readers how catastrophic other settlement attempts had been: "And if any deeme it a shame to our Nation to haue any mention made of those inormities, let them peruse the Histories of the Spanyards Discoueries and Plantations, where they may see how many mutinies, disorders, and dissentions haue accompanied them. . . ."[20] By invoking the "historical" *leyenda negra*, or Black Legend, of Spanish conquest in the Americas, Smith embeds one narrative to contrast with his own, creating apologetics for the failures of Jamestown by showing the much worse failures of others. Then he presents the imagined narrative of what Jamestown without him might have been in order to show how successful a leader he was. "Now whether it had beene better for Captaine Smith . . . to haue abandoned the Countrey with some ten or twelue of them, who were called the better sort," writes Smith, leaving the rest of the settlers "to the fury of the Salvages, famine, and all manner of mischiefs, and inconveniences . . . I leaue to the censure of all honest men to consider."[21] He defends his actions by implying that if he erred, it was on the side of charity, not selfishness.

These examples suggest that what readers presently often see as Lane's unconscious declaration of his failures as a leader are, in fact, rhetorical devices accepted—perhaps even expected—by sixteenth- and early-seventeenth-century readers. While it makes good twentieth-century fiction, we must be careful about accepting Inglis Fletcher's condemnation of Lane as a bad rhetorician and, therefore, a bad leader. We ought not say, as do two of Fletcher's characters, "Lane is indeed a fool. . . . His talk in London is certainly a fool's talk. He has nothing to tell but what he might have done, *if*————[.]" "I know. A weak man soothes himself by excuses. A strong man takes the blame."[22] We should instead recognize that Lane fashions himself for himself in his rhetoric, the typical rhetoric of his day for creating the identity of a good leader. Whether he truly was a good leader can be determined only by examining his writings—along with other evidence—in the light of the rhetorical conventions of the time.

NOTES

1. Fletcher purposely spells the name *Greenvile* here because she has noted earlier in the work that Lane pronounces the name as such, *Green vile*.

2. Inglis Fletcher, *Roanoke Hundred* (Indianapolis: Bobbs-Merrill, 1948; reprint, New York: Bantam, 1972), 381-382.

3. Paul Green, *The Lost Colony: A Symphonic Drama of Man's Faith and Work* (1937; reprint, New York: Samuel French, 1980), 34.

4. David Beers Quinn, *Set Fair for Roanoke: Voyages and Settlements, 1584-1606* (Chapel Hill: University of North Carolina Press, 1985), 87.

5. Quinn, *Set Fair for Roanoke*, 87.

6. A notable exception is David Stick in his *Roanoke Island: The Beginnings of English America* (Chapel Hill: University of North Carolina Press, 1983). Stick avoids the issue of judging what Lane was "really like" by presenting his known actions and, wherever necessary, noting the source of information about Lane, whether an unknown author of a report that is "highly critical of the governor" about his choice to abandon the colony or Lane himself, who clearly would slant the information in his own favor. Stick, *Roanoke Island*, 148.

7. Richard Hakluyt, *The Principall Navigations, Voiages, and Discoveries of the English Nation* (London: George Bishop and Ralph Newberie, 1589), Hakluyt Society Extra Series, No. 39 (Cambridge, U.K.: Hakluyt Society and the Peabody Museum, 1965).

8. Choanoke: a Native American province along the Chowan River.

9. Hakluyt, *Principall Navigations*, 261-262.

10. Hakluyt, *Principall Navigations*, 739.

11. Hakluyt, *Principall Navigations*, 742.

12. Stephen Greenblatt, *Renaissance Self-Fashioning: From More to Shakespeare* (Chicago: University of Chicago Press, 1980).

13. This is a simplification of the ten items that Greenblatt lays out as "a set of governing conditions common to most instances of self-fashioning." Greenblatt, *Renaissance Self-Fashioning*, 8-9.

14. Hakluyt, *Principall Navigations*, 262-263.

15. Thomas Hariot, *A Briefe and True Report of the New Found Land of Virginia* (London: [R. Robinson], 1588); reprinted in Quinn, *Roanoke Voyages*, 1:320-321.

16. Quinn, *Roanoke Voyages*, 1:320-321.

17. Quinn, *Roanoke Voyages*, 1:322.

18. Quinn, *Roanoke Voyages*, 1:319.

19. John Smith, *The Generall Historie of Virginia, New-England, and the Summer Isles: with the names of the Adventurers, Planters, and Governours from their first beginning An: 1584 to this present 1624* (1624; reprint, Murfreesboro, N.C.: Johnson Publishing, n.d.).

20. Smith, *Generall Historie of Virginia*, 50.

21. Smith, *Generall Historie of Virginia*, 50.

22. Fletcher, *Roanoke Hundred*, 449.

Fig. 2. *The Finding of the Croatan Tree*, painted in 1935 by Sidney Newbold, hangs in the Virginia Dare Room in the Alumni House at the University of North Carolina at Greensboro. (Photo by Dan Smith, courtesy of the University of North Carolina–Greensboro Alumni Association.)

The Genteel Heroine:
Virginia Dare One Hundred Years Ago

Kelley Griffith

The most elegant building at my school, the University of North Carolina at Greensboro, is the Alumni House. Built in 1934, it is Georgian in style and gracious in its accommodations. It was designed not just for alumni activities but for formal and dignified events that are special to the university. The central and largest room in the building, the place where we hold most such events, is the Virginia Dare Room. At each end of the room there is a large mural. The one that everyone looks at, because the chairs are facing that way, is called *The Baptism of Virginia Dare* (see Figure 1, Frontispiece). The other is called *The Finding of the Croatan Tree* and depicts the moment when John White and his men discovered the tree with the word "CROATOAN" written on it (see Figure 2). The murals were painted in 1935 by Sidney Newbold.

In a sense this room is the heart of the university, and Virginia Dare inhabits it like a goddess in her temple. She is a fitting goddess for UNC-G, which was established originally as a college for women. Not only was Virginia Dare the first English person born in the New World, she was a native of what became North Carolina, and she was female. But what else might she have represented to those who founded the school in 1892 and to the students who came there in the years after? Or, more generally, how would people have told her story one hundred years ago?

To answer these questions, I propose to look at the literary treatments of Virginia Dare published around the turn of the twentieth century. Anyone studying imaginative writings about Virginia Dare owes a large debt to Robert D. Arner, whose essay "The Romance of Roanoke: Virginia Dare and the Lost Colony in American Literature," published in 1978, surveys this literature.[1] It is from this article that I have gleaned the five works I would like to discuss here. In chronological order of publication they are E. A. B. Shackelford's *Virginia Dare: A Romance of the Sixteenth Century* (New York: Thomas Whittaker, 1892), Sallie Southall Cotten's *The White Doe: The Fate of Virginia Dare: An Indian Legend* (Philadelphia: Lippincott, 1901), William Farquhar Payson's *John Vytal: A Tale of the Lost Colony* (New York: Harper, 1901), William Thomas Wilson's *For the Love of Lady Margaret: A Romance of the Lost Colony* (Charlotte: Stone and Barringer, 1908), and Mary Johnston's *Croatan* (Boston: Little, Brown, 1923).

All of these works belong to a genre of literature that I call the Genteel Romance. Near the end of the nineteenth century, the most heated literary controversy in the United States was between the proponents of "realism" and the proponents of "romance." Defenders of romance asserted that "realism" was merely "literary photography" and dealt with unappealing and even degrading subject matter. Defenders of realism, such as William Dean Howells, argued that "romance" was not only untrue to reality but damaged readers' understanding by giving them a distorted view of life. Today we see realism as having clearly won the argument. The most admired American literature from this period—works by Howells, Henry James, Mark Twain, Kate Chopin, Edith Wharton, and Stephen Crane, among many others—emerged from the realistic movement. Yet in the 1890s, just when realism seemed to be triumphing, the forces of romance staged so successful a counterattack that realism seemed for the moment to have lost not only the battle but the war as well.

The romances written during that period mirror the cultural ethos that George Santayana called the "genteel tradition." Santayana maintained that a schizophrenia separated the intellectual life of America from its vital, energetic, practical life. One half of the American mind "has floated gently in the backwater, while, alongside, in invention and industry and social organization the other half of the mind was leaping down a sort of Niagara Rapids."[2] American intellectuals, he said, disapproved of the untidiness of business, industry, and politics and retreated into a fantasy world in which people of good family were revered, morality was absolute, people had free will, Providence guided all human actions, America was the greatest nation on earth, and everything turned out for the best.[3] The art of the genteel tradition, he said, was imitative and decorative, like "those candlesticks, probably candleless, sometimes displayed as a seemly ornament in a room blazing with electric light."[4]

Although enormously popular at the time, the genteel romances are mostly third-rate works whose authors—people like F. Marion Crawford, S. Weir Mitchell, Winston Churchill, Maurice Thompson, Thomas Nelson Page, Richard Harding Davis, Mary Johnston, Paul Leicester Ford, Charles Major, and George Bar McCutcheon—have mostly been forgotten. But although these works may no longer find an appreciative audience, they nonetheless do "cultural work." Their popularity and the seriousness with which critics and readers took them suggest that they reflected the values and tastes of a large number of American readers.

One manifestation of the sudden rebirth of romance was the numerous critics who vigorously attacked "bad" fiction (realism) and defended "good" fiction (romance). In magazine articles and book reviews, they spelled out the qualities that good fiction should have. Preeminently, fiction should represent the "ideal." By this, they meant that fiction should avoid "mere materialism"[5] and "should strive to portray society not solely as it is but as it is hoped it will be in that 'possibly better' state suggested by present improvement."[6] To accomplish that purpose, authors should tell a "good story," one filled with suspense, action, "adventure," exotic locales, noble heroes, pure heroines, and demonic villains.[7] The hero, especially, should represent "the possible reach and the occasional achievement of the human soul."[8]

Fiction, furthermore, should exclude objectionable materials—mere "fact," or "instincts," or "passions," or the "sordid."[9] Most objectionable to the genteel critics was a frank treatment of sexuality, which they felt was shockingly prevalent in European realistic fiction. Instead, fiction should deal only with the "essentially spiritual element in sex."[10] As for purely physical sex, "There are things too low to be spoken of, which indeed become low by being spoken of."[11] In response to claims that romance was just escapist fare, its defenders said that romance should be relevant to American life by "purifying" and "idealizing" American democracy.[12] Some even called for heroic actions in imperialistic ventures such as the Spanish-American War. Such endeavors would allow Americans to *live* romance, not just write or read it.[13]

The authors who actually wrote genteel romances used a number of easily recognizable conventions to manifest the "ideal." Most important were those conventions that invoked medieval chivalry: heroes who are brave, adept with sword, and courtly to women; heroines who are pure, beautiful, and asexual; dastardly villains who strive to deprive the hero of his family inheritance and marry the heroine; a plot in which the hero pleads for the heroine's affections and beats off nefarious attacks by the villain. The climax of the plot is an all-or-nothing sword fight between hero and villain, followed by the heroine's acquiescence to the hero's ardent appeals for her favor. The appropriate setting for these narratives is the pre-industrial past, a time when chivalric behavior was supposedly practiced and when people fought with swords. But although Genteel Romances pretended to be about an idealized past, they in fact provided paradigms for modern society and suggestions about what the United States should do and be. In spite, for example, of the critics' high-flown rhetoric about democracy, the romances themselves were profoundly anti-democratic. In them, the upper classes alone are capable of genuine chivalry. They are culturally and biologically superior to ordinary people and should, therefore, rule over them. This social and political hierarchy applies even to the United States, where the founding fathers— Washington, Adams, Jefferson, Hamilton—are presented as homegrown aristocrats.

In keeping with this anti-democratic drift, the Genteel Romances were often racist. Many of them did not deal directly with race, but whenever white characters encounter dark-skinned people, "chivalry" is almost always coextensive with the "Anglo-Saxon race" and is a code word for domination of whites over nonwhites. The most notorious and extreme example of such racism is the trilogy of romances written by Thomas Dixon about the post-Civil War period in the South: *The Leopard's Spots* (1902), *The Clansman* (1905), and *The Traitor* (1907).[14] *The Clansman*, the best known of these today, celebrates the rise of the Ku Klux Klan and is the basis for D. W. Griffith's film *The Birth of a Nation* (1915).

The five books about Virginia Dare mentioned above feature elements common to the Genteel Romance. In Shackelford's *Virginia Dare: A Romance of the Sixteenth Century*, the Indians venerate Virginia for her spirituality. As she grows to young womanhood she becomes a paragon of Christian virtue. She and Manteo's son, Iosco, fall in love. But not until Iosco proves willing to live by Christian values will she marry him. This book is unique among the five for actually allowing Virginia to marry an Indian.

Cotten's *The White Doe: The Fate of Virginia Dare: An Indian Legend*, a long narrative poem, recounts the supposed Indian legend about Virginia's metamorphosis into a white doe. Like Shackelford's, Cotten's Virginia grows up to embody "civilization" and thus earn the Indians' reverence. Just when she and an Indian brave, Okisko, seem close to marrying, a jealous magician turns her into a white doe. Okisko's attempt to return her to human form ends tragically. She dies before they can declare their love. At the end, Cotten improbably casts the story as a parable of American "progress."

Payson's *John Vytal: A Tale of the Lost Colony* begins in London with a sword fight in which Vytal, with the help of the poet Christopher Marlowe, protects the love of his life, Eleanor White, from rapacious villains. Vytal, Eleanor, Marlowe, and the villains all end up on the same ship sailing to Roanoke Island. Much to his chagrin, Vytal finds Eleanor already married to Ananias Dare, who in this narrative is a drunkard, coward, miser, rapist, and traitor. After John White leaves for England, Vytal and Eleanor lead the colony to safety, Ananias conveniently dies, Vytal and Marlowe fight the Spaniards, and, at the last possible moment, Vytal and Eleanor are free to marry. Although by this point Virginia Dare is still a child, she seems headed toward an alliance with Manteo's son, Dark Eye. She is called White Doe and is "always clad in white draperies, loose and clinging" and goes "barefoot, hatless, and unrestrained."[15]

Wilson's *For the Love of Lady Margaret: A Romance of the Lost Colony* is another swashbuckler that likewise begins with a whopping sword fight. The aristocratic hero fights pirates, Spaniards, demented family members, and traitorous English, all on behalf of his pure but coy lady love. As in most of these narratives, the gentlefolk use archaic language that signals chivalric elevation: words like *thee, thy, thine, ye, an* (for "if"), *'twere, naught, mayhap,* and *hast.* By the time this narrative begins, the "Lost Colony" is already lost. The hero accompanies John White on his return to Roanoke Island, where instead of the "Lost Colony" the hero finds his lady love taken captive by the villains. With the help of Manteo and an Indian princess, he rescues her and returns triumphantly to England. John White gives us our only glimpse of Virginia Dare when he worries that she may have been slain by the "savages."[16]

In Johnston's *Croatan* the colonists settle with Manteo's people in the North Carolina foothills, where Virginia grows up to embody spiritual and "Anglo Saxon" virtues. She is taken into captivity by the Shawnee, who carry her to their settlement over the mountains and revere her as a prophetess. The English youth who rescues and ultimately marries her revels in tales about King Arthur and St. George and the Dragon. He calls his quest for Virginia his chivalric "*devoir.*" Of these five authors, Johnston was the best known. She began her writing career with two very popular romances—*Prisoners of Hope* (1898) and *To Have and to Hold* (1900).

If we extract and combine the Virginia Dare story from these five books, we end up with something like the following: The settlers arrive. Virginia is born. John White leaves. After much uncertainty and debate, the settlers join Manteo's tribe at Croatan. Virginia begins to grow up. As a child, she learns Indian ways but is always apart from and different from the Indians. Her mother or other English people teach her how to read. She learns Bible stories, hymns, and psalms. The Indians venerate her for her spirituality. Her signature is whiteness: she is the White Doe, with blue eyes and golden hair, who always dresses in white and looks like an "angel."[17] The place where she grows up is Edenic. It is "the new world of romance and beauty,"[18] "an island with beauty abloom," saturated with "languid perfume."[19] Virginia accords perfectly with this paradise. She is "light and aerial," "a gossamer spirit," a "butterfly," one of the "wild ferns and unnamed blossoms of the field."[20] She and her Indian playmates are "deer, revelling in their forest freedom," "sylvanites" who live in an "Eden unbounded."[21]

When she reaches young womanhood, the question looms: Whom will she marry? A white person or an Indian? Will she marry at all? The Indians in these narratives are nothing like the real Indians described by Arthur Barlow, Thomas Hariot, and John White. They are Noble Savages: the "Fearless Red Hunter," "Lithe as the antelope," whose "birthright" is the forest.[22] They could serve "as a model for some picture, representing savage beauty."[23] Yet despite their nobility and oneness with nature, they are still "the rude, untutored savage."[24] They are inferior to the Europeans and subservient to them. Wilson's depiction of Manteo is typical: Manteo "dogged my [the hero's] footsteps, as though he were a tame animal and I his master."[25] Even the one Indian deemed a fitting mate for Virginia (in Shackelford's tale) must first become "Western" before he can marry her.

And therein lies the answer to what Virginia Dare will do for the rest of her life. Her mission, her career, will be to bring civilization to the barbarians and to preserve it among the surviving whites. The concluding scene of Shackelford's *Virginia Dare* transforms her into a missionary heroine who arrives at Manteo's village just in time to disrupt a demonic Indian worship service and help an Anglican priest convert all the Indians to Christianity. The priest watches her "pick up one brown little boy, who was scarcely more than a papoose, and hold him close to her heart."[26] To the Indians in Cotten's *The White Doe*, she "Seemed divinely 'dowed with reason./She, the heir of civilization,/They, the slaves of superstition,/Gave to her a silent rev'rence/Growing better with such giving."[27] Her Indian suitor loves her and gives her "all his heart's rude homage."[28] Mary Johnston's Virginia feigns madness so that she will not have to marry one of her Shawnee captors. At the end of the narrative, she and her "golden haired" lover pledge "not to let England, not to let Christendom, die from remembrance. They [are] bent that the sixteenth century of Europe should not perish, overlaid and smothered by primeval forest and the barbarian." Their children and children's children "must know, must remember!"[29]

The story I have recounted here fits the conservative values about society, race, and the roles of women that pervaded America one hundred years ago. We can guess that many women who attended the Woman's College of the University of North Carolina envisioned themselves conforming to a pattern something like Virginia Dare's life. They would bring culture and religion to their students, to their husbands and children, and, possibly as missionaries, to the dark-skinned, benighted peoples of the world. Compare this pattern to that represented in two recent novels about Virginia Dare: Sonia Levitin's *Roanoke: A Novel of the Lost Colony* (New York: Atheneum, 1973) and

Harry Scott Gibbons's *Tall Woman: The Story of Virginia Dare* (New York: Bantam, 1984). Both these works reflect a new set of assumptions at the turn of our century. As with the Virginia Dare of a hundred years ago, the protagonists of these novels learn the Native American way of life. But this time they find it superior to the European or English. When forced to choose, they take Native American rather than Western culture.

Since Virginia Dare ceased to exist in the historical record when she was only a few weeks old, storytellers have almost free rein to reinvent her story. What will her story be in the future? Perhaps a hint lies in the many stories about her contemporary, Pocahontas. Literary critic Philip Young claims that the retellings of Pocahontas's story make her into a national archetype, the founding "grandmother" of the nation.[30] The stories about Virginia Dare also tap archetypal sources. But in contrast to Pocahontas, she becomes a kind of "daughter" of the nation. We, as her surrogate parents, fear for her safety when she's an infant. As she grows into childhood, we want to see her safe and well brought up—learning the skills necessary to cope in the wilderness but at the same time learning good values. When she becomes a young woman, we worry about whom she should marry and what her career might be—whether as wife, mother, teacher, or leader. These "family" considerations make her story not just national but "personal." They probably account for her story's appeal over the years, and my guess is that they will determine its future structure. Whatever forms it may assume, the story will no doubt speak to the beliefs, needs, and passions of those who tell it, hear it, and read it, just as it did a hundred years ago.

NOTES

1. Arner revised this article and published it as a booklet, *The Lost Colony in Literature* (Raleigh: America's Four Hundredth Anniversary Committee, North Carolina Department of Cultural Resources, 1985).

2. George Santayana, "The Genteel Tradition in American Philosophy," in *The Genteel Tradition: Nine Essays by George Santayana*, ed. Douglas L. Wilson (Cambridge: Harvard University Press, 1967), 39-40.

3. George Santayana, "The Genteel Tradition at Bay," in *The Genteel Tradition*, 169, 175.

4. George Santayana, "The Moral Background," in *The Genteel Tradition*, 81.

5. Walter Taylor Field, "A Plea for the Ideal," *Dial* 14 (April 1, 1893): 206.

6. Richard Burton, "The Persistence of Romance," *Dial* 16 (December 16, 1893): 380.

7. Burton, "Persistence of Romance," 380.

8. Hamilton Wright Mabie, "The Two External Types of Fiction," *Forum* 19 (March 1895): 46.

9. Mabie, "Two External Types of Fiction," 44.

10. B. A. Crackanthorpe, "Sex in Modern Literature," *Nineteenth Century* 37 (April 1895): 614.

11. James Ashcroft Novel, "The Fiction of Sexuality," *Contemporary Review* 67 (April 1895): 494-495.

12. William Morton Payne, "The Great American Novel," *Dial* 21 (December 1896): 318-319.

13. Maurice Thompson, "The Critics and the Romancers," *Independent* 52 (August 9, 1900): 1920.

14. *The Leopard's Spots: A Romance of the White Man's Burden—1865-1900* (New York: Grosset and Dunlap, 1902); *The Clansman: An Historical Romance of the Ku Klux Klan* (New York: Doubleday, 1905); *The Traitor: A Story of the Fall of the Invisible Empire* (New York: Doubleday, 1907).

15. William Farquhar Payson, *John Vytal: A Tale of the Lost Colony* (New York: Harper, 1901), 275.

16. William Thomas Wilson, *For the Love of Lady Margaret: A Romance of the Lost Colony* (Charlotte: Stone and Barringer, 1908), 206.

17. E. A. B. Shackelford, *Virginia Dare: A Romance of the Sixteenth Century* (New York: Thomas Whittaker, 1892), 108.

18. Shackelford, *Virginia Dare*, 157.

19. Sallie Southall Cotten, *The White Doe: The Fate of Virginia Dare: An Indian Legend* (Philadelphia: Lippincott, 1901), 23.

20. Payson, *John Vytal*, 215.

21. Payson, *John Vytal*, 275.

22. Cotten, *The White Doe*, 24.

23. Wilson, *For the Love of Lady Margaret*, 234.

24. Cotten, *The White Doe*, 43.

25. Wilson, *For the Love of Lady Margaret*, 204.

26. Shackelford, *Virginia Dare*, 196.

27. Cotten, *The White Doe*, 43.

28. Cotten, *The White Doe*, 47.

29. Mary Johnston, *Croatan* (Boston: Little, Brown, 1923), 280.

30. Robert S. Tilton, *Pocahontas: The Evolution of an American Narrative* (Cambridge, U.K.: Cambridge University Press, 1994), 178-179.

Climate For Colonization

Joyce Youings

My task is to speak in general terms about the economic and social climate in England when Sir Walter Raleigh was preparing to follow up Philip Amadas and Arthur Barlow's exploratory voyage in 1584. This is a tall order, as even such a small island off the edge of Europe nurtured a society of great complexity and an economy of great regional variety. All I can do in the space available is to highlight the main ongoing features and to draw particular attention to the situation in the early 1580s.

Rural Employment

The great majority, perhaps as many as 90 percent, of Queen Elizabeth's subjects lived very close to the land, either in villages (that is, small rural communities) or, especially in the upland regions of the West and North of England, in hamlets (that is, groups of three or four farms). Only a minority lived in total isolation from their neighbours as most farming families do in England today. In each case they derived their sustenance primarily from their own labour, whether that was devoted predominantly to arable or pastoral farming or, the most rewarding, a combination of both. It depended, of course, on the local terrain, i.e., soil conditions, which varied enormously, even within relatively small areas, and on the weather, which determined not only long-term possibilities but also short-term fluctuations in the quality of the harvest. These in turn dictated not only how well individual households lived, but also how much cash income they could generate by meeting market demand for grain, meat, dairy produce, hides, skins, and, particularly, wool. Only thus could they pay their annual rent to their landlord and the occasional entry fine for new or renewed tenancies. But for most of Tudor England's tens of thousands of small family farmers, those occupying up to ten or fifteen acres of arable land, cash came very largely from part-time labour on the larger farms in the neighbourhood. Younger sons in particular, and also daughters, either worked as "day-labourers" or went off in their teens to live as resident farm servants. Even eldest sons left home until their fathers died or became too old to work the farm and their heirs could move back and marry. Over half of the age-group fifteen to twenty-four lived in other people's households. Farming households were therefore usually small and rarely comprised more than two generations. The same applied to many other sectors of the English people: foreign observers thought it eccentric and indicative of a want of familial affection!

Supplementary employment, largely seasonal, was also available in the extractive and manufacturing industries, most of which were rural-based: tin mining in the South West, lead mining in Somerset, stone quarrying in many parts of the country. Almost universally, but especially in the highland regions, the combing, spinning, and weaving of wool, thread, and cloth occupied whole farming families in such hours as were left after work on the land was complete. This, of course, could be done at home. The entrepreneurial talent built up over the centuries to organise the essentially rural manufacture of woollen cloth was phenomenal: the rich clothier was no figure of fiction, but in certain areas, notably in parts of Yorkshire and the South West, the various processes involved in cloth making were organised around local markets whose craftsmen-suppliers operated on a weekly cash basis. To those in government circles in Westminster, the cloth "interest," which provided so much employment, was always paramount.

One must not forget, too, that from farms on or near England's long coastline many people went fishing to supply their own and others' enormous demand for this cheap food. Some farmers signed on seasonally as merchant seamen, and it was common for wills in the maritime counties to contain bequests, not only of farm implements but also of such items as bosuns' whistles and shares in boats. Even ships' masters would arrange to be home to help their wives with sheep-shearing and the harvest. Tudor country people were extraordinarily multi-skilled, and their diversified economy provided them with considerable protection against the vagaries of both the harvest and the market. Was Barlow, perhaps, a man equally at home on land and at sea?

Rise of the Larger Farm

So much for the smaller rural fry, whose degree of security on the land they farmed ranged from that of the tenant "at will," virtually at the mercy of his landlord, through a great variety of customary tenures that enjoyed considerable protection from manor courts, to those, in some parts of the country quite numerous, who could call on the Common Law to defend their freehold. But the sixteenth century also brought a great increase in England of the larger, and usually more specialised, farms. Most villages, in fact, were characterised by the existence of a half dozen or more farms of one hundred acres or more (of arable land) and many more acres of upland pasture. Especially in the vicinity of urban markets their owners concentrated on livestock farming and the production of meat and raw hides. Much of their land was leasehold, which gave them a degree of medium-term security, but they often accumulated a fair bit of copyhold and even freehold, in the process dispossessing their smaller neighbours. A favourite method was to foreclose on cash loans to needy neighbours. They were not so much old-fashioned enclosers as new-fashioned engrossers. What distinguished them was the scale of their operations and their concentration on agriculture, employing rather than being employed. Indeed, governments were nervous of their control of the labour market. These larger-scale landholders, rather than the small farmers, together with many gentlemen, were alive to news of new farming techniques coming in from the Continent, especially in the 1570s, or at least were successful in improving grain yields by the use of extraneous fertilisers. They first used lime to good effect in about 1578. Indeed, the 1570s and 1580s saw the nearest thing in Tudor England to an "agrarian revolution," though if Arthur Barlow told his friends in East Budleigh that he could take them where they could grow three crops a year, they would have told him to pull the other leg! New methods tended to increase the polarization of the farming community by putting more money into the pockets of only the larger farmers. The "yeomen," as they had come to be called, tended to dominate local affairs, monopolising the offices of churchwarden and, toward the end of the century, of Overseer of the Poor. Under the eyes of the thin scatter of the justices, they were the ones who kept the peace, it being in their interests to do so. In that sense governments relied upon them, not least because they were more inclined than their humbler neighbours to stay where they were. Moreover, they were better able, even than some gentlemen, and certainly than ordinary husbandmen, to buy farms for their younger sons or send them into such profitable callings as trade or the law.

Towns and Trade

In this great sea of English countryside, the towns played a vital role by virtue of their facilities for processing, fashioning, and distributing the products of the fields and pastures. Through them countrymen were linked with the wider world, even with foreign nations. Their economy was chequered, so much so that some historians, taking too literally the towns' own cries for help, have described the sixteenth century as one of "crisis." The towns were not only very different from rural communities; they also ranged both in size and character from enlarged villages that had acquired urban accessories such as markets, fairs, and hostelries, to the score or so of large provincial cities, and so to London, which was in a category of its own. Their more established residents, depending on their degree of organisation by local craft guilds, generally followed one full-time occupation, though not always throughout their working lives. On the whole, town dwellers were far less "handy" than their country cousins, and part-time employment was largely unskilled. But polarisation of wealth was even more pronounced than in rural communities. Especially in London, the richest inhabitants, merchants engaged in overseas trade, were very rich indeed. By and large the bigger the town, the more institutionalised its government, with tighter controls over people's activities. Apprenticeships to local craftsmen lasted roughly seven years, from about seventeen years old to the extraordinarily advanced age of twenty-four, and in the case of merchants even longer. The government believed that towns were potentially more tractable but was concerned at the expansion of their population, which from the middle of the sixteenth century was greater than that in the countryside. In fact, one anomaly of English society in the early modern period is that, in spite of the far greater constraints and regimentation of urban life, Tudor people at every level of society were drawn to it in seemingly ever-increasing numbers, especially to the larger towns and to London preeminently. They came for many reasons. The one that would probably have sprung most quickly to the lips of contemporary commentators was pressure of population on rural employment.

Population Movements

Contemporaries saw and historians agree that in the course of the sixteenth century the English population rose substantially, increasing by about 50 percent between 1500 and 1600, and by at least 30 percent during Elizabeth's reign. It sounds like a lot, though it is marginal compared with population growth in many parts of the world today. But the most important point to grasp is that in Tudor England—and well-informed contemporaries knew this—growth was from a low base: today's population technocrats tell us that while it rose from about 2.75 million in 1541 to over 4 million in 1601, two centuries earlier, before the Black Death of 1349, the country had supported, without more than occasional pressure on resources, whether of employment or food, considerably more people than it did even in 1600. The continuing fall from 1350 to 1450 had had very pronounced social and economic effects in town and country alike. The tide had slowly turned toward the end of the fifteenth century, but even in the 1530s Henry VIII's advisers had warned him that he ruled over a "penury" of people, a dangerous situation for a king prepared to take on the military might of his European neighbours. It is ironic that Queen Elizabeth, who dreaded above all the financial expense of war, was warned about the dangers of an excess of people.

In fact, at least as far as the country as a whole was concerned, she had little cause to worry. In simple terms a rise—or fall—in the number of mouths to be fed depends on the relationship between birthrates and death rates. Where particular places are concerned—villages, small towns, large towns and cities, and even whole counties and regions—there is also the factor of movement into and out of them. This was only marginally important nationally, the arrival of overseas immigrants toward the end of the century actually affecting only certain towns, including London. Birthrates, the demographers tell us, are largely determined by such factors as the number of children per marriage, which in turn depends to a great extent on the age at which men and women marry. We now know that ordinary people married late in Tudor England, men on average in their late twenties, women in their middle twenties—late, that is, in terms of childbearing. Even so, that still left the possibility of raising a baker's dozen. In fact, few marriages resulted in more than three or four children reaching their teens. What is more, a considerable number of men and women, especially resident domestic and farm servants, remained single all their lives. Had there not been other limiting factors, though, the population could still have reached at least the highest medieval levels by 1600.

That it did not was to a great extent due to levels of mortality. Of only marginal importance was the death of infants. Infant mortality remained fairly high, but women who lost babies, because they did not have to breast-feed them for the traditional two and even three years, would more quickly conceive replacements. The great early-modern killer was epidemic disease, principally bubonic plague and, more rarely, the sweating sickness to which young men and women were particularly vulnerable.

Plague was not new, of course, but its outbreaks were more frequent in Tudor England than in previous times. Epidemic diseases were, in fact, a far greater immediate cause of premature death than starvation, although a run of bad harvests weakened people's resistance to disease. Harvest failures were made worse—not only by poor facilities for transporting bulky goods to areas of greater need (and higher prices) but also by the natural propensity of farmers to hoard their produce, both for local and family consumption and, more reprehensibly, in the hope that prices in local markets would rise still further.

Mortality, for whatever cause, as compared with the birthrate, was far higher in towns than in rural communities, and especially so in large cities, with London suffering worst of all. The prosperous little cloth-making town of Crediton in Devon lost through plague in 1571 nearly a quarter of its total population, and London in 1563 about the same proportion, a massive twenty thousand people. In the countryside not only was the death rate not quite so high and the outbreaks not so frequent, but there was also a degree of catching up as young people, able to obtain vacant farms, married earlier. That happened more rarely in the towns, where sheer weight of numbers produced a longer wait for dead men's shoes.

Migration

The effect of the more frequent, and more devastating, outbreaks of epidemics in the towns of Tudor England would have been to destroy many of them altogether had it not been for the replacement process already mentioned which, it is believed, more than balanced the mortality, namely inward migration. That phenomenon often took place in stages, starting with movement from countryside to neighbouring town and proceeding from the provincial towns to London, always, that is, from the north and west to the southeast. Men and women came to London (some four thousand to five thousand a year in the 1580s) from as far away as Yorkshire, though not very many moved to the metropolis from the southwestern counties. In fact, recent research has shown that most of the migrants who failed to find a niche in London and who were arrested by the authorities as vagrants came, or claimed to have come, largely from the adjacent Home Counties. Successful or not, most were young (i.e., in their teens) and male, and they came for a variety of reasons. Only to a very limited extent were they driven out of their places of birth by actual unemployment; most, like Dick Whittington (who was a gentleman, remember), came to better themselves. A high proportion were younger sons looking for better prospects than had been available at home, including studying to be a lawyer. A large number came to take up formal apprenticeships already arranged by their families and could expect a comfortable and relatively secure future, though some met with disappointment and ran away, or failed to make the grade. Others, especially women, had employment arranged for them by or with relations as resident domestic servants, the largest by far of the categories of London's employees. By no means all who found themselves hailed before the magistrates as "vagrants" within the meaning of the law had arrived as the rogues and vagabonds of popular literature. Still less did they come in gangs with a common and alien culture. Far more came with hope of employment than because they had heard that London had more to offer by way of charity. But that did not stop their begging (which was illegal), stealing, and, even worse in the eyes of the powers-that-be, being "idle" and "masterless." In every town and city, London in particular, enormous efforts were indeed made, by a combination of public and private charity, to relieve the most desperate and, by less humanitarian ways, to be rid of the problem. Vagrants were not, so far as I know, sent to sea, but those like Raleigh who obtained commissions to impress seamen were enjoined to seek out the unemployed. They perhaps were the fortunate. The unlucky (some six hundred a year in the early 1580s) were herded into the former royal palace of Bridewell, the chief institution in London at which some attempt was made to provide work, so far as possible competing only with the import trades (in the making of wool cards, for example). But it was a losing battle, and particularly in London's inner suburbs from Clerkenwell around to Southwark, and also to the west in Holborn and even Westminster, countless men and women lived, bore children, and died in the streets or hidden in the warrens of cellars. Thus, in spite of such a high mortality from disease, and to a certain extent from hunger, London's population increased at a far higher rate than that of the country at large, from 3 percent of the rising national total in 1545 to 6 percent by the later 1590s. All the larger English towns had their complement of deserving and undeserving poor, but their problems were largely containable. London's was not: the superabundance of people about which the queen was warned was not so much a national problem as one that lay very largely at her own back door.

The very year of her accession had seen the problem, if such indeed it was over the country as a whole, very nearly solved. The rise in the country's total population had really gotten firmly under way in the 1540s—whether because of a lowering of the age of marriage or less virulent outbreaks of plague, or indeed for other reasons, we do not know. This continued during the early 1550s and then went suddenly into reverse in the years 1557-1559 as a result of a great and almost universal outbreak of a viral infection akin to influenza. Even in rural areas death rates trebled, especially among young adults, leading to an overall decrease of population of about 6 percent. Arthur Barlow's arrival in May 1559 must have brought particular joy to his family in East Budleigh, an omen of better times under a new queen, perhaps coinciding with his father's taking possession of a vacant farm. Mortality in east Devon had been particularly severe. The 1560s and 1570s were to be, for the most part, good years. In 1583 the younger Richard Hakluyt, with tongue slightly in cheek, looked back on twenty-seven years (not entirely coincidentally the exact length of the queen's reign to that date!) not only of good harvests but of "seldom sickness." It was indeed almost true, but the corollary was a return to population growth, a national increase in the decade 1576-1586 of more than 11 percent, higher than at any time since the late

1540s. But for our purposes the important thing is the very speedy recovery, in terms of births, between 1559 and 1564, so that in the early 1580s England was full of men and women in their early twenties, especially in London. The metropolis was also, as throughout the sixteenth century, home to thousands of "strangers" from overseas. How many of them sailed in 1584 with Amadas and Barlow?

Underemployment

And yet, as Hakluyt knew very well, this larger population had no need to be destitute. Even in the 1580s there were still, in every part of England, hundreds of acres of waste (that is, land once cultivated and capable of being put to good use), as well as marshes and fen that could have been, and later were, reclaimed. Even Hakluyt, while at pains to stress the increase in population, declared that England could support a fivefold increase in numbers. Foreign observers said that the English were lazy—Devonians certainly were—and that if so minded, they could provide a surplus of grain sufficient to upset altogether the reliance of their export trade on woollen cloth. English commentators such as the astute Sir Thomas Smith, who was so keen on Raleigh's projects in Ireland, were more inclined to argue that at the root of the problem of migration, especially toward the end of the sixteenth century, lay lack of sufficient alternative full-time employment to farming. Apart from small-scale industries limited to supplying a fixed local demand, there was little, in fact virtually no, large-scale industrial development available to mop up surplus rural labour except the almost universal involvement in cloth making. Such as there was—tinworking, quarrying, and in the seaports shipbuilding—was under-capitalised and, as already indicated, supplied mostly by part-time labour. There were a few new industries by Elizabeth's reign, such as the making of brass cannons in the Weald (or forest) of Sussex and Kent, and of window glass in the former county, but on the whole they were not labour-intensive. Joan Thirsk and others have shown that Elizabethan England was full of new ideas and new "projects," but few had progressed or spread very far, and many had suffered through their promoters' seeking, and being favoured with, royal grants of patents of monopoly. Also, apart from those industries necessarily based in the countryside, the rest, both old and new, such as soapmaking and metalworking, were sited in London near the main national markets for consumer goods. Inevitably, as in our own day, they exerted a fatal attraction. Perhaps it would have been too much to hope for some liaison between the rural industrial entrepreneurs and the "governors" of the newly established, largely urban, and significantly named "Houses of Correction." Were their unfortunate inmates the people the Peckhams had in mind in 1583 when they advocated shipping to the New World "a great number of men [and women, and even children] which do now live idly at home," there to be set on work? If so, they would have met opposition from those "protectionists" who thought that England already imported too many foreign wares.

Rural theorists did envisage, though, for "those persons as are no men of art or science," employment "in matters of husbandry."

The Better Sort

Most of what I have said already has been about the lower and middling orders, but Elizabethan society, in spite of all we hear about the "rise of the gentry" (that is, the middling landowners), was becoming increasingly polarised, with the gentry nearer the upper end, both economically and socially. Landownership was still, as it had been in medieval times, not only the chief criterion for social status—both the qualification for and the objective of political power, both locally and at the central government level—but also the chief source of income. Most of the great medieval feudal landed empires had changed hands, but, often broken apart and reassembled, they still existed, augmented by much of the landed property of the monasteries, torn apart by Elizabeth's father and distributed subsequently among every degree of landowner, from the peerage downward. Some new gentry estates were actually built up from scratch on monastic lands, but not many. For the most part the former church property had been paid for at the current market price, but with creeping inflation, depending on the length of existing leases and hence on the scope for raising rents, it had proved a good investment. Well over half had been dispersed by the Crown before Elizabeth's accession, and some of what was left was sold before she died, but by 1558 it was no longer anything like a buyers' market, even if the Crown had ever been a soft touch where its lands were concerned. It is interesting to compare the handsome grants of land in the South West (almost entirely ex-monastic) made to John Lord Russell in 1539 to establish his local authority with the queen's extreme stinginess toward Raleigh in a not-dissimilar situation in 1584. Even had she been minded to be generous, the property was not readily available. Much has been said about the economic straits of the Elizabethan aristocracy, but they were not as easily parted by the queen from their estates as were her bishops, and it was not the queen's intention to do more than clip episcopal wings. The greater part of the land of England was still in the ownership of the nobility and gentry, and under Elizabeth it may even have been increasing.

So what about those waiting on the sidelines? Raleigh's needs for an endowment were as desperate as those of younger sons at every level of society, including his own half brother, Sir Humphrey Gilbert. Even leasehold and copyhold tenancies had to be bought by farmers at the expense of increasingly substantial entry fines. Once in possession there were opportunities at every tenurial level for playing the land market, but, not only for Raleigh but for all his countrymen seeking betterment, the difficulty was to get a foot in. That meant finding ready money. At that time the only sure way to do that was to capture a well-endowed bride.

Along with entry into the land market, other opportunities for material advancement were limited by lack of capital, or just not grasped by those who could raise the wind. As already indicated, there was some industrial investment, largely via partnerships between needy landowners and city moneyed men, notably in mining and metallurgy. Even the nobility diversified into new crops such as woad, and all farmers were under great pressure to grow hemp, but most of them lacked the marketing expertise to realize a really good return on their money. Not until the next century did England become truly industrialised—that is, not until men with ideas stopped looking to the Crown for financial help.

Overseas Trade

To a certain extent, but not perhaps as much as the metropolitan and provincial merchants would have argued, full employment, and lack of popular unrest, especially in the chief clothing regions, depended upon the country's ability to find foreign markets, especially for its main product, woollen cloth. The 1550s had seen a disastrous falling off, especially in the export of broadcloths from London to the Low Countries, on which the city's merchant adventurers had concentrated for two centuries. Apart from a further trade slump in the early 1570s, though, the situation had recovered by 1580, and Londoners were trading very profitably with Spain right up to the outbreak of hostilities in 1585 and, indeed, beyond. By and large, English overseas trade in the 1570s and 1580s was steady. As war with Spain loomed, many, even in London and certainly in some of the provincial ports, actually welcomed the prospect of indulging in legalised piracy, a quicker way to get rich than the hard slog of traditional merchandising. For them an all-out challenge to Spanish New World supremacy could not come too soon. There were also, however, whole communities of merchants, including many in London, whose only wish was to be allowed to carry on normal trade along customary and proven routes. Such, for example, was the powerful Exeter Company of Merchants trading to France. John Hooker, their spokesman, had no room for transatlantic nonsense, especially any financed from the profits of cloth and wine patents, which must have made life a little uncomfortable for the widowed Katherine Raleigh, Walter's mother, then living near Exeter city centre. And while many of the London merchants continued to concentrate their energy on an all-out onslaught on aliens engaged in trade in London, especially the Easterlings and even the Italians, many of the provincial merchants just as ruthlessly invaded the Londoners' preserves in Russia and the Baltic, the Mediterranean, and even West Africa. The Turkey, Barbary, and Guinea Companies were all creations of the 1580s. Their members would put their money wherever they saw their own best interests, and only the prospect of spices, silks, and all that had beckoned so many to seek a shorter route to the Far East via the Northwest Passage was likely to attract the majority of English merchants to the New World. Was there any real hope of finding, so far south, a market for thick English broadcloth, which was all that the leading clothiers had to offer? As for the lighter-weight Devonshire kerseys, as Philip Amadas's Plymouth friends would have told him, there were markets in plenty in a friendly Spain. Truly, of all the many arguments put forward by the promoters of New World settlement, that which promised new transatlantic openings for overseas trade was probably the least convincing.

BIBLIOGRAPHIC NOTE

The following works have been consulted and are suggested for further reading on the subject: A. L. Beier, *Masterless Men: The Vagrancy Problem in England, 1560-1640* (London: Methuen, 1985); R. A. Houlbrooke, *The English Family, 1450-1700* (London: Longman, 1984); David Palliser, *The Age of Elizabeth*, 2d ed. (London: Longman, 1992); Paul Slack, *The Impact of Plague in Tudor and Stuart England* (London: Routledge, 1985); Joan Thirsk, *Economic Policy and Projects: The Development of a Consumer Society in Early Modern England* (Oxford: Clarendon Press, 1978); and Joyce Youings, *Sixteenth- Century England* (Oxford: Clarendon Press, 1978).

Who Came to Roanoke?

William S. Powell

We have the names of close to 300 people who were involved with Sir Walter Raleigh's efforts to establish an English colony on the Atlantic coast of North America between 1584 and 1587. We know something in detail about a few of them, but the vast majority are known only as names in a list. A reconnaissance expedition arrived in 1584 under the direction of Philip Amadas and Arthur Barlowe and was followed in 1585 by a colony of 107 men under Ralph Lane, which remained almost a year. This second expedition sailed under the direction of Sir Richard Grenville. In July 1587 a colony of 117 men, 17 women, and 9 boys—the famous "Lost Colony of Roanoke"— landed, again guided during the voyage by Grenville, to be governed by John White and a body of assistants named by Raleigh. Of the 12 assistants, 3 remained in England and 2 (Governor White and pilot Simon Fernandez) soon returned to England. Still another assistant was killed by Indians after less than a week.

Since it is this last group, the "Lost Colony," that seems to capture the attention of more people than do the other Roanoke expeditions, let me set the stage by giving a few figures about them, deduced largely from the list of names. There were 80 single men (or at least men without women of the same surname). There were 11 families consisting of just a husband and wife and 2 families with one child each. There were apparently 4 men who brought their sons, or perhaps they were younger brothers. There were 6 single women and 3 children with no apparent relatives among the other colonists. Incidentally, all the children were boys and, judging from a comment made by John White, one of the children with his mother was so young that he was still nursing. White wrote that at an island "called Santa Cruz . . . some of our women and men, by eating a small fruit like greene Apples, were fearefull troubled with a sudden burning in their mouthes. . . . Also a child by sucking one of the womens breasts, had at that instant his mouth set on such aburning, that it was strange to see how the infant was tormented."[1] Finally, two children were born in August 1587, soon after the colonists reached Roanoke—Virginia Dare and a Harvey child.

For four hundred years people have speculated as to just who these people were. We can only guess *why* they came and for the most part we can only *wonder* who they were. Nor do we know what became of most of them—even those earlier ones who returned to England. Here we have the basis of a mystery. Over the centuries many historians, genealogists, novelists, and other writers have tried to solve the puzzle of their fate. It now looks as if we are on the verge of finding some clues that may help answer a lot of the questions.

The pioneer in this search was Prof. David B. Quinn, who collected, edited, and prepared for publication all of the known records of Raleigh's attempts at colonization on England's behalf. Published in two volumes in 1955 as *The Roanoke Voyages*, Professor Quinn's work contains the basic documents together with additional identifying material. I also played a very minor role in trying to identify the people of Roanoke. In 1949 I made a preliminary investigation at the Library of Congress and in 1956 held a Guggenheim Fellowship that enabled me to spend the better part of a year in the British Isles doing research. Some of my tentative conclusions were published in an article, "Roanoke Colonists and Explorers: An Attempt at Identification," in the April 1957 *North Carolina Historical Review.*

More recently lebame houston, Olivia Isil, and others have formed a research team and spent many months in Great Britain seeking facts and clues toward identifying the Roanoke explorers, financial supporters, and colonists. Members of the team have been local experts in England on the history of the sixteenth century, handwriting of the period, legal terminology, and civil and church archives. These professionals have begun a program to comb contemporary records of various kinds wherever they can be found. Although their work is far from complete, they have shared their findings to date with me so that I can combine them with my earlier notes and suggest to you who some of the Roanoke colonists were.

A hindrance that has plagued all of us is that we must work with little more than names of persons, without their birth or death dates, places of residence, occupations, or other clues. As a rule, surnames in the sixteenth century had descended regularly from father to child for less than 250 years, and, indeed, English records on into the eighteenth century contain instances of people without surnames—merely single or descriptive names. Several men and one woman are identified in the records we use by only one name—Captain Aubrey, Captain Boniten, Chapman, Coffar, and others, which are perhaps surnames. Some are recorded only as Daniel or Robert—Christian names. The St. Andrew's, Plymouth, register includes such entries as "John a duchman" and "Christofer a dutcheman." Such entries have hindered our efforts at identification even further. For example, among the men who remained a year with Ralph Lane was a Master Allen; later a Morris Allen was a "Lost Colonist"—were they the same person? A Haunce Walters was another of Lane's men, yet four years later John White mentions that Hance the Surgeon was with him searching for the "Lost Colonists"— does this represent one or two people?

Neither spelling nor handwriting was standardized at that time, and a name might appear one way one time and another the next. Nor was there a great variety of surnames among the Roanoke colonists; forty-two family names among all the known colonists and explorers are borne by from two to four individuals. There were even fewer Christian names, and a middle name was excessively rare. The earliest instance I have discovered of the use of a middle name occurred just ten years before the date of the "Lost Colony."

Among the nearly 280 people counted among the explorers, crew, and colonists who actually reached Roanoke Island during the six-year period under consideration, it appears that at least twenty-two were not English-born. Three others bore names that do not seem to be British—Shaberdge, Skevelabs, and Smolkin. Nine nationalities apparently are represented: German, Spanish, Portuguese, French, Irish, Scottish, Danish, Flemish, and Welsh. The Germans were mining specialists who had worked in the tin mines of Cornwall and elsewhere in England. The Spanish and Portuguese were pilots; the Dane, Martin Laurentson, was a member of the Grenville expedition in 1585. A letter from Frederik II of Denmark to Queen Elizabeth said that Laurentson "intends to devote his attention to the art of naval warfare," and Frederik requested that he be put in the charge of a skilled naval officer for that purpose.[2] Two of the German mineral experts have been carefully studied. Both Joachim Ganz and Daniel Hochstetter, members of the Lane colony, were sons of distinguished families with scientific and industrial backgrounds.

Fourteen of the transatlantic passengers made the voyage more than once. John White came the maximum number of times—five. Simon Fernandez came three times, and Philip Amadas, twice. Only two of the "Lost Colonists," however, had been to Roanoke before. Seven of the men who had been with Ralph Lane returned for a second time. In 1590, when John White returned to seek the colonists left in 1587, he had with him six men who had been to Roanoke previously.

The few facts that I am going to give you and the many assumptions and guesses concerning some of the Roanoke colonists are based on the recent findings of the research team of lebame houston, Olivia Isil, and their staff, and on David Quinn's research and my own of a few years back. Much of it comes from entries in parish and guild registers and other manuscript records in England and from printed primary sources. While care has been taken to consider location and date in attributing our statements, we cannot at present be absolutely certain in every case that this information applies to the Roanoke colonists—it could be to someone else of the same name and time. We certainly hope that it is correct and that it can soon be proven beyond a doubt to apply to these early North Carolina residents.

One John Anwike was christened September 17, 1556, at St. Peters, Cornhill, London, a parish from which many other Roanoke colonists appear to have come. This was an area occupied by many merchant-tailors, armorers, upholsterers, bakers, and grocers. Anwike is a rare family name, but one Edmund Anwike was one of the crew on a West Indian voyage in 1582-1583, and the will of Thomas Anwike was submitted for probate in 1591.

Those of us who have been trying to identify these people are convinced that family relationships are important and may prove to be unexpected sources of information. A Valentine Beale was one of the colonists who stayed with the Ralph Lane colony for the year 1585-1586. Another Valentine Beale, son of Stephen, was christened at St. Matthew's Church, Friday Street, London, February 19, 1597; he could have been a nephew or other relative of the colonist, and perhaps both were born on St. Valentine's Day. Interesting speculation, of course, but more significant is the fact that a Robert Beale was brother-in-law to the powerful Sir Francis Walsingham. And Walsingham was governor of the mines of Keswick in Cumberland

and others in Cornwall; some German miners from them were among the Roanoke colonists. Another member of the Lane colony was Thomas Philips, chief agent of Walsingham, and Beale's and Philips's names are included together in the list of colonists. To add further to the interest in association is the fact that pilot Simon Fernandez was described as "Mr. Secretary Walsingham's man." This all remains to be sorted out, but I have a feeling that in time we're going to have a lot of new things to say about the significance of the Roanoke ventures. The question has been raised as to whether some of these people might have been "spies" for Walsingham. In 1587 a Roger Beale married Agnes Powell, and Edward and Wenefrid Powell became "Lost Colonists." What kind of network might have been laid? Is the answer to the riddle of the "Lost Colony" concealed in family or business relationships?

Marke Bennet and William Berde, both "Lost Colonists," are described in contemporary records as a husbandman and a yeoman respectively. Richard Berry was of the same group, and someone of his name, described as a "gentleman," had been a muster captain in 1572.

Thomas Bookener or Buckner was a Lane colonist whose London home was in Threadneedle Street near the Royal Exchange, and his parish church was St. Christopher's nearby. It was at Bookener's that Thomas Harriot died, and he was mentioned in Harriot's will.

Not surprisingly among Lane's men who stayed a year there was a shoemaker—John Brocke. Francis Brooke, treasurer of the 1585 expedition, seems later to have been a naval captain who commanded several privateer vessels. And John Fever was a basket maker, undoubtedly a useful occupation in the colony, with corn to be carried and fish weirs to be made.

William Brown is a common enough name, but one of that name was a London goldsmith prior to 1587, at which time the name appeared on the roll of the "Lost Colony." Since England hoped to find gold in the New World and artifacts of the goldsmith's trade have been found at the site, this William Brown may have practiced his trade at Roanoke.

Another 1587 colonist was Anthony Cage, and one of that name had been sheriff of Huntington in 1585. The Cage family was large, prominent in a number of endeavors, and wealthy. Anthony was a favored name for many generations. Anthonys lived and had business in Friday Street and were members of St. Matthew's parish there. They appear to have been related to the Warren family with "Lost Colony" connections, and Ananias Warren was Cage's grandson, suggesting a Cage/Dare association. Later there were also Cage connections with Jamestown and New England.

John Clarke commanded the *Roebuck*, one of Raleigh's ships on the 1585 crossing, but, of course, did not remain with the colony. Nevertheless, he and Philip Amadas did accompany Sir Richard Grenville on an expedition across Pamlico Sound. His father left him a considerable sum of money and the lease of a Thames wharf.

William Dutton was one of the "Lost Colonists." He may well have been the William Dutton, Esq., whose license to marry Anne Nicholas of St. Mildred, Bread Street, was issued October 2, 1583. She was the daughter of Sir Ambrose Nicholas, sometime Lord Mayor of London. William Dutton, armiger, of Gloucester, possibly the father of the "Lost Colonist," contributed £25 toward the defense of England on the eve of the expected attack by the Spanish Armada.

Men bearing the same name as two other "Lost Colonists," James Hynde and William Clement, according to contemporary manuscripts now in the Essex Record Office, had been in prison together in Colchester Castle near London for stealing. This should not be unexpected, as Ralph Lane referred to his company as "wylde menn of myne owne nacione."[3] Perhaps to be considered as at the other end of the scale on this list was Thomas Ellis; before leaving home in Exeter he had been a member of the vestry of his parish church, St. Petrock, which still stands on the main business street of Exeter. The boy, Robert Ellis, likely was his son. The apparently unattached boy, William Wythers, possibly was the vestryman's nephew, as one Alice Withers had married a Hugh Ellis in 1573. An infant William Withers was christened in St. Michael Cornhill on March 25, 1574, making him thirteen at the time of the "Lost Colony." The plot further thickens, however. Adjacent to St. Michael Cornhill was St. Peter's, the parish of the prominent Satchfeilde family of bakers and grocers and next of kin of Ananias Dare. Moreover, John Withers, a merchant-tailor of St. Michael's who died in 1589, was the son-in-law of John Satchfeilde of Guildford, Surrey. Thus, there appears to be a viable three- or even four-family connection: Dare, Ellis, Satchfeilde, Withers.

One Henry Greene, a member of the very first expedition, the one headed by Amadas and Barlowe, was a graduate of Corpus Christi College, Cambridge, and it has been suggested that he was of the family as the ancestor of Gen. Nathanael Greene of Revolutionary War and Guilford Courthouse fame.

One of Lane's men, Rowland Griffin, was convicted and sent to prison in 1594 for robbery. On the other hand, John Harris, a member of the same expedition, was knighted in 1603 at the coronation of James I.

There may have been at least two college students among the Roanokers. Thomas Luddington, one of Lane's men, was a fellow of Lincoln College, Oxford, while Thomas Harriot, another Lane colonist, was a fellow of Corpus Christi College, Cambridge, from 1579 to 1586 and held the master's degree from the same college.

Thomas Hewet may have been the lawyer of the "Lost Colonists." At any rate, he had a law degree from Oxford University. Robert Holecroft of Westminster, one of the Lane colonists, once appeared in court representing several dock and river workers.

It is possible that one of Lane's men recruited a colonist for his college. Both William White and Richard Wildye were graduates of the same Oxford college, and it appears that young Thomas Hulme, a member of the same expedition, entered their college the year following his return from Roanoke. Richard Ireland of the same colony entered Christ Church College, Oxford, two years later and eventually was headmaster of Westminster School.

It may have been thought that there would be a need for a particular official to serve with the Lane colony. At any rate Lane had with him Christopher Marshall, described as "one of the Waiters in the port of London," and a waiter at a port was a customs collector.

"Lost Colonist" William Nicholes may have been a tailor. A "clothworker" of that name was married in London in 1580, and in 1590 we find the grant of a license to someone else "to occupy the trade of a clothier during the minority of George Nicholles, son of Wm. Nicholles." I wonder if a place was being held for the orphaned son of a "Lost Colonist."

George Raymond, who came over in 1585, was a captain in the Royal Navy at the time of the Spanish Armada threat. In 1591 when he sailed on an expedition to the West Indies, he was described as a "gentleman captain and privateer promoter."

Anthony Rowse was a member of Lane's expedition. A man of the same name had been a member of Parliament the year before and afterward was sheriff of Cornwall for several years. He was knighted in 1603 and, at the death of Drake, was executor of his estate. At the other extreme was Richard Sare of the same expedition, described simply as a laborer. Considering the significance of rank and position at that time, I have my own opinion as to which man would have been more valuable in such an expedition.

John Spendlove, later a "Lost Colonist," was described on a 1585 muster list as a "gentleman" and reported present with his horse.

John Stukely came over in 1585. One of this name was Sir Richard Grenville's brother-in-law and the father of Sir Lewis Stukely, who had an unfortunate role in the downfall and death of Sir Walter Raleigh.

John Twyt was one of Lane's men, and one John Twyt was a London apothecary in 1580. We do not know whether this represents one man or two, but an apothecary would certainly have filled a potential need with the colony.

Both Benjamin and John Wood were with the Amadas and Barlowe initial trip in 1584. Later a Benjamin Wood had an interesting career at sea and was a noted navigator and captain. He fills a niche in the annals of British naval history for his attempt to reach China. He was known to have arrived at the Malay Peninsula but was later lost at sea. John Wood had already been a muster captain and, after returning home, became one of the "Jurates" of the town and port of Sandwich. He was knighted in 1603 at the coronation of James I.

While doubt may be cast on the association of some of these people with the Roanoke ventures, there are others about whom there is no doubt at all. Philip Amadas was born in Devonshire, England, and at the age of nineteen, while a member of Raleigh's household, was chosen by Raleigh to explore the coast of America and select a site for a settlement. He returned to America the following year and remained a year under Ralph Lane. A few years ago there were reports in the press that his family home near Plymouth had been identified; the family coat of arms was carved in stone above a fireplace.

Arthur Barlowe was another young man in Raleigh's personal service who took part in the 1584 search for a site. It was he who kept the journal of the expedition on which we depend for so much valuable information. Ralph Lane was the leader of the 1585-1586 colony of men sent over to lay the foundation of Raleigh's permanent settlement. It was composed only of men, a few of whom may have been of the gentry class, but most must have been skilled craftsmen and specialists. We know from the comments of Thomas Harriot, however, that some of them were reluctant to work and were disappointed in what they found. Lane was a professional soldier and a distant relative of Queen Elizabeth. The queen recalled him from service in Ireland and placed him at Raleigh's service, but she continued to pay him. Unfortunately Lane returned home with his colony prematurely, and it did not accomplish its objective. He later served as sheriff of Kerry in Ireland, was knighted in 1593, and died in 1603 in Dublin, where he is buried.

Thomas Cavendish, who furnished and commanded a ship for Sir Richard Grenville's fleet that brought the Lane colony over in 1585, is one of England's great naval heroes. He sailed around the world in 1586-1587, making many discoveries in the south Pacific, and while on a second such voyage in 1592 died at sea.

An extremely interesting report exists on an early experience of Abraham Cocke (or Cooke), captain of the *Hopewell* during John White's 1590 return search trip to Roanoke. Cocke later achieved notoriety as a privateer captain. The High Court of Admiralty records reveal that he had been a seaman aboard the *Minion*, which was trading to Brazil in 1581. At Bahia he fell out with the captain, Stephen Hare, over the matter of victuals and went ashore and did not return to England with the ship. In 1587 he was captured by one of Cumberland's ships while he was serving as a pilot aboard a small Portuguese vessel. Cocke had married and settled down in Brazil, but following his "capture" returned to England. In 1589 he commanded the *May Morning* and the *Dolphin* on voyages to the coast of Brazil.

Marmaduke Constable, a member of Lane's expedition, bears such a famous name that he poses an inviting problem for the researcher. He is likely to have been the one who had just been graduated from Oxford and was nineteen or twenty years old. We presume that he was one of the wild and unruly young men who gave Lane a hard time. Soon after returning to England following the year in Virginia, Marmaduke Constable was summoned to appear at Star Chamber as the leader of an armed gang of twenty ruffian-like and vagrant persons accused of tearing down hedges; cutting up the earth; and driving away, hurting, and wounding "beasts and cattle." Whether for sure this was the colonist, we do not yet know, but it certainly fits Ralph Lane's comments about some of them. We know a great deal about the various Marmaduke Constables, but they cannot all be sorted out yet. In time we are likely to be able to prepare a rather full biography of him—and perhaps even to have a portrait to illustrate it.

Sir Francis Drake is no problem, as he has been the subject of numerous biographies and appears as a character in novels, motion pictures, and television productions. He stopped by Roanoke Island when the Lane colony was there and picked up the men in 1586 to return them home. Afterwards he sailed around the world, attacked Spanish shipping, and was a hero at the defeat of the Spanish Armada.

Edward Gorges, who came to Roanoke Island with Sir Richard Grenville in 1585, was a cousin of Sir Ferdinando Gorges, later Lord Proprietor of the Colony of Maine; his mother and Sir Walter Raleigh were first cousins. A graduate of Magdalen College, Oxford, Gorges was later employed by Queen Elizabeth as a personal messenger to Henry IV of France, and he was knighted by her successor, James I. He is buried in St. Margaret's Church, Westminster, not far from Sir Walter Raleigh. A portrait of him was sold some years ago but probably could be located.

Thomas Harriot, mathematician and astronomer, spent a year investigating the coastal region between what is now South Carolina and the District of Columbia. He examined the plants and trees, the soil, and the native people, and joined with John White in mapping the area. His book, *A Briefe and True Report of the New Found Land of Virginia*, published in 1588, gave Europeans their first information about this part of America. It introduced them to the products of the New World and undoubtedly played a role in luring many people to become settlers a few years later. And Harriot himself has been the subject of many biographies.

George Howe was one of the "Gentlemen of London" who was made an assistant in the government of the Cittie of Raleigh in the 1587 "Lost Colony." Also present was a boy, George Howe, most likely his son and certainly not yet of age. The senior Howe was killed by Indians on July 28, 1587, just six days after the arrival of the colonists, when he was crabbing and strayed away from the settlement. One George Howe was a member of the painter-stainer company, as was Gov. John White, which suggests that had events developed more favorably, there might have been even more watercolors to delight us. An interesting possible family connection is that one of the Lane colonists, Thomas Rattenbury, was married to one Elizabeth Howe.

Abraham Kendall was a veteran navigator and renowned mathematician who was with the Lane colony. He commanded a ship as part of the 1578 Frobisher expedition to Greenland, during which John White executed some watercolors. He undertook a voyage to the Strait of Magellan in 1589, and in 1594-1595 he was in the West Indies. Sir Robert Dudley, for whom Kendall once worked, considered him one of the most expert mariners produced by England. He may have been related to the "Master Kendall" who also was with the Lane colony, but we can't be sure.

Edward Kettel, a Lane colonist, bore an excessively rare name in England, so he may have been the son of the celebrated Dutch painter Cornelius Kettel. Cornelius's name appears in the *Returns of Aliens in London*, and he was dwelling in the parish of Saint Andrew Undershaft in 1573. Four others of the name lived in an adjacent parish from which a number of Roanoke colonists are believed to have come. It has been supposed that young Edward Kettel may have been an apprentice of John White's.

In cases where a man and a woman bore the same surname among the "Lost Colonists," it has been assumed that they were husband and wife. Edward and Wenefrid Powell are examples. The baptism of one Edward Powell is recorded in the register of St. Margaret's, Westminster, January 2, 1563; another baptism of an Edward Powell occurred at St. Martin-in-the-Field, Westminster, on March 13, 1569. The marriage of Edward Powell and Wenefrid Gray is recorded in St. Nicholas Church, Deptford, Kent, just outside London, January 10, 1584. While Edward is a common sixteenth-century name, Wenefrid is not, and the combination of Edward and Wenefrid Powell makes it rather likely that they are indeed the "Lost Colonists." An Edward Powell was with Sir Francis Drake on the West Indian voyage of 1585- 1586 that stopped at Roanoke Island to relieve the Lane colony. Edward Powell was the scribe and recorder of the *Tiger* journal and was probably in the personal service of its captain, Christopher Carleill, who just happened to be Sir Francis Walsingham's stepson. Perhaps Edward decided in 1586 that he liked America and returned in 1587.

Jacob Whiddon, who was with Grenville in 1585 when he brought over Ralph Lane and his colony, was a trusted servant and follower of Sir Walter Raleigh. Raleigh spoke of him as "a man most valiant and honest." Raleigh dispatched Whiddon to explore the Orinoco River, and Whiddon was with Raleigh on the latter's voyage to South America in 1595. He died and was buried on the Island of Trinidad in the West Indies.

David Williams, if I have correctly identified the one who was a Lane colonist, was a young Welsh lawyer recently called to the bar and later an outstanding London lawyer and judge. He served in Parliament for one year immediately prior to coming over and for three years after he returned. In 1603 he was knighted. When I last inquired, a portrait of him was in storage while some repairs were being made at the home of a descendant.

All of us who have attempted to identify the Roanoke colonists have been struck in many cases by the fact that both explorers and colonists, leaders and followers, were related by blood or by marriage. Some were surely friends or acquaintances because they were neighbors who lived in the same parish or adjoining parishes. Edward Kelly and Thomas Wise, for example, both members of Lane's colony, lived about two and a half miles from each other in Devon. Some were employed by the same person—Atkinson, Fernandez, and Russell are all spoken of as being in the service of Sir Francis Walsingham. Four others apparently were members of the same military unit—and as I have already hinted, two may have served time together in prison. Professor Quinn concluded that several of the men he investigated worked together on the Thames River.

Two of the single women among the "Lost Colonists" are interesting as they have surnames very much like those of two of the men. Because of the absence of uniformity in handwriting and spelling, it may be that Audrey T-A-P-P-A-N and Thomas T-O-P-A-N were husband and wife, as were Joan W-A-R-R-E-N and

Thomas W-A-R-N-E-R. Further support for the latter case exists in the 1584 marriage record of a mariner named Thomas Warner and Johanna Barnes.

I can make some reasonable guesses about several others of the single women— Agnes Wood, for instance. In 1549 one Robert Woode of St. Bride's Church, Fleet Street, London, married Johanna Toppan. Might this Agnes Wood have been their daughter and related to the Tappan/Topans? Or perhaps she was the Agnes Traver who married John Wood in London in 1577. John Wood had come to Roanoke in 1584; now there may have been some reason for his wife to come.

Or what can we say about the single woman Jane Pierce? In Ireland, Henry Piers, who died in 1623, was the husband of one Jane Jones. Could this Jane Pierce have been their daughter and therefore related to Griffin, Jane, and John Pierse, who were also among the same body of colonists? Yet another possibility exists. In 1568 one Jone Pierse, a Portuguese, was registered as an alien in London. She was identified as the sister of men named Simon and Fornando and the tenant of one Frauncis White. When we see the names Simon, Fornando, and White in connection with the Roanoke colonists, they immediately suggest a relationship. This Pierce woman lived within sight of the Tower of London in the parish of All Saints Barking. In the parish register regularly for between thirty and seventy years will be found the following names represented among the Roanoke colonists: Archard, Backhouse, Bailey, Borden, Chapman, Constable, Cooper, Deane, Dymoke, Evans, Fullwood, George, Platt, Pratt, Hardin, Harvye, Harriot, Ireland, Nichols, Powell, Sampson, Sares, Snelling, Stone, Stevens, Wade, Wright, and John White. Jane Pierce might have felt quite at home among such people.

One final association. Jane Mannering was a very common name in a distinguished family, so it will be difficult to sort her out. Yet the grandmother of Humfrey Newton, another of the "Lost Colonists," was Katherine Mainwaring. The question then occurs to me: were Jane Mannering and Humfrey Newton perhaps first cousins, grandchildren of Katherine?

But what about the other single women? Maybe they were looking for husbands among their fellow colonists, or perhaps they already had husbands among the fifteen to eighteen men left at Roanoke by Grenville the previous year. The colony had departed suddenly under unfortunate circumstances, and these men, out on reconnaissance, had been abandoned. Did their wives take this opportunity to join them in America?

Why were there three boys with no apparent connection to any of the adults? Perhaps their fathers were among those abandoned the year before—or, of course, they could have been nephews or grandsons of colonists, and we have just not yet discovered the relationship. Young Thomas Humfrey may well have been the son or brother of Richard Humpfrey of the Lane colony. Young Thomas Smart, who came alone with the 1587 colony, may well have been the son of the Thomas Smart who was with the Lane colony. The boy William Wythers may have been associated with the

Tayler (Taylor) family—John and Thomas Taylor had been with the Lane colony; Clement and Hugh were with the "Lost Colony"; and John returned in 1590 with John White to search for the "Lost Colony." And the implied family association continued in 1592 when one Robert Taylor married Elizabeth Wythers.

Now having mentioned a selection of typical Roanoke colonists, let me add that in recent years three "new" colonists have turned up. These are three whose names do not appear in the standard records—Hakluyt, Harriot, or Quinn. (1) Richard Butler is discussed in James A. St. John's *Life of Sir Walter Raleigh*, published in 1868 in London. His record was found in the general archives of Simanca in a report he made on May 1, 1593, about his service to Sir Walter Raleigh with the Amadas voyage. (2) The second source is the inscription on the tomb of Robert Masters, Gentleman, who traveled to Virginia and afterward about the globe with Thomas Cavendish. His tomb is in the little church of Burghill in Herefordshire, where he died in 1619. (3) The third man is anonymous, but he was a young clergyman of the Anglican Church who, when he learned of the Amadas and Barlowe expedition, sold everything he had and joined the company to take the Christian religion to the natives of America.

If we had relatives at a lonely outpost—perhaps a space station on Mars—and the sending of supplies to them depended first upon the speedy defeat of an enemy who threatened to invade our shores, I expect we would support all possible means of defense. In England there survives a list of persons who subscribed toward the defense of the country at the time of the threatened attack by the Spanish Armada in 1588. A comparison of this list with the names of the Roanoke colonists reveals that 38 men and 1 woman with the same family names contributed from £25 to £100 each to England's defense. This represents an enormous sum of money. Of those names, only 9 were represented among the colonists and explorers *before* 1587. But 29 contributors had the same family names as "Lost Colonists," and 15 even had the same first name as well, making me feel that in these fifteen cases, at least, it was the father of a colonist who contributed so generously. While it is difficult to put a monetary value on love, this generosity suggests to me that there must have been some colonists who were from families of more than average means.

The identities of many colonists remain uncertain. While these hardy pioneers were undoubtedly cut from uncommon fabric, the majority carry relatively common English names. Thus, for every Devon smuggler or Yorkshire cattle thief who bears a colonist's name, a learned Oxford clergyman or respectable London merchant may be found who bears exactly the same name at or close to the same time. We anticipate that further research will reveal more of these willing pioneers to have been worthy predecessors of the kind of people who now occupy the land in which they had such faith.

NOTES

1. David Beers Quinn, ed., *The Roanoke Voyages, 1584-1590: Documents to Illustrate the English Voyages to North America Under the Patent Granted to Walter Raleigh in 1584*, 2 vols., Hakluyt Society Second Series, No. 104 (London: Hakluyt Society, 1955; reprint, New York: Dover, 1991), 2:517-518.

2. Quinn, *Roanoke Voyages*, 1:226.

3. Quinn, *Roanoke Voyages*, 1:204.

The Search for Ananias Dare

William S. Powell

Until fairly recently we knew very little about Ananias Dare, and we still don't know all we'd like to—or surely all that we're going to learn in the future. If you have seen Paul Green's symphonic drama *The Lost Colony*, you will recall that Dare was a member of Sir Walter Raleigh's colony that arrived at Roanoke Island in July 1587. He was one of the nine "Assistants" who together with Gov. John White were granted coats of arms and came over to form the government of the Cittie of Raleigh in Virginia, as the settlement was named. Dare's wife was Elinor White, daughter of Governor White of the colony, and he was the father of Virginia Dare, the first English child born in America. Nothing further concerning Dare appears in the meager records of the colony, so I hope you have not fallen under the spell of the drama to the extent that you believe anything else about him from the play.

Over the years, many people have wished they knew more about Dare and the nearly three hundred other people directly involved in the efforts made between 1584 and 1590 by Sir Walter Raleigh to plant a colony on the South Atlantic coast of North America. Prof. David B. Quinn was the dean of the searchers after the Roanoke colonists, of course, and it is to him that the greatest debt is owed for many of the basic facts that we do know. Following him came several others who were able to add a few facts and many suppositions.

I believe it was the late professor Louise Hall of Duke University who discovered that Dare was described in 1586 as a tiler and bricklayer. Despite the fact that being a tiler and bricklayer might be considered a lowly occupation, it was an honorable one, and it had its own guild. In a document pertaining to the colony drawn up for Sir Walter Raleigh, Dare was classified as a "gentleman late of London." The fact that Dare's name appears third in the list of colonists, undoubtedly prepared after the English practice and arranged in some kind of formal order that we don't yet understand, suggests that his status was rather high among the colonists and lends credence to the reference to him as a gentleman.

Like most of the other surnames represented among the various groups associated with the sixteenth-century Roanoke voyages, that of Ananias Dare was published in the records for the first time in Richard Hakluyt's account printed in the 1589 edition of his *Principal Voyages and Navigations*. Dare is not a family name that shows up in any of the books on English surnames that I have examined, but a name that comes close appears in John Stow's *Survey of London*, published in 1598. There it is recorded that a monument to one William Dere (D-E-R-E) was in St. Augustine's Church near St. Paul's. This Dere was one of the sheriffs in 1450. Three men named Dare—William and Richard in 1541 and 1543 and Marke in 1565—are found in London parishes. The family name is also mentioned in the *Returns of Aliens Dwelling in the City and Suburbs of London from the Reign of Henry VIII to that of James I*, compiled by R. E. G. and Ernest F.

Kirk. That source records one Gautier [Walter] Dare, a printer ["typographus"] and a native of Rouen, France, living in Blackfriars in the East End of London in 1562.[1] We don't know anything about this printer named Walter Dare, but his Christian name raises questions about a possible connection with Sir Walter Raleigh. Marie, daughter of Gilbert Dare, was baptized February 13, 1596, at St. Mary Colechurch, London, leading one to wonder if Sir Humphrey Gilbert, Raleigh's half brother, might have been recognized in the name. Since Raleigh and Gilbert were associated in schemes for New World settlement, it is natural to speculate whether these Dares were related to each other or otherwise connected with Gilbert and Raleigh.

Ananias Dare's Christian name has also puzzled me. Ananias does not appear in any of the books on English given names that I have been able to consult. It's a biblical name, of course, but the man of that name described in the Book of Acts was dishonest, and the word *ananias* is now cited in dictionaries as an allusion for "liar." I wonder why Christian parents would have named a son Ananias. Nevertheless, the name Ananias *Daw* occurs six times in the parish register of Black Torrington, Devon—the earliest in 1640. Given the many ways of writing the letter *R* in sixteenth-century handwriting, it is easy enough to confuse an "AR" with an "AW"—so these may have referred to other Ananias Dares rather then Daw.

On January 17, 1587, arms were granted for the projected Cittie of Raleigh in Virginia, for Gov. John White, and for each of the assistants in its government. Dare's was described as "A Feelde Gules, A Crosse engrailde, between fower Fuzzels Argent." In simpler language, this describes a shield bearing a cross with fluted or wavy edges on a red background with a silver diamond-shape in each of the four quarters. There apparently is nothing in this design to suggest anything about Dare's origin or ancestry, although it is very similar to the arms granted to Roger Bailey, whose name occurs just ahead of Ananias Dare's in the list.

My own interest in seeking biographical information on the Roanoke colonists began in 1949 when I was able to spend some time in Washington at the Library of Congress searching for information about the members of Raleigh's "Lost Colony" of 1587 in published records there. In 1956 I held a Guggenheim Fellowship that enabled me to spend nearly a year in London and elsewhere in England, Scotland, and Ireland not only to continue the work but also to include in my search for biographical information the names of persons from exploratory expeditions and colonization efforts made between 1584 and 1587—that is, before the "Lost Colony."

Although I was able to suggest some interesting suppositions about a great many colonists, the single most exciting fact that I found about Ananias Dare was that he left a son, John Dare, in England. Under English law, an unaccounted-for absence of seven years was necessary for a ruling of presumed death. In 1594 the requisite number of years had passed after the last contact with the Roanoke colony. It was then that a relative of the young John Dare petitioned the court on his behalf that he be given his father's property. The document stated that Ananias had been a member of St. Bride's

Church, Fleet Street, London—which is not far from St. Paul's Cathedral. Finally, in 1597, after three years had passed and John Dare was clearly more than ten years of age, the petition was granted.

The mother of John Dare is not named, but the child was described as legitimate. I doubt that he was the son of Elinor White Dare, however, or he would have been among the boys who accompanied the 1587 colonists. The only subsequent reference to a John Dare that I discovered was to one living in 1622 in Essex, where he was a surveyor. During several later trips to England I was unable to find any additional information about a possible John Dare descendant in Essex.

From time to time I receive letters from people named Dare, particularly in England, who have tried without success to trace a connection with Ananias. One of the most intriguing correspondents, however, was a pilot named Dare who flies a small plane in Australia taking tourists to see Ayers Rock. He wrote that his father, born in England, had told him of a family tradition connecting them with the Raleigh colony. Needless to say, no proof has been forthcoming.

On several expeditions to Great Britain during recent years, lebame houston and Olivia Isil have made a more thorough search than anyone previously was able to make. Their discoveries of forthright facts, as well as additional clues and hints, which they expect in time will provide further information, are exciting. They have shared their research notes with me, and I am able to relay to you some recently discovered facts about Ananias Dare.

William Bateman Sr., they discovered, was a citizen of London and a member of the tiler and bricklayers' guild, as was Ananias Dare. Bateman's will, dated March 15, 1586, was probated on June 25, 1586. Bateman, a wealthy and influential member of the guild, owned considerable rental property in and around London, including some in the parish in which one John White (not the "Lost Colony" governor, however) and a William Dare lived. Included in the will was a bequest to Ananias Dare; this 1586 bequest of money is the earliest reference to Ananias. It is of further interest because it associates Dare with a number of men of substance in London who were also remembered by Bateman.

Further evidence of Dare's status is revealed in a three-part indenture drawn up on March 7, 1589, after Ananias was already in America. It involved the participation of three groups of men with colonial interests. Sir Walter Raleigh composed one part; nineteen London merchants formed another; and a revised list of Assistants for the Cittie of Raleigh comprised the third. All of them were investors in the colony in America. Dare's standing, cited in the grant of arms as a gentleman of London, was repeated in the indenture, which described him as "late of London. gentleman." This was an assignment by Raleigh to "divers gentlemen of London, to continue the action of planting in Virginia." Dare's name continued to appear third in the list, following that of Governor White and Roger Baylye.

The next document in chronological order with information on Ananias Dare is one I have already mentioned: that having to do with the administration of his estate. On April 26, 1594, a commission was issued to Robert Satchfeild of London, Ananias's next of kin, to administer the goods, rights, and credits of Ananias. Richard Goodall, notary public and procurator, swore to confirm the process. Ananias is clearly described as being a resident of the Parish of St. Bride, Fleet Street, the parish church of which has probably been visited by many of us—and which has a modern memorial to Virginia Dare.

For some unknown reason, Satchfeild's administration was revoked on June 27, 1595, and transferred to John Nokes, identified as a blood kinsman (although not next of kin) of Ananias Dare, with John Robinson, notary public, as young John Dare's procurator. In both cases John Dare is described as "natural and lawful." We are left for the present to wonder who his mother might have been—there is no marriage register for St. Bride's at this date. If she was Elinor White Dare, why was the boy not taken with them to the New World? Thanks to the houston-Isil research team, we now know that Elinor was eighteen when her daughter, Virginia, was born, so if John were her son, she was a very young mother. If Ananias were a widower, his first wife, judging by the presumed age of John, must not have been dead very long.

Future searches into the identity of Ananias Dare's relatives, Robert Satchfeild and John Nokes, and of the procurators Richard Goodall and John Robinson may also be rewarding. Evidence exists that there was an inventory of Ananias Dare's estate, but the document itself is apparently temporarily misfiled among the records in the Guildhall Library in London. To know what property he left would surely be useful in gathering additional information about him.

The research team has begun to look for the Christian name *Ananias* among other contemporary families bearing the same surnames as other Roanoke colonists. This may reveal kinship among them. The name, as has already been suggested, was rarely used, yet one Ananias Warren was christened in a parish adjacent to St. Bride's, and there was a Warren among the Lost Colonists.

To pursue the search for the identity of Ananias Dare, a list has been prepared of the members of the tiler and bricklayers' guild during the period 1568-1600 preparatory to making a search of their wills for Dare references. This list may also facilitate a further search for the identity of Satchfeild and Nokes. Equally as careful investigation is anticipated in a search for the marriage record of Ananias and Elinor White Dare, as well as information about the whole list of colonists.

NOTE

1. R. E. G. Kirk and E. F. Kirk, eds., *Returns of Aliens Dwelling in the City and Suburbs of London from the Reign of Henry VIII to that of James I*, 4 vols. (London: Huguenot Society of London, 1900-1908), 1:290-291.

Simon Fernandez, Master Mariner and Roanoke Assistant: A New Look at an Old Villain

Olivia A. Isil

Most modern scholarship casts Simon Fernandez, at best, in the role of a seagoing ne'er-do-well. At his worst, he is cast in the role of an arch-villain with a wickedly selfish personal agenda who abandoned an entire colony to their fate in the wilderness. In this presentation, I will depart from the more traditional views of Fernandez and offer what I hope will be an objective analysis of his factual, recorded career, as compared to highly subjective, contemporary narratives and their unfortunate historical legacy. It is my intention to dismantle certain preconceived ideas that are not grounded in fact but, rather, in misunderstanding and misinterpretation of known primary and secondary sources. I would like to present Roanoke scholars with a fresh canvas, a broader brush, and the challenge to paint their own picture of Fernandez. The image that emerges might be very surprising.

In order to understand the persona of Simon Fernandez, Master Mariner and Roanoke Assistant, he must be viewed against the dynamic socioeconomic and political backdrop of sixteenth-century Europe. By the time Elizabeth Tudor ascended the throne in 1558, Spain held an economic and political stranglehold over the rest of Europe. That supremacy resulted in part from the vast wealth being extracted from its holdings in the Americas. England's economic survival, indeed its very survival as a nation, depended on overseas expansion, increasing its own holdings, and gaining the wealth and power necessary to challenge Spain's dominance in Europe and in the Americas. In order to achieve those ends, England had to gain more experience in the emerging science of navigation. Though highly skilled as coastwise navigators, the English were aware of their shortcomings as blue-water sailors. They began looking to Portugal, the first of the great maritime world empires and the acknowledged master in the science of navigation, for the help they needed to hone their own skills. During the reign of the Tudors, astute Englishmen, their eyes on the future as well as on the yet untapped resources of the New World, began hiring experienced Portuguese pilots and navigators from whom they could learn. Simon Fernandez was such a man.

The factual career of Fernandez can be found recorded in primary source documents: Calendars of State Papers (Foreign and Domestic) from the reign of Elizabeth I; Chancery Proceedings; Acts of the Privy Council; Records of the High Court of the Admiralty; and the Vincent, Calthorpe, Harleian, and Cotton Manuscripts. Essentially government records, without frills or literary graces, they are cut-and-dried legal documents—factual, to the point, and presumably objective.

Additional sources of information on Simon Fernandez dating from the period are the narratives found in the chronicles of information gatherers such as John White, Richard Madox, Richard Hakluyt, and Raphael Holinshed. They are subjective sources—one person writing about another as seen through the distorting prism of personal opinion, cultural bias, jealousy, and a host of other emotions. Succeeding generations have formed impressions of Fernandez based almost exclusively on subjective narratives rather than on his actual, recorded career. This is indeed unfortunate. While the prevailing impression of the pilot undoubtedly carries some shades of reality, it continues to obscure some highly relevant and significant factual information.

Virtually nothing is known with certainty about Fernandez's origins. It is generally accepted that he came from Terceira in the Portuguese Azores, settled in England sometime before 1570, and eventually became an English subject. While over the centuries the mariner's name has been given many Anglicized forms—Fernando, Ferdinando, Fernand, Fardinando—he was a literate man who signed his name in a clear, bold hand: Simão Fernandez.

Fernandez's name first appears in the English State Papers in 1571. The record indicates that he was in partnership with John Callis, one of the most notorious pirates of the Elizabethan age, and that the pair were operating out of Bristol, England, and Pennarth, Wales. To say that Fernandez was a pirate is to say, simply, that he was a businessman. The government's official stance on piracy was contradictory. While the Crown deplored piracy in principle, it was always willing to turn a blind eye—to borrow a metaphor from the age of Nelson—to piracy when it served royal or national interests. Thus English pirates, considered to be villains when they preyed on their own country's shipping, were magically transformed into privateers, those patriot-heroes authorized by the Crown to attack the enemies of England. Pirates—and Fernandez was no exception—were frequently under the patronage and protection of influential men, high government officials who themselves underwrote the illegal but enormously profitable ventures. The queen herself was known to have lent ships to, and taken her share of loot from, expeditions aimed at Spanish and French shipping. Conflicts of interests, both personal and national, frequently stretched the distinguishing line between outright piracy and licensed privateering perilously thin. As a pirate-entrepreneur, Simon Fernandez participated in a flourishing business network, no better or worse a man than many others of his time.

A veritable catalog of piratical crimes is documented in the records for the reign of Elizabeth: captured pirates being released from jail by town mayors; brokers negotiating deals between pirates and their victims for the return, at a price, of their recently stolen goods; and respectable merchants discreetly fencing pirate loot in their shops. Jailed many times for piracy during the 1570s, Fernandez found one influential patron after another to procure his bail and subsequent liberty to roam profitable sea lanes. William and Henry Herbert, the powerful earls of Pembroke, were frequently responsible for setting Fernandez at large. In 1576 alone, persons fined for "trafficking with pyrats" included the Lord Mayor of Dartmouth; the Lieutenant and Deputy Customs Searcher for the Port of Plymouth; the Deputy Vice-Admiral of Bristol; the High Sheriff of Glamorganshire; William Winter, a relative of the Surveyor of the

Navy; William Hawkins, brother of the Treasurer of the Navy; and Henry Knollys, son of the queen's own vice-chamberlain and a member of her Privy Council. Knollys owned the *Oliphant* (*Elephant*), a vessel frequently leased by Fernandez for his piratical activities. To say simply that English piracy flourished in the last half of the sixteenth century is a gross understatement. It had, in fact, become a recognized and respected profession. Social mobility in Elizabethan England was such that men who amassed fortunes as pirate-privateers—Drake, Hawkins, Grenville, Raleigh, Gilbert, Frobisher— rose meteorically in the service of queen and country, achieving knighthoods, respectability, and the esteem of their fellow citizens as well as that of succeeding generations of historians.

It appears, however, that old habits die hard, and once a pirate, always a pirate. Sir Francis Drake couldn't resist taking a ship for spoil during the thick of the Armada engagement. Martin Frobisher was outraged—not because Drake had broken off with an enemy who was knocking at England's back door but because he was denied his own share of the loot. The distraction of a fellow squadron commander and brother pirate making off with fifteen thousand gold ducats was almost unbearable. After making a colorful speech that someone had the wit to record for posterity, Frobisher managed to concentrate on the business at hand, distinguished himself in the engagement, and, as a result, earned his own knighthood. Frobisher's third officer during the Armada engagement was none other than Simon Fernandez. Although he never achieved knighthood or the respect of twentieth-century historians, Fernandez was a valued member of an illustrious company of Elizabethan sea dogs.

The factual career of Fernandez as recorded in the Spanish State Papers continues: in 1579 he was the master of the royal ship *Falcon*, with Walter Raleigh as captain, bound on a venture to the West Indies. Don Bernardo de Mendoza, the Spanish ambassador, reporting from London to Philip II on the sponsorship and plans of "Onpegilberto" (Humphrey Gilbert) for a reconnaissance voyage to the Indies, wrote that "they are taking with them one Simon Fernandez, a thorough-paced scoundrel who has given them and is giving them much information about that coast which he knows very well." A fragmentary account of that venture in the Holinshed Chronicles records that the expedition ran short of supplies and that after "many tempests and fights" the *Falcon* returned to Plymouth without having reached the Indies.

The English State Papers record that in 1580, again under the patronage of Sir Humphrey Gilbert, Fernandez undertook a reconnaissance voyage to Norumbega, roughly the area of Newfoundland and present-day Maine. By that time, Fernandez's reputation as a pirate was such that, despite Sir Humphrey's venture being authorized by letters patent from the queen herself, he was obliged to enter into a bond of £500 for the good behavior of the master and his crew. Reputation notwithstanding, the intrepid master and his crew brought back the hides of very large animals thought to be bison and also collected valuable information regarding the natives and natural resources found in those northerly latitudes. It was reported that "Simon Fernandez,

Mr. Secretary Walsingham's man went and came to and from the said coast within three months in the Squirrel, a little frigat of viii tuns burthen without any other escort and arrived at Dartmouth where he embarked when he began his voyage. . . ." That Fernandez crossed the North Atlantic in such a tiny vessel with a ten-man crew and without a larger consort must be viewed with some degree of admiration, albeit grudgingly, for the seamanship such an undertaking required. Attempting the same voyage in the *Squirrel* some two years later, Sir Humphrey Gilbert perished in the waters off the Azores.

In November 1580 Fernandez visited John Dee, noted scientist and astrologer, in order to give him an account of the voyage and to loan him his sea chart that a copy might be made for Dee's extensive library. It should be noted that the queen's principal secretary, Sir Francis Walsingham, and Elizabeth herself were in frequent contact with Dee. The copy of Fernandez's sea chart is now in the British Museum's Cotton Manuscript. A note on the map reads: "The counterfeit map of Master Fernandez Simon and his sea chart which he lent unto my Master at Mortlake Anno 1580 November 20. The same Fernandez Simon is a Portugale, and born in Terceira being one of the Isles called Azores." Some scholars have suggested that Fernandez plagiarized this sea chart. In all probability this notion stems from nineteenth-century misunderstanding of archaic wording and the fact that the Fernandez sea chart is known to be based on a map that dates from the mid-sixteenth century. In preparation for a dangerous voyage across the North Atlantic on behalf of an important patron, a master mariner, even one as seasoned as Fernandez, would visit a reliable cartographer to obtain an existing map of the unfamiliar sea route. The master would add personal notations on winds, currents, distances covered, and other relevant data collected during his particular voyage. The end product was a sea chart of a specific voyage. The copying, buying, and selling of annotated maps had been standard operating procedure for centuries. Fernandez did nothing devious or underhanded in basing his sea chart on an existing map. Maps based on the voyages of Giovanni da Verrazzano along the eastern seaboard of North America during the late 1520s, errors and all, were used by English colonizing ventures well into the seventeenth century. Finally, it should be noted that Dee's secretary's use of the word *counterfeit* does not imply fraud. The sixteenth-century usage of *counterfeit*, now obsolete, simply meant to imitate or copy without the intent to deceive.

The factual, recorded career of Fernandez continues: in 1582 the earl of Leicester—the queen's own beloved Robin—began an enterprise to establish an English spice trade with the Molucca Islands. Martin Frobisher was to lead the expedition, and Simon Fernandez was to co-pilot the fleet along with Thomas Hood. The Cotton Manuscript contains an undated and fragmented letter to Frobisher from Fernandez indicating that the pilot was overseeing the final fitting-out of the galleon *Leicester*, the earl's own ship and admiral, or flagship, of the fleet. The letter reflects a good grasp of English vernacular. It is written with style, ease, good humor, and a certain rough grace. For reasons not entirely clear, Frobisher was discharged from command and replaced by Edward Fenton, with Fernandez staying on as co-pilot. The long-suffering Spanish ambassador in London again wrote to King Philip: "the pilot of the principal ship is a Terceiran Portuguese called Simon Fernandez, a heretic who has lived here for some years and is considered to be one of the best pilots in the country. . . ."

Mendoza's use of the word *heretic* has given rise to an idea that Fernandez was Jewish or perhaps a Moor. In the grand scheme of things, this represents a minor point. However, it does illustrate the confusion that can arise from taking a word out of its sixteenth-century context and putting a twentieth-century spin on it. Anyone who was not Catholic was, by Mendoza's definition, a heretic. One contemporary reporter, in fact, described Fernandez as a Lutheran.

The Privy Council appointed Richard Madox, Fellow of All Souls, Oxford, as co-chaplain and instructed him to keep a detailed record of the expedition. Madox recorded what he considered relevant information in a personal diary that he wrote in a system of code, convoluted cross-referencing, and marginalia. Madox, who likewise sailed aboard the galleon *Leicester*, described the pilot as being a "braggart, a glutton, coward . . . a ravenous thief with talons more rapacious than any vulture. . . ." The chaplain used Latin pseudonyms in his diary to describe merchants and members of the ship's company: Fernandez the Swine, Fenton the Deceiver, and Hood the Buffoon. Other unsuspecting shipmates were labeled parasite, swell-head, stupid, braggart, and one described as a "fyzzeling [farting] tale-bearer."

Few escape Madox's critical scrutiny—he even comments jocularly on a fellow chaplain's sexual proclivities—but Fernandez bears the brunt of the chaplain's diatribes: "he makes observations in Portuguese translating ineptly into English, they come out in a swill of many languages and everywhere abound in barbarisms, solecisms, and hyperbatons . . . these he sells as his own and boasts of himself as a notable author, inventor, rather he should be called a perverter of books, an extorter of readers and tormentor of writers. . . ."

The Oxford educated clergyman-scholar viciously and personally attacks everyone around him—one Latin marginal note reads: "tales not without flavor." With its mean-spirited digressions and preoccupation with its author's own puerile wit, the diary tells us more about Madox himself than any of the other members of the expedition. Madox's credibility as an objective observer and source of information is questionable. Certainly, his layman's opinion of Fernandez's skill as a pilot must be dismissed totally. Despite Madox's vilification, Fernandez did not lose the confidence and respect of the earl of Leicester, Sir Francis Walsingham, the Privy Council, or any of the other influential investors in the voyage. Quite the contrary. High-placed patrons continued to increase Fernandez's responsibilities by involving him in the all-important ventures for overseas expansion and colonization.

Fernandez's name next appears in a narrative in conjunction with Sir Walter Raleigh's ventures to Virginia beginning in 1584, the so-called Roanoke voyages. The

1584 expedition co-leader, Arthur Barlowe, presents a highly literate account of the fateful contact between the native North Americans and the English reconnaissance party, as well as of the structure of native society and of Roanoke's natural resources, but has little to say about members of the expedition. Fernandez is mentioned only in the context of being master and pilot of the admiral and as having been a member of the party that made initial contact with the natives on Roanoke Island.

During the expedition to Roanoke in 1585 under the leadership of Ralph Lane, the anonymous author of the *Tyger* journal reported that "the Tyger grounded on the bar due to Fernandez's carelessness. . . ." Implicit in this report is the seed of an idea: that Fernandez intentionally grounded the ship. The vessel was ultimately floated off the bar, beached, and saved, but not before the colony's stores of corn, salt, rice, and other needed supplies were destroyed or seriously damaged by water. In a letter to the queen's principal secretary, Sir Francis Walsingham, dated August 12, 1585, Lane, a professional soldier with demonstrated leadership abilities, described the grounding of the *Tyger* and the loss of its stores. Far from blaming Fernandez for the serious accident to the flagship, Lane took the opportunity to praise the pilot for his skill and faithfulness to duty: "the best harbor of all the rest is called Ferdinando discovered by the master and pilot of our fleet, your honor's servant Simon Ferdinando who has truly carried himself with great skill and great government all this voyage not withstanding this great cross to us all. . . ."

Despite the contempt of the anonymous author of the 1585 *Tyger* journal, Fernandez was chosen once again to be the chief pilot of the fleet taking colonists— men, women, and children—to what was to be a permanent settlement in Virginia. In addition, Fernandez was one of twelve men appointed to assist John White in governing the newly formed colony and, along with the governor and other assistants, was granted armorial bearings.

Acting under the patent granted to him by the queen on March 25, 1584, Sir Walter Raleigh incorporated the Governor and Assistants of the Cittie of Raleigh in Virginia. William Dethicke, Garter Principal of Arms, was instrumental in the actual granting of arms to the new city. Within that grant were incorporated individual grants of arms to the governor and each of his assistants. Three drafts survive, each more definitive than its predecessor—a possible indication of proofing and rewriting. Two of the surviving drafts are owned by the College of Arms in London and one by Queen's College, Oxford. The final grant is lost. Logically, it would have been given to Gov. John White and may have been lost on Roanoke along with his armor, maps, and frames. Since the drafts do not agree on all points, it is clear that changes were made in the final grant. The heraldry contained in the surviving drafts leaves many questions unanswered. However, the arms of Simon Fernandez are simple and unambiguous: "a field argent, two bars wavy azure, On a canton gules three fuzels of the first." The fuzels argent on a field gules that appear on Fernandez's arms, as well as those of the governor and other assistants, refer to the patronage of Sir Walter Raleigh. The two wavy bars on an azure field unmistakably refer to Fernandez's profession—mariner.

In the Queen's College manuscript of the Grant of Arms, Simon Fernandez is described as a "gentleman of London." Whether he was made a gentleman in order to meet the minimum qualifications for bearing arms or whether he had attained that social standing prior to 1587 is not known. It must be said that sixteenth-century armorial grants conformed to the upward social mobility of the time. For a price, traditional rules for granting arms were ignored. In a 1602 manuscript titled, "The York Herald's Complaint," George Brooke, York Herald, complained that William Dethicke granted coats of arms to families unworthy of armorial bearing. York used an outline of arms granted by Dethicke to William Shakespeare to illustrate his point. However, there is no reason to assume that Fernandez was poor or socially unworthy because he was a mariner. He had influential friends and patrons, some close to the queen herself, so there is good reason to believe the opposite.

John White's narrative of the 1587 voyage reflects an open, ongoing, and bitter conflict between himself and the pilot-assistant. Fernandez's dismal reputation is rooted in the fertile ground of that critical and damning narrative. It may never be known with certainty whether the bad blood between the two antagonists began during the days of preparation for the 1587 expedition or was a holdover from previous reconnaissance voyages. But their relationship during the long and arduous voyage to Virginia was strained from the start.

Roanoke scholars and historians have accused Fernandez of usurping John White's authority. In order to understand fully the interfacing of their respective roles, sixteenth-century maritime tradition must be taken into consideration. White evidently sailed as captain of the *Lion*, the admiral or flagship of the small fleet of three vessels. Fernandez was the master of the *Lion*, as well as pilot for the fleet. The captain of a vessel was the absolute authority over every aspect of shipboard life and activity—the moral arbiter responsible for law and order while at sea. Everyone aboard the ship, mariner and landsman alike, was subject to the captain's authority. The captain might well be the merchant who owned the ship, an agent of the company, or any appointee so designated— in other words, a landsman with neither knowledge nor experience of the sea.

On the other hand, by definition, the ship's master was a professional mariner— skilled, able, and experienced. He was responsible for instructing the helmsman on the courses to be taken, commanding the boatswain with regard to the trimming of sails, and overseeing all other technical aspects of sailing and maneuvering the ship. As pilot, Fernandez had the further responsibility of plotting courses for all ships of the fleet, a skill that required knowledge of astronomy, mathematics, and cartography. The title of ship's master was not an empty one, while that of captain could be, under certain circumstances. Yet the ultimate authority aboard the *Lion* was not its master, Simon Fernandez, a professional mariner, but the colony's governor, John White, an artist by guild affiliation and trade. Although this Atlantic crossing was probably the third for

Governor White, he was by no means qualified as a shipboard leader, and, indeed, some might argue the same case for his leadership abilities on land.

White and Fernandez had been shipmates or at least co-participants in two expeditions to Roanoke prior to 1587. In both instances, Fernandez, as pilot of the fleet and master of the admiral, held a position of great responsibility and influence, while John White, not yet "Governor and Gentleman," acted a considerably less exalted role. This third expedition's reversal of fortunes may have created an impossible situation between Fernandez and White, one not likely to be ameliorated by a long ocean voyage aboard a cramped ship. White as captain, governor, and probable recruiter was no doubt preoccupied with the colonists, who crowded the holds and decks of the 120-ton merchantman. In all probability, Elinor, the governor's own nineteen-year-old pregnant daughter, was aboard the *Lion*, as was her husband, Ananias Dare, one of the twelve assistants of the colony. How this struggle for control and preeminence must have rankled White's and Fernandez's nerves!

The first in a long series of John White's charges against Simon Fernandez is dated May 1587: "Simon Fernandez master of our admiral lewdly forsook our flyboat leaving her distressed in the Bay of Portugal." On June 22, 1587, while anchored at Santa Cruz (St. Croix), the governor along with six others went ashore for fresh water. According to White's narrative, upon heading back to the ship by another way, the group came upon "certain potsheards of savage making, made of the earth of that island: whereupon it was judged that the island was inhabited with savages, though Fernandez had told us for certain the contrary."

A week later, at Ross Bay along the coast of St. Johns, where "Fernandez promised we should take in salt," another incident took place. White relates that when all was in readiness to go ashore for the salt, Fernandez changed his mind, saying that he did not know whether this was the right place and that if the pinnace went into the bay, the tide being treacherous, he did not know whether he could maneuver it back out again without endangering both ship and occupants. White then described the following scene: "Whilst he was thus persuading, he caused the lead to be cast, and hauling craftily brought the ship in three fathom and a half of water, he suddenly began to swear and tear God in pieces, dissembling great danger, crying to him at the helm, bear up hard, bear up hard. So we went off, and were disappointed of our salt by his means."

White relates that on the seventh of July in the Caicos Islands, while a group of the colonists occupied themselves usefully in hunting, fowling, and seeking salt, "Fernandez solaced himself ashore with one of the company. . . ." How the pilot solaced himself the governor does not specify, but his inference of inappropriate behavior is clear enough. Whether Fernandez dallied with one of the unattached women colonists, spent a lazy, tropical afternoon ashore with an agreeable native woman, or roistered with a brother mariner is inconsequential. Far more interesting and deserving of scrutiny is the governor's continual nit-picking. His narrative reveals that White was preoccupied, almost pathologically, as was Madox, with Fernandez's every move and cried foul against him for every misadventure, however trivial, that chanced to occur. With great passion and intense rhetoric, White casts himself in the role of stalwart hero—the star of the narrative—largely through vilifying the foreign-born Fernandez. In print, if not in fact, the governor strives to bolster his own image as a strong and decisive leader. This raises a number of thorny questions: Did White cast blame on a convenient scapegoat in order to hide his own inability to maintain control? For whose eyes did Governor White intend his narrative, with its long recitation of Fernandez's alleged misdeeds? What did he hope to achieve?

White writes that on the sixteenth of July "the fleet fell within the maine of Virginia, which Simon Fernandez took to be the Island of Croatoan where we came to anchor and rode there two or three days: but finding himself deceived he weighed and beared along the coast where in the night, had not Captain Stafford been more careful in looking out than our Simon Fernandez, we had been all cast away upon the breach, called the Cape of Fear, for we were come within two cable lengths upon it: such was the carelessness and ignorance of our Master." With its implicit charge of deceit and negligence, this passage of White's rings a familiar bell. One may only speculate on the identity of the anonymous author of the *Tyger* journal.

The governor's narrative continues:

The two and twentieth of July we arrived safe at Hatorask [Port Ferdinando], where our ship and pinnesse anchored—the Governor went aboard the pinnesse accompanied with forty of his best men, intending to pass up to Roanoke forthwith, hoping there to find those fifteen Englishmen, which Sir Richard Grenville had left there the year before ... meaning after we had done so to return to our fleet and pass along the coast to the Bay of Chesapeake according to the charge given us among other directions in writing under the hand of Sir Walter Raleigh: but as soon as we were put with our pinnesse from the ship. A gentleman by the means of Fernandez, who was appointed to return to England, called to the sailors in the pinnesse charging them not to bring any of the planters back again, but leave them on the Island, except the Governor and two or three such as he approved, saying that the summer was far spent, whencefore he would land the planters in no other place. Unto this were all the sailors both in the pinnesse and ship persuaded by the Master, wherefore it booted not the Governor to contend with them, but passed to Roanoke. ....

Financial infrastructure, authority, and the power behind the 1587 voyage are central to this highly significant passage from the narrative. Barely mentioned by traditional scholarship, the passage raises a series of highly relevant questions that, to date, have not been addressed. Who was the "gentleman" of whom White speaks? Was he a personal representative of Raleigh or one of the other important backers of the expedition? Did he have carte blanche to make autonomous on-the-spot decisions despite "directions in writing under the hand of Sir Walter Raleigh"? The gentleman in question was obviously so influential that "it booted not the governor" to contend with him. Governorship notwithstanding, White apparently lacked the authority or the means to dissuade him. A decision had been made, and further discussion on the location of the landing site was futile. "A gentleman by means of Fernandez" charged the sailors to leave the planters on the island. These words may be taken two ways: that Fernandez called to the sailors in the pinnace on behalf of the "gentleman" and persuaded them to do his bidding; or that the "gentleman" made his decision "by means of Fernandez," that is, by his influence. Since the "gentleman" was aboard the flagship during the three-month voyage, he had to be well aware of the conflict between the captain-governor and the pilot-assistant. The unnamed gentleman would have had ample opportunity to hear both sides before making up his mind and giving final word on the landing site.

This seems the appropriate time to address the issue of financial backers and their incentive for investing in the voyages. Fernandez is frequently singled out as the privateer—the only privateer—whose self-serving interests came into direct conflict with colonization and thus contributed to the failure of the colony. It was Sir Walter Raleigh himself who encouraged financial investors by combining colonizing schemes with privateering enterprises. Returns on colonization schemes were long-range and risky. By comparison, returns on privateering ventures were substantial—occasionally they were spectacular—and quickly in hand. Sixteenth-century Roanoke Island, with its lush vegetation, virgin forests, and bountiful harvests from the sounds, was indeed "Raleigh's Eden." Protected by a long, low string of barrier islands and ever changing shoal water, it was also ideally suited as a base from which the English could prey upon Spanish ships as they lumbered their way north from the Caribbean with the homeward-flowing currents of the Gulf Stream. With their holds bulging with silver and gold, the cumbersome galleons of the treasure fleet were like so many plump sitting ducks to race-built English ships. On the return trip to England, after depositing Raleigh's 1585 military colony on Roanoke, Sir Richard Grenville captured a fortune in Spanish booty, a turn of events that no doubt pleased investors in the expedition, as well as encouraged others to fatten their own purses by joining the colonizing scheme. Fernandez is frequently assigned the sole responsibility for landing the colonists on Roanoke Island so that he could get about the business of privateering. The words of Governor White and the presence of an unnamed gentleman of means seem to put a different twist on this matter. It is quite clear that the mystery man had more authority than either White or Fernandez. It is not known who he was, but apparently he had high stakes in the combined venture. Did he really want to plant the colony along the comparatively open shores and deepwater anchorages of the Chesapeake Bay, a location that invited Spanish detection and chase? Did Raleigh? Raleigh continued to reap his share of the spoils from privateering long after his interest in the Roanoke colony had waned. When John White finally returned to relieve the colony on Roanoke Island in 1590, it was with a privateering squadron.

The narrative continues, and on the twenty-fifth day of July the flyboat, which Fernandez had "lewdly forsaken" in the Bay of Portugal, landed safely at Hatorask, a scant three days behind the other ships:

The flyboat, and rest of our planters, arrived all safe at Hatorask to the great joy and comfort of the whole company: but the Master of our Admiral grieved greatly at their safe coming, for he purposely left them in the Bay of Portugal, and stole away from them in the night, hoping that the Master thereof, whose name was Edward Spicer, for that he had never been in Virginia, would hardly find the place, or else being left in so dangerous a place as that was, by means of so many men of war, as at that time were abroad, they should surely be taken or slain: but God disappointed his wicked pretenses. . . .

White's next reference to Fernandez is by implication. On the twenty-first of August, in the midst of preparing the flyboat and the *Lion* for their return to England, "a storm at the northeast arose . . . our Admiral then riding out of the harbor, was forced to cut his cables and put to sea, where he lay beating off and on six days before he could come to us again, so that we feared he had been cast away, and the rather, for that at the time of the storm took them, the most and best of their Sailors were left aland." White seems to be implying that Fernandez returned only for the skilled manpower necessary to work his own ship on its homeward, privateering voyage. On the other hand, the return of the *Lion* and its master might indicate that he was not as hostile to the colony as the governor would have us believe. As an assistant and probable investor, Fernandez had his own money tied up in the venture and had as much—if not more—to lose than anyone if the colony failed.

At last, on the twenty-seventh of August, the governor having been constrained by the colonists to return to England for supplies boarded the flyboat, which "already had weighed anchor and rode without the bar, the Admiral riding by them." Fernandez rode at anchor just offshore in the admiral for more than five weeks. Such a delay hardly reflects an overeagerness to get on about the business of privateering, nor does it bolster the case for Fernandez's having abandoned the colony. And where was the unnamed "gentleman" all this time—ashore with the governor and the colonists or aboard the admiral with its master? Did the mystery man return to England aboard the flyboat with White, or did he go privateering with Fernandez? At this point, scholars may only wonder whether the mystery man kept a log or a personal diary.

While those returning to England prepared to get under way, an accident with the capstan resulted in serious injury to twelve men aboard the flyboat, only five of whom were able to "stand to their labor." Totally out of character in this instance, Governor White did not document the name of the flyboat's master, nor did he impute blame for this life-threatening accident. Despite the battered condition of the crew, they were "able to keep company with the Admiral" until the eighteenth of September, when "wherefore understanding that the Admiral meant not to make haste for England, but linger about the Island of Terceira for purchase [taking booty], the flyboat departed for England with letters, where we hoped by the help of God to arrive shortly."

On the sixteenth of October, following a series of storms, great sickness, and near starvation, the flyboat landed on the west coast of Ireland. After two weeks spent in attending to the needs of his sick and exhausted crew, White shipped out aboard the *Monkey*, bound for Southampton:

The 8th. we arrived at Hampton where we understood that our consort the Admiral was come to Portsmouth and had been there three weeks before: and also that Fernandez the Master with all his company were not only come home without any purchase, but also in such weakness by sickness, and death of their chiefest men, that they were scarce able to bring their ship into the harbor, but were forced to let fall anchor without, which they could not weigh again, but might all have perished there, if a small bark by great hap had not come to them to help them. The names of the chief men that died are these, Roger Large, John Mathew, Thomas Smith and some other sailors, whose names I know not at the writing hereof. AD 1587.

This ends the narrative as seen through the eyes of and written by the hand of John White, artist and governor. The White narrative survives as the only known source of information on the 1587 colony. It is possible that somewhere in the nether regions of an obscure muniment room in England or Wales rests another version of that fateful venture as seen through the eyes of another, written by his hand and bearing the bold signature of Simão Fernandez.

The next known references to Fernandez occur in the English State Papers and in the Harleian Manuscript. They date from the time of the Armada. The *Triumph*, the queen's own galleon of 900-1,100 tons and reputed to be the largest ship on either side during the Armada of 1588, was captained by Martin Frobisher, one of four men commanding a squadron. Frobisher's second-in-command was a Lieutenant Eliot, possibly the Laurence Eliot who was with Drake on the circumnavigation. The third officer aboard was Simon Fernandez, the boatswain. As such, Fernandez was responsible for the manual operation of the ship, setting and reefing sails, raising and lowering anchors, repairing canvas, transmitting the captain's orders to the crew, and seeing that those orders were carried out properly—a considerable effort in defense of his adopted country with a foreign invader at its door.

In a post-Armada survey of ships carried out at the Chatham dockyards, Fernandez was one of four out of a total of twenty-five boatswains who could write his own report. The *Triumph* had been in the thick of the action for more than a week and had engaged the Spanish flagship off Gravelines. Fernandez reported that the *Triumph* had lost but a single longboat. He noted that his old sponsor and captain, Frobisher, had made off with some prized souvenirs, the ship's silk ensigns, and that they would have to be replaced at some expense.

In 1589-1590 Sir Walter Raleigh and Gov. John White secured investors for an attempt to relieve the colonists left on Roanoke Island. The agreement was a three-part indenture between Raleigh, the nineteen investors, and the governor and his assistants. While Fernandez's name appeared therein as having been one of the original Roanoke assistants, he is not mentioned as part of the relief attempt that was being planned. Had Fernandez been censured in light of White's vindictive report? In view of Fernandez's demonstrated abilities and faithful services to England, as well as his continued patronage by powerful connections, this scenario does not seem likely. Another fight was brewing with Spain, and Fernandez may have simply lost interest in colonizing ventures, particularly ones that included his old nemesis, White.

Shortly after the heir to the throne of Portugal disappeared during the Battle of Morocco in 1578, King Philip II annexed Portugal and its entire empire. The possession of the islands of the Azores, Canaries, Cape Verdes, and the Madeiras poured a steady stream of wealth into the open coffers of Spain. In 1590 Sir Martin Frobisher and Sir John Hawkins mounted an English attempt to blockade the Iberian peninsula by capturing the strategic Atlantic islands of the Canaries and the Azores. Simon Fernandez served in that campaign as master of the 300-ton *Foresight*, captained by William Winter. It is not known whether Fernandez survived that engagement, but this is the last known reference to the Roanoke pilot by name in the records.

The following entry, "A Note Of Australia Del Espiritu Santo," dated 1605, appears in *The Writing and Correspondence of the Two Richard Hakluyts*, by Richard Hakluyt: "Simon Fernandez, a Pilot of Lisbon told me Richard Hakluyt before other Portugals in London, the 18th of March 1604: that he having been in the Citie of Lima in Peru, did perfectly understand that four ships and barks departed from the said citie of Lima about the year 1600, in the month of February towards the Philippines...."

It is not known whether this man is Fernandez of Roanoke. If they were the same man, it does not seem likely that his name would be mentioned without some small reference to Roanoke, a project that had fascinated the Hakluyts. Nor does it seem likely that Fernandez, a naturalized Englishman of Portuguese extraction and a constant thorn in the side of the Spanish, would settle in Lisbon under Hapsburg rule.

In his *Historie of Travell Into Virginia Britania*, William Strachey refers to "an olde plotte" shown to him by Lord De La Warr, "wherein by a Portingall our seat is laid out and in the same, 2 silver mines pricked downe." A logical assumption would be that the map represented a potential settlement site on the Chesapeake Bay or James River. Since, at this juncture, we know of no other Portuguese involved in the Virginia enterprise, it remains suggestive that the "olde plotte" was a sketch map based on Fernandez's firsthand knowledge of the area.

While the narrative of 1587 has had an enormous influence in forging Fernandez's reputation, there has been another influence, more compelling and more insidious than the passionate rhetoric of John White. For sixty-four production seasons, every night from mid-June until Labor Day, Simon "Fernando," reborn in the fertile mind of playwright Paul Green, leaps from the shadows of history onto the stage of Waterside Theatre on Roanoke Island. The swarthy, semi-crazed "Fernando" is played as the quintessential villain. As the drama *The Lost Colony* unfolds, the black-hearted, black-bearded, black-clad "Fernando" bellows, swaggers, shakes his fists, spits, frightens children, insults women, kicks dogs, crosses blades with the gallant Ananias Dare, slaps beloved Old Tom, and grins malevolently as the English attack a peaceful gathering of Native Americans. Ultimately, it is Green's double-dealing "Fernando" who betrays the colonists to the Spanish and abandons them to their fate in the wilderness. Such is the stuff of which symphonic dramas are made. Paul Green's portrayal of "Fernando" is generally accepted without question, despite the fact that in 1937 the playwright stated that he interpreted the historical data available to him and changed it when it suited his dramatic purpose. With great artistic license, Green places White and Fernandez in the roles of antagonists: the courtly, grief-stricken English grandfather vs. the uncouth, bellowing, foreign-born bully. As a Spanish ship anchors off the bar, ragged, starving colonists drag themselves off into the forest primeval—still singing—to meet their heroic destinies. The capacity house is left with an image of Elinor White Dare—in the spotlight, *en tableau*—a beautiful, tragic young mother, tears streaming down her face, her baby daughter clutched to her breast. At that moment, the real-life Fernandez and his theatrical doppelganger become fused into one—where does fiction end and historical reality begin? Is it any wonder that Simon Fernandez, the man you love to hate, comes up short once again? Voltaire, that great cynic of a later century, said it best: "History is the lie that everyone agrees upon."

The sins attributed to Fernandez, of both omission and commission, comprise an impressive list. The more grievous allegations, such as his incorrigible privateering habits, his incompetence as a pilot, his usurping authority, his ill will and overt attempts to compromise the safety of the colonists, and, finally, his abandonment of the 1587 colony, have been discussed earlier in this paper. One last question remains to be addressed: was Simon Fernandez in the pay of Spain or sympathetic to its cause? It has been well documented that a Terceiran pilot by the name of Fernandez worked with the Spanish at St. Augustine in the 1570s. However, this man was Domingo Fernandez—our man Simon Fernandez was occupied elsewhere, as the records on English piracy bear out. The final answer to this vexing question rests with Sir Francis Walsingham, a longtime sponsor and patron of Simon Fernandez. Walsingham, Queen Elizabeth's Principal Secretary and member of her Privy Council, was a highly intelligent, disciplined, formidable machine of a man, who spoke many languages. A consummate diplomat, he possessed an uncanny grasp of international politics. The queen, his intellectual equal, was often a guest at his manor house in Surrey. He was Elizabeth's omniscient "Spymaster." Walsingham's raison d'être was to protect his queen from her enemies, both foreign and domestic. His network of spies and information gatherers was all-encompassing. Walsingham, the archetypal Puritan, loathed Spain on general principle and, more specifically, on religious grounds. After eighteen years of intricate plots and counterplots, it was the relentless Walsingham who fashioned the web that finally ensnared Mary, Queen of Scots, and brought her to the scaffold. He was a master of duplicity who played cat-and-mouse games with spies and double agents before pouncing on them for the kill. Refined and cultivated as he was, Sir Francis had few scruples about sending enemies of the Crown to the bloody horrors of a traitor's death. The continued patronage of such a man as Walsingham attests powerfully to Fernandez's loyalty.

As a historical character, Fernandez does not quite fit the Hollywood mold of a swashbuckling, Elizabethan sea dog—the embodiment of virtuous and patriotic manhood, risking all for queen and country. But neither was he a rogue and villain merely on account of his calling or his foreign birth. Of all the diverse types serving English overseas expansion, privateers such as Fernandez, driven by dreams of gain, glory, and social prominence and perhaps by a smattering of loyalty, may have pulled hardest in the yoke—if not always in the right direction. While succeeding generations have called his loyalty into question, Simon Fernandez cannot—must not—be dismissed as a petty villain. He indubitably had highly placed patrons, some close to the queen herself, who trusted him in those turbulent days when England's survival as a nation hung in the balance. Fernandez, a skilled and experienced pilot who could read and write, employed his considerable knowledge of navigation to facilitate, in no small measure, the planting of an English-speaking America.

BIBLIOGRAPHIC NOTE

Manuscript sources for this essay come from the following manuscripts in the United Kingdom: the Acts of the Privy Council, Public Record Office, London; the Calthorpe Manuscript transcript, the Historic Manuscripts Commission, London; the Chancery Proceedings, Public Record Office, London; the Consistory Court Wills, the Guildhall, London; the Cotton Manuscript, the British Library, London; the Harleian Manuscript, the British Library, London; the Queen's College Manuscript, Queen's College, Oxford; the Records of the High Court of the Admiralty, Public Record Office, London; the State Papers (Foreign, Colonial, and Domestic) from the Reign of Elizabeth I, Public Record Office, London; the Vincent Manuscript, the College of Arms, London.

Other primary sources used are Richard Hakluyt's *Principal Navigations*, in particular the 1903-1905 Glasgow edition (Glasgow: Maclehose, 1903-1905); Richard Madox's *An Elizabethan in 1582: The Diary of Richard Madox, Fellow of All Souls* (London: Hakluyt Society, 1976); William Strachey's *Historie of Travell Into Virginia Britania* (London: Hakluyt Society, 1953); and the collection of William Monson's writings in *Naval Tracts of Sir William Monson* (London: Navy Records Society, 1902-1914).

Secondary sources used include Philip L. Barbour's edition of *The Complete Works of Captain John Smith (1580-1631)*, 3 vols. (Chapel Hill: Institute of Early American History and Culture and University of North Carolina Press, 1986); the *Dictionary of National Biography* (London: Oxford University Press, 1938); C. L'Estrange Ewen's *The Golden Chalice: A Documented Narrative of an Elizabethian Pirate* (Paignton, U.K.: Cecil Henry L'Estrange Ewen, 1939); Francis Hawks's *History of North Carolina* (Fayetteville: E. J. Hale and Son, 1857-1858); *The International Genealogical Index*; my own "Piracy, Privateering and Elizabethan Maritime Expansion," in *Roanoke Revisited* (Manteo: Times Printing Co., 1993), and "Simon Fernando of Plymouth, London and Roanoke, The Man You Love to Hate," in *The Croatan: Official Program Guide to THE LOST COLONY* (Manteo: Roanoke Island Historical Association, 1994); R. E. G. Kirk and E. F. Kirk's edition of *Returns of Aliens Dwelling in the City and Suburbs of London from the Reign of Henry VIII to that of James I*, 4 vols.

(London: Huguenot Society of London, 1900-1908); John Knox Laughton's edition of the *State Papers Relating to the Defeat of the Spanish Armada, Anno 1588*, 2 vols. (London: Navy Records Society, 1894); John Hobson Matthews's edition of the *Cardiff Records*, 6 vols. (Cardiff: Corporation of Cardiff, 1898-1911); Samuel Eliot Morison's *The Northern Voyages, 500-1600* (New York: Oxford University Press, 1971); Benjamin F. DeCosta's "Simon Ferdinando and John Walker in Maine," *New England Historical and Genealogical Register* 174 (April 1890): 149-158; George Brunner Parks's *Richard Hakluyt and the English Voyages* (New York: American Geographical Society, 1928); David Beers Quinn's *England and the Discovery of America, 1481-1620* (New York: Knopf, 1974), *North America from Earliest Discovery to First Settlements, The Norse Voyages to 1612* (New York: Harper and Row, 1977), *North American Discovery Circa 1000-1612* (Columbia: University of South Carolina Press, 1971), "Preparation for the 1585 Virginia Voyage," *William and Mary Quarterly*, 3d ser., 6 (April 1949): 208-236, *The Roanoke Voyages, 1584-1590*, 2 vols. (London: Hakluyt Society, 1955), and *The Voyages and Colonising Enterprises of Sir Humphrey Gilbert* (London: Hakluyt Society, 1940); G. V. Scammell's "England in the Atlantic Islands, 1450-1650," *Mariner's Mirror* 72 (August 1986): 295-317; David Stick's *Roanoke Island: The Beginnings of English America* (Chapel Hill: University of North Carolina Press, 1983); L. A. Vigneras's "A Spanish Discovery of North Carolina in 1566," *North Carolina Historical Review* 46 (October 1969): 398-414; Hugh Williamson's *The History of North Carolina*, 2 vols. (Philadelphia: Thomas Dobson, 1812); and Justin Winsor's *English Explorations and Settlements in North America, 1497-1689* (Boston: Houghton, Mifflin, 1884).

Manteo and Wanchese in Two Worlds

Michael Leroy Oberg

Following a brief encounter with English explorers along the Carolina Outer Banks in the summer of 1584, Manteo, a native of Croatoan, and Wanchese, of Roanoke Island, traveled to England with the expedition's leaders, Philip Amadas and Arthur Barlowe. Both Indians would return one year later with the soldiers and settlers sent by Sir Walter Raleigh to colonize what he, at least, considered this "New Found Lande" of "Virginia." Manteo, by English standards, would remain steadfastly loyal to Raleigh's settlers for the next three years, disappearing from the historical record with the "Lost Colonists" in 1587. Wanchese, however, would quickly rejoin his people and oppose both continued native interaction with the settlers and successive English attempts to plant colonies in the region.

Both men's stories are important because they reveal potentially so much about the nature of the early Anglo-Indian exchange. Native American history ought not to be divorced from its broader transatlantic context, and Manteo and Wanchese clearly became members of an Atlantic community, confronting Englishmen at home and in England, viewing their relationship with Raleigh's settlers through lenses crafted of native material.[1] The sparse documentation surviving from Raleigh's Roanoke ventures can allow one, albeit tentatively, to reconstruct something of what Indians saw when they looked at the English. After their transatlantic voyage, Manteo and Wanchese responded in dramatically different ways to the colonists. It seems incumbent upon us to explain why.

A further point worth noting: the Roanoke voyages ended in failure, and none of Raleigh's colonies took root. In fact, after going ashore at Roanoke in 1584, 1585, 1586, and 1587, Raleigh's transitory voyagers never gave English names to the places they visited. While English colonists two decades later would plant "Jamestown" in Virginia, and the Pilgrims would settle "Plymouth," Raleigh's settlers explored "Roanoac," "Dasemunkepeuc," "Aquascogoc," and "Choanoac."[2] The importance of this point should not be underestimated. Because the English unquestionably failed in their efforts to plant colonies at Roanoke, students of the ethnohistory of early America who look there can free themselves from the teleological fallacy that views all Indian-white relations in terms of the ultimate demise of native peoples. They can escape as well from the dichotomies so common to studies of European colonization: modern vs. traditional, exploiter vs. exploited, and civilized vs. savage. At Roanoke Island there took place an intercultural encounter from which natives and newcomers learned difficult lessons about each other in an arena in which neither was clearly dominant. The divergent paths followed by Manteo and Wanchese allow us a revealing window into that encounter.

What do we know about these two individuals? The existing sources suggest that Manteo and Wanchese both held positions of high social status within their communities. Manteo's mother may well have been the leader, or *weroansqua*, of the Croatoans; throughout Wanchese's career he seems to have remained in close contact with the Roanoke *weroance* Wingina and to have served him in an advisory capacity. As among the culturally analogous Powhatans, natives who demonstrated great valor in war could earn a position as consultants to their rulers. Clearly in 1587, one year after Wingina's death, the English identified Wanchese as one of the leaders of the Roanoke community in a pair of attacks upon English settlers.[3] The precise relationship between the Roanokes and Manteo's Croatoans is not clearly recorded, but it appears to have been close. We cannot say for certain what Manteo was doing at Roanoke. The records simply will not allow us to draw a firm conclusion. Both Manteo and Wanchese, however, owing to their status and their positions as advisers to powerful individuals, may well have been suited for their roles as diplomats and observers, travelers to England who would report to their people about all that they witnessed and all whom they encountered.[4]

Manteo and Wanchese, I would suggest, traveled to England on a mission. They entered the English orbit from an intensely spiritual universe. The extant English sources—and no native voice was recorded at Roanoke—reveal a surprisingly great deal about Carolina Algonquian spirituality. Carolina Indians, according to Thomas Harriot, believed "that there are many Gods which they call Mantoac, but of different sortes and degrees; one onely chiefe and great God, which hath beene from all eternitie."[5]

This "chiefe and great God" probably was not the focus of much Carolina Algonquian religious activity. The Powhatans of Virginia worshiped a like figure whom they called Ahone, a kind deity so beneficent that he required neither offerings nor ritualized observance. The Powhatans directed the bulk of their religious activity toward diverting the wrath of an evil god called Okeus, who would deliver misfortune upon communities if not properly appeased.[6] The *Kiwasa* of the Carolina Algonquians, described by Harriot and drawn by the artist John White, clearly was a similar figure.[7]

Like their neighbors throughout the Eastern Woodlands, Carolina Algonquians believed that the universe was suffused with power, or *mantoac*, and that rituals were an important means for acquiring that power. But power existed in many forms, and some things and beings possessed more power than others, as Harriot's statement above suggests. Historian Gregory Evans Dowd has pointed out in his study of religious awakenings in eighteenth-century Eastern Woodland communities that "nothing was more important for life than power." Those who had it would fight well in battle, hunt successfully, and raise an abundant harvest. As in the Eastern Woodlands, so it was along the Carolina coast. Power was necessary for survival.[8]

No direct evidence exists to identify how Manteo and Wanchese came to join the English, and much of what follows admittedly is conjectural. We can, at heart, venture only informed guesses as to why they crossed the Atlantic. I would suggest, however, that indigenous concepts of power—beliefs about *mantoac*—are central to understanding their unfolding relationship with the English.

The Roanoke Indians in 1584 quickly and readily engaged in trade with Arthur Barlowe's expedition. "There came," Barlowe wrote, a "great store of people, bringing with them leather, corrall, divers kindes of dies very excellent, and exchanged with us."[9] Granganimeo, the brother of Wingina, reflected his people's great interest in this trade, which likely informed his decision to extend to the English an invitation to settle on the island. Interest in trade may also have made travel with these strangers to their homeland an intriguing option. Such was the case with Uttamatomakin, an Indian sent by Powhatan to report on England in 1616. The technology demonstrated to the Carolina Algonquians by the English suggested that they were a powerful people, and the Roanokes sought especially to acquire those elements of English material culture that manifested *mantoac*.

Harriot understood the Roanoke concept of *mantoac* in terms analogous to the English "god," perhaps a not unreasonable misunderstanding. But to Carolina Algonquians, *mantoac* signified a power higher than that of human beings, an immediate and pervasive sacred power that could manifest itself both in things and beings. For instance, Granganimeo, according to Barlowe, hung around his neck "a bright tinne dishe" that he had acquired from the English, "making signes that it would defende him against his enemies arrowes."[10] Clearly Granganimeo believed that that object evinced a significant degree of beneficent power. English items manifested power, which made them both useful and attractive to the Indians. As Harriot wrote after the 1585 expedition: "Most things they sawe with us, as Mathernaticall instruments, sea compasses, the vertue of the loadstone in drawing yron, a perspective glasse whereby was showed manie strange sightes, burning glasses, wildefire woorkes, gunnes, bookes, writing and reading, spring clocks that seeme to goe of themselves, and manie other thinges that we had, were so straunge unto them, and so farre exceeded their capacities to comprehend the reason and meanes how they should be made and done, that they thought they were rather the works of god then of men, or at the leastwise they had ben given and taught us of the gods."[11]

English technology played a vital role in shaping Carolina Algonquian perceptions of the colonists, whom they viewed as powerful people bearing magical and perhaps otherworldly items permeated with *mantoac*, a power that allowed them, in Bruce White's apt phrase, "to do things that ordinary human beings could not."[12] Indians on the Outer Banks, then, had good cause for taking interest in the English explorers who began to penetrate their world in the sixteenth century.

In England Manteo and Wanchese learned English from Thomas Harriot and taught him, in turn, the rudiments of Carolina Algonquian. Harriot, "being one that have beene in the discoverie, and in dealing with the natural inhabitantes specially imployed," developed apparently a very good understanding of the native language, at least enough to begin developing an alphabet for it. Manteo and Wanchese learned English well enough so that by the end of 1584 they could serve as interpreters, and they provided important testimony on Carolina Algonquian social structure that enabled Arthur Barlowe to complete his report on the 1584 voyage.[13] The pair, it should be noted, also served an important promotional function. Raleigh used them to generate interest among investors in his overseas venture and to rally support for a parliamentary confirmation of his rights in America.[14]

Manteo and Wanchese returned to America with the fleet that departed from Plymouth in April 1585, anchoring near Wococon Island, some distance south of Roanoke, on the twenty-sixth of June. Things began badly for the colonists. The expedition's flagship, the *Tyger*, commanded by Sir Richard Grenville, ran aground near Wococon. Though the ship was saved, salt water poured into the hold, ruining the provisions on board and leaving the colonists with food sufficient for only twenty days. The colonists arrived too late in the year to plant their own crops. Unless they could obtain food from the Indians, they faced the prospect of starvation.[15]

Undeterred, Grenville fitted out smaller ships to explore the Pamlico Sound and the Carolina mainland. On the third day of July, Grenville sent word to Wingina that the English had arrived. It is likely that Wanchese accompanied the Englishmen who sailed on this short voyage; he would not return to the English. Three days later, "Master John Arundell was sent to the mayne, and Manteio with him," perhaps to look for Wanchese. Arundell must also have sailed to Roanoke. Manteo and Arundell returned to Wococon in time to accompany a larger expedition, which departed on the eleventh in three boats and which included the colony's governor, Ralph Lane, Harriot, Amadas, White, and some sixty men.[16] On the twelfth this party reached the palisaded village of "Pomeioke." One day later they reached Aquascogoc, and on the fifteenth Secotan, where the explorers "were well intertayned there of the Savages."[17] White made numerous drawings at Secotan, and Harriot conversed there with the villagers on matters of religion in some detail.[18]

To do so, Harriot would have found an Indian interpreter indispensable, and he probably had Manteo with him, though we cannot be certain. If Manteo accompanied the group, he would have learned about, or perhaps even witnessed, the English attack on Aquascogoc, which took place on the sixteenth. One of the party's three boats, under the command of Amadas, returned to the village to demand the return of a silver cup reportedly stolen by an Indian. Not receiving it, one crew member recorded, "we burnt, and spoyled their corne, and Towne, all the people being fledde."[19]

Whatever its significance, the attack at Aquascogoc does not appear to have seriously affected initial relations with the Roanokes. By the twenty-first, the expedition had returned to Wococon, whence the English fleet quickly "wayed anker for Hatoraske." On the twenty-seventh, as they anchored along the Outer Banks, Manteo, and perhaps others, made the quick trip across to Roanoke. Two days later, Granganimeo extended an invitation to the colonists to settle on the island, and by early August they had established the foundation for a fortified base on the northern tip of Roanoke, not far from Wingina's village.[20]

The colonists, with the help of Manteo, quickly reestablished friendly relations with the Roanoke Indians. The surviving records indicate a significant degree of interaction between natives and newcomers, consequently placing a premium on the talents of those capable of bridging the cultural divide. In the colony's early months, Manteo and Harriot played a crucial role in mediating and brokering a tenuous middle ground on the Carolina Outer Banks.[21]

It would not last. Hungry English settlers placed increasingly dangerous pressure on Carolina Algonquian subsistence systems, especially during the lean months of winter and early spring. It is not at all surprising that relations between natives and newcomers began visibly to deteriorate in the early months of 1586. It would be wrong, however, to focus solely on events at Roanoke in terms of an Algonquian subsistence crisis, for such an explanation cannot account for the behavior of Manteo, Wanchese, Wingina, and other natives in the face of English settlement. If technology convinced some natives that the English had access to powerful and attractive items that were more "the works of god than of men," the power of the English could manifest itself as well in malevolent forms. Indians on the Outer Banks weighed both considerations as they confronted the colonists.

Carolina Algonquians were both frightened and impressed by the power of English disease, which quickly began to ravage native communities on the Outer Banks. In some villages the English entered, Harriot wrote, "the people began to die very fast, and manie in short space: in some towns about twentie, in some fourtie, in some sixtie, & in one six score, which in trueth was very manie in respect of their numbers." Disease, according to Harriot, the Indians considered "the worke of our God through our meanes, and that wee by him might kil and slaie whom wee would without weapons and not come neere them." In Indian eyes the English controlled an enormously powerful force—"invisible bullets," they called it—that devastated native communities and so impressed the Indians that "some people could not tel whether to thinke us gods or men."[22]

The English settlement was small, barely one hundred men, but it did much damage. Throughout the early contact period, even cursory contact with Europeans could launch horrible epidemics in native communities.[23] That devastation, and the widespread belief among Indians on the Outer Banks that the English were more powerful than they, generated divisions within the Roanoke community. English power, it seemed, could both harm and help Indians. Though the Roanoke Indians could agree that they had declined relative to the English, they divided over how best to respond.

At the two extremes were Manteo and Wanchese. Manteo anglicized fully, and no evidence suggests that he ever wavered in his cooperation with, and identification with, the English. His motives for doing so cannot be reconstructed with any certainty. It seems likely, however, that he found both status and security through cooperation with what he probably recognized as the more powerful English. Wanchese quickly abandoned the English and appears to have been deeply hostile toward the colonists.

Perhaps he had seen enough during his year in England to ameliorate any affection he entertained toward them. Certainly he no longer was impressed by English power and thought that the colonists were the source of his people's problems.

Others, who had not gone to England, wavered between these two poles, trying to secure their people's survival in an arena of rending social change. For instance, Ensenore, described as a "savage father" to Wingina, along with Granganimeo, apparently accepted that the English were more powerful than they and hoped to secure their survival through careful accommodation to, and cooperation with, the colonists.[24] Ensenore, for example, certainly feared the power of the English. According to Harriot, Ensenore was among those who "were of the opinion that we [the English] were not borne of women, and therefore not mortal, but that we were men of an old generation many yeeres past, and risen againe to immortalitie."[25] According to the colony's governor, Ralph Lane, Ensenore warned those "amongst them that sought our destruction" that instead they "should finde their owne, and not be able to work ours." Fearing what he believed to be extremely powerful, otherworldly beings, "dead men returned into the world againe . . . that . . . doe not remayne dead but for a certaine time, and that then . . . returne againe," Ensenore was convinced of the impossibility of killing the English.[26]

Ensenore's warnings that the English "were the servants of God" and that the colonists "were not subject to be destroyed by them" clearly carried some weight with Wingina, who may have been among those Roanokes who, in the spring of 1586, sought the assistance of English prayers to combat the effects of drought. Certainly, at Ensenore's urging, he planted a crop of corn for the English and helped them construct fishing weirs. Unlike Manteo and Wanchese, whose experiences with the English had formed for them strong impressions of the English and the way natives should interact with them, Wingina, Ensenore, Granganimeo, and others felt their way along slowly. They tried to understand the sources of English spiritual power and to incorporate that power into their accustomed ways of living. This they did through joining the English in praying, singing psalms, and other activities. They assessed carefully how best to protect the interests of their communities when confronted by visitors who had the power to do things that Indians could not.

In this atmosphere of acute social and cultural dislocation, some Roanokes beseeched the English to send disease among their native enemies so that they "might in like sort die."[27] Others sought the assistance of English prayers—English rituals— to preserve their corn during a period of drought, "fearing that it had come to passe by reason that in some thing they had displeased us."[28] Many, searching for moorings amid a maelstrom of change, hoped to halt the epidemiological onslaught visited upon their communities through active participation in the public rituals of English Christianity. "When as wee kneeled downe on our knees to make our prayers unto god," Harriot wrote, "they went about to imitate us, and when they saw we moved our lipps, they also dyd the like." If the English caused the disease by shooting their "invisible bullets" at the Indians, and if the English were not affected by disease, it made sense to seek protection through English means.[29]

Wingina, according to Harriot, joined the English in the rituals of prayer and the singing of psalms, "hoping thereby to be partaker of the same effectes which wee by that meanes also expected." When on two occasions he became "so grievously sicke that he was like to die, and as he lay languishing, doubting of anie help by his owne priestes," Wingina called upon the English "to praie and bee a meanes to our God that it would please him either that he might live, or after death dwell with him in blisse."[30] Others, believing strongly in a connection between English power and the Bible, desired "to touch it, to embrace it, to kisse it, to hold it to their breasts and heades, and stroke over all their bodie with it." To Harriot, a man full of sincere philanthropic intentions for the Indians, such behavior demonstrated the natives' "hungrie desire of that knowledge which was spoken of."[31] Harriot, as acute an observer as he was, missed the point. Those Roanokes who joined the English in prayer desired Christianity less than they did access to the power that enabled the English to remain alive on the Outer Banks while Indians suffered.

For Wingina, this effort appears to have been profoundly disillusioning. Buffeted in a world of rapid change, Wingina experimented with English cultural forms in order to secure the power that preserved and bestowed so many benefits upon the settlers. English power, however, provided few answers for beleaguered Algonquians, and Wingina moved rapidly away from the accommodationism of Granganimeo and Ensenore and toward Wanchese's more openly hostile position. Deaths from disease continued, and Granganimeo and Ensenore were among the casualties. The rains never came. Lane's hungry settlers placed increasingly dangerous pressure upon limited Roanoke food supplies. Like Wanchese, Wingina concluded that his people's problems stemmed from contact with the English. English power manifested itself in malevolence, in death and suffering. Harriot noted that "there could at no time happen any strange sicknesse, losses, hurtes, or any other crosse unto them, but that they would impute to us the cause or meanes therof for offending or not pleasing us."[32] After the death of Ensenore in April, according to Lane, Wingina, along with "certaine of our great enemies," including Wanchese, "were in hand again to put their old practises in ure against us."[33] Wanchese and Wingina likely viewed the English, once feared and respected for the power they demonstrated, as the source of their community's problems, a violent and pestilential people who placed great strains on Roanoke food supplies. Led by Wingina, the Roanokes abandoned the island and moved to the mainland village of Dasemunkepeuc, dooming the English colony. Their intent, as Lane correctly realized, was "starving us, by . . . forbearing to sowe."[34] In June 1586, after launching an attack that killed Wingina, the English, with little food and less hope of obtaining any, abandoned Roanoke Island.

In the wake of the English departure, Wanchese maintained considerable influence among the remnants of Wingina's people at Dasemunkepeuc and continued to organize opposition to the English. Late in the summer of 1586, he apparently led the attack that killed a small group of English sailors from a relief expedition left by Grenville to hold Roanoke Island after Lane's departure. In 1587 he led the attack that killed George Howe, a high-ranking colonist at what ultimately came to be known as the "Lost Colony." Thereafter he disappeared from the historical record.

Manteo, through all of this, remained loyal to the English. In 1586 he accompanied an expedition led by Gov. Ralph Lane into the Albemarle Sound and Roanoke River, and he returned again to England in June 1586 when the English abandoned the colony. In 1587 he returned to Roanoke Island again with the ill-fated colonists led by the artist and explorer John White. Raleigh hoped that White's explorers would settle on the Chesapeake Bay. Manteo would remain at Roanoke Island, serving Raleigh as a sort of feudal lord maintaining English title to the region until Raleigh was again ready to establish a base in the region. On August 13, 1587, Manteo was "christened in Roanoak, and called Lord thereof, and on Dasamonguepunke, in reward for his faithful service."[35] The christening of Manteo is revealing in what it tells us about Raleigh's understanding of an Anglo-American empire. Indians would play a vital role in Raleigh's nascent brand of English imperialism.[36]

White's colonists, of course, did not move on to the Chesapeake. Simon Fernandez, the expedition's irascible pilot, deposited the colonists like so much unwanted luggage at Roanoke. There, at White's behest, Manteo worked to patch up relations between the English and neighboring Indians. The legacy of bitterness left by Lane's expedition the year before made this a formidable task. Even Manteo's Croatoans fled from the English at first sighting, begging them not to steal their food, a measure of the desperate tactics Lane resorted to for feeding his hungry settlers.[37] To retaliate for the killing of Howe, the English attacked Dasemunkepeuc, hoping to catch Wanchese and his followers. Manteo helped lead the attack. The Roanokes, however, had abandoned Dasemunkepeuc after the murder of Howe and fled inland. A group of Croatoans—Manteo's kinfolk—then occupied the hastily abandoned village. It was these upon whom the English attack fell. The cruel irony here is that Manteo, who behaved himself during the attack, according to John White, "as a most faithfull English man," failed to recognize until too late his own native kin sitting around the fires at Dasemunkepeuc.[38]

What to make of all this? The story of the Anglo-Indian exchange was not simply one of conquest, as the ultimate failure of Raleigh's colonizing ventures makes clear. The history of Indians during the early contact period is a transatlantic one, something too few historians recognize: Indian allies would play an essential role in Raleigh's American empire; hostile Indians would be its undoing. Indians closely watched the English and, by all accounts, sought initially to incorporate these powerful men, and elements of their culture, into their communities. Some, I would suggest, wanted to learn more or were sent to learn more. There was no united response to English colonization. Manteo found advantage and, perhaps, social advancement and status through maintaining close association with the English. This did not come without cost, as the attack at Dasemunkepeuc revealed. Wanchese, however, watching and observing, ultimately saw in the English a threat to the Roanoke Indians that must be avoided or, if necessary, countered through violence.

NOTES

1. See, for example, the following fine studies: Ian K. Steele, *Warpaths: Invasions of North America* (New York: Oxford University Press, 1994) and *Betrayals: Fort William Henry and the "Massacre"* (New York: Oxford University Press, 1990); Eric Hinderaker, *Elusive Empires: Constructing Colonialism in the Ohio Valley, 1673-1800* (New York: Cambridge University Press, 1997); Peter C. Mancall, *Valley of Opportunity: Economic Culture along the Upper Susquehanna, 1700-1800* (Ithaca: Cornell University Press, 1991), and Peter C. Mancall, ed., *Envisioning America: English Plans for the Colonization of North America, 1580-1640* (Boston: St. Martin's, 1995); and James H. Merrell, "The Customes of our Countrey," in *Strangers within the Realm: Cultural Margins of the First British Empire*, ed. Bernard Bailyn and Philip D. Morgan (Chapel Hill: University of North Carolina Press, 1991), 115-156.

2. David Beers Quinn, ed., *The Roanoke Voyages, 1584-1590: Documents to Illustrate the English Voyages to North America Under the Patent Granted to Walter Raleigh in 1584*, 2 vols., Hakluyt Society Second Series, No. 104 (London: Hakluyt Society, 1955; reprint, New York: Dover, 1991), 2:841-872.

3. Quinn, *Roanoke Voyages*, 2:527-528; David Beers Quinn, *Set Fair for Roanoke: Voyages and Settlements, 1584-1606* (Chapel Hill: University of North Carolina Press, 1985), 39; Karen O. Kupperman, *Roanoke: The Abandoned Colony* (Totowa, N.J.: Rowman and Allanheld, 1984), 118.

4. On native social structure, see the discussion in Stephen R. Potter, *Commoners, Tribute and Chiefs: The Development of Algonquian Culture in the Potomac Valley* (Charlottesville: University Press of Virginia, 1993), 14-16, and Helen C. Rountree, *The Powhatan Indians of Virginia: Their Traditional Culture* (Norman: University of Oklahoma Press, 1989), 101.

5. Quinn, *Roanoke Voyages*, 1:372.

6. Rountree, *The Powhatan Indians of Virginia*, 35-136; Frederic Gleach, *Powhatan's World and Colonial Virginia: A Conflict of Cultures* (Lincoln: University of Nebraska Press, 1997), 36.

7. Quinn, *Roanoke Voyages*, 1:424-425, 2:888; Paul Hulton, *America 1585: The Complete Drawings of John White* (Chapel Hill: University of North Carolina Press with British Museum Publications in Association with America's Four Hundredth Anniversary Committee, North Carolina Department of Cultural Resources, 1984), plate 38, fig. 25.

8. Gregory Evans Dowd, *A Spirited Resistance: The North American Indian Struggle for Unity, 1745-1815* (Baltimore: Johns Hopkins University Press, 1992), 3.

9. Quinn, *Roanoke Voyages*, 1:103.

10. Quinn, *Roanoke Voyages*, 1:100.

11. Quinn, *Roanoke Voyages*, 1:375-376.

12. Quinn, *Roanoke Voyages*, 1:378.

13. Quinn, *Roanoke Voyages*, 1:103-104, 119, 321; Vivian Salmon, "Thomas Harriot (1560-1621) and the English Origins of Algonkian Linguistics," *Historiographia Linguistica* 19 (May 1992): 25-56; W. A. Wallace, *John White, Thomas Harriot, and Walter Ralegh in Ireland*, Durham Thomas Harriot Seminar Occasional Paper No. 2 (Durham, U.K.: Durham Thomas Harriot Seminar, 1985), 15.

14. G. R. Batho, *Thomas Harriot and the Northumberland Household*, Durham Thomas Harriot Seminar Occasional Paper No. 1 (Durham, U.K.: Durham Thomas Harriot Seminar, 1983); Quinn, *Roanoke Voyages*, 1:127-128.

15. Quinn, *Roanoke Voyages*, 1:176-177, 201.

16. Quinn, *Roanoke Voyages*, 1:189-190.

17. Quinn, *Roanoke Voyages*, 1:190.

18. See Hulton, *America 1585*, plates 36-42.

19. Quinn, *Roanoke Voyages*, 1:191.

20. Quinn, *Roanoke Voyages*, 1:191-192.

21. Richard White, *The Middle Ground: Indians, Empires, and Republics in the Great Lakes Region, 1650-1815* (Cambridge, U.K., and New York: Cambridge University Press, 1991).

22. Quinn, *Roanoke Voyages*, 1:378-380.

23. Peter B. Mires, "Contact and Contagion: The Roanoke Colony and Influenza," *Historical Archaeology* 28 (1994): 30-38.

24. Quinn, *Roanoke Voyages*, 1:275.

25. Quinn, *Roanoke Voyages*, 1:379-380.

26. Quinn, *Roanoke Voyages*, 1:278.

27. Quinn, *Roanoke Voyages*, 1:378.

28. Quinn, *Roanoke Voyages*, 1:377. Recent dendrochronological research has confirmed that drought-like conditions existed at Roanoke during the time of the Roanoke ventures. (See David W. Stahle et al., "The Lost Colony and Jamestown Droughts," *Science* 280 [April 24, 1998]: 564-567.)

29. Quinn, *Roanoke Voyages*, 1:425.

30. Quinn, *Roanoke Voyages*, 1:376-377.

31. Quinn, *Roanoke Voyages*, 1:377.

32. Quinn, *Roanoke Voyages*, 1:378.

33. "put their old practises in ure against us": Quinn notes that *in ure* means "into effect." (*Roanoke Voyages*, 1:280 n. 8.)

34. Quinn, *Roanoke Voyages*, 1:280-281.

35. Quinn, *Roanoke Voyages*, 2:531.

36. This is the central point of my *Dominion and Civility: English Imperialism and Native America, 1585-1685* (Ithaca: Cornell University Press, 1999).

37. Quinn, *Roanoke Voyages*, 2:526.

38. Quinn, *Roanoke Voyages*, 2:530.

Investment in the Roanoke Colonies and Its Consequences

David Beers Quinn

It may be useful, to begin with, to suggest what the promoters of the Roanoke expeditions hoped for, which led them to support the expeditions of 1584 and 1585 and, to a certain degree, the later ones as well.

Richard Hakluyt set out his hopes of what should be the objectives of the American expeditions in his "Discourse of Western Planting" in October 1584, which was to see a large and growing English community established in North America so as to create another England overseas. Such a community would produce goods that would allow England to dispense with other sources of supply and make it independent of most foreign countries commercially. In return, the colony would provide a base from which woolen goods (England's most important produce) could be sold to the native inhabitants, as well as to the growing colonial population. Hakluyt considered that all sorts of Mediterranean and subtropical products could be produced in the new colony and that its vast timber supplies could supply another of England's major needs, timber to build its ships. He hoped, in the end, to create a self-contained empire of the North Atlantic. Some of those objectives would be achieved in the very long run, but ignorance of what North America, in the parts to be first settled, was really like impeded their accomplishment. No one had then explored those regions. In addition, Hakluyt hoped that the new colonies would help weaken England's great enemy, Spain, in that the local inhabitants, when Christianized, and the colonists too, would attack the Spanish empire in the Caribbean and that the colonies themselves would serve as bases for English ships to attack the Spanish fleets carrying treasure and so many other valuable things from the Spanish empire to Europe. Only a few of those objectives were attainable at the time, and only if Queen Elizabeth would devote her money and ships to their achievement, but this was largely wishful thinking, too. Walter Raleigh, Sir Richard Grenville, and, above all, the adventurous Sir Francis Walsingham, the queen's principal secretary of state, shared in Hakluyt's hopes; all were prepared to risk some appreciable part of their private fortunes to realize them.

The missing element here is minerals. There was some skepticism about finding valuable minerals outside the Spanish possessions after the failure of Martin Frobisher to find gold in the far north in 1577 and 1578.[1] But the prevailing theory was that gold did not "grow" in cold countries but only nearer the tropics or at least in warm climates, so that there might indeed be gold in the regions to which the new colonizing ventures were directed. But gold was not the only mineral attractive to Englishmen: they had done much to develop the mining of iron and, still more, copper and lead deposits in England, with considerable, though mixed, success. Potential mineral discoveries, therefore, could attract a certain amount of money to a new venture, though nothing like the vast sum, for those days, of £30,000 promised, if not all paid, for the Frobisher ventures. Copper, indeed, had special attraction, since demand for it was growing.

We all realize how fortunate we are that Richard Hakluyt left us such full and graphic records of the Roanoke voyages, so that they have become, in a real sense, the heritage of the people of North Carolina and the beginnings of both its modern history and the history of English settlement in North America in general.[2] What is not so well realized is that the records are edited narratives, trimmed of extraneous detail and hiding specifics that would tell us how the expeditions were planned and who, apart from the three I have mentioned, inspired and financed them—indeed made them possible. For only one Elizabethan expedition whose purpose included colonization do we have full details of the subscribers' financing and of the ships' fitting out. This is for the Frobisher expedition to Baffin Island in 1578, which involved planning a colony, as well as mining for fool's gold. We know a good deal about who backed the expeditions of Sir Humphrey Gilbert in 1578 and 1583, even if their precise contributions remain uncertain.[3] For the Roanoke voyages we have almost no information of this kind outside the narratives, though a certain limited amount can be put together or at least guessed at.[4] Even though I and others have sought long and hard for specific detail, not a great deal has come to light. You cannot therefore expect me to give what apparently does not exist, a full account of my subject—namely, by whom and to what extent the expeditions were supported.

Raleigh, who had owned a privateer since 1582, lost no time in sending off Philip Amadas and Arthur Barlowe to America in 1584. They were both Devon men whom he knew well, and one of their barks may well have been Raleigh's privateer (a polite name for a pirate ship), Simon Fernandez having been a pirate and narrowly escaping execution in 1577. Their reconnaissance was brisk and not costly—it did not cost Raleigh more than a few hundred pounds, and he would not have needed outside assistance. It is worth noting that Barlowe brought his vessel home with his report, as well as, I am inclined to believe, Thomas Harriot and the two Indians—Manteo and Wanchese—while Amadas and Fernandez went off attempting to find a ship to rob in the vicinity of the Azores, though we do not know if they did so.

Manteo's proficiency in English, which amazed and inspired possible contributors to the next colonizing venture in December, was one of Raleigh's propaganda lines, along, I believe, with copies of Barlowe's glowing report. Then, when Raleigh had got himself elected to Parliament, he was able to carry his propaganda further. He probably drew up his bill to give statutory effect to his patent with Walsingham's approval, though with little hope that the queen would accept it, but it would help him gain the support of rich men in both houses.[5] The House of Commons put the bill through its paces and eventually sent it to a committee. There, Raleigh reckoned on getting subscribers and supporters. Sir Francis Drake was there, for example, and ready to help (though perhaps not to subscribe very much—he had his own plans for a bigger expedition under way). Sir Richard Grenville was a vital associate enlisted at that time. Sir Philip Sidney wished to go but drew back, though he certainly subscribed. Thomas Cavendish, a rich young man from Suffolk, not only wished to go but was willing to mortgage some land to fit out a ship to take part in the expedition. Anthony Rowse, a west country M.P., likewise declared his willingness to go. Who else, we do not know, but a note taker added that on the committee were "many that were to go in that journey."[6] Walsingham and Sir Christopher Hatton, both royal officials, were undoubtedly supporters and subscribed as well. The bill was, of course, rejected in the House of Lords, as Raleigh knew it would be, since it infringed on the queen's prerogative, but it picked up at least one subscriber there, Lord Howard of Effingham, who was shortly to become Lord High Admiral and a vital ally of Raleigh's maritime activities for many years.

Although Walsingham undoubtedly urged Queen Elizabeth to support the venture substantially, largely as a means to forestall a Spanish attack on England and to weaken that adversary's overseas empire, she, rightly, responded cautiously. She proved willing to give Raleigh money and privileges worth considerable amounts, but she did not intend to involve herself to any extent directly in the venture. She did agree to accept the name *Virginia* for the colony (her major contribution to later American nomenclature); in return she knighted Raleigh in January 1585[7] and allowed him to have one of her ships, the *Tiger* (though we do not know on what terms), powder from the Tower of London, and perhaps other contributions of this sort involved in equipping the ship.[8] She gave him the unpopular privilege of impressing ships, men, and stores for the expedition, although we do not know to what extent he used it.[9] She also put a little cash (£120) into equipping two ships that were to follow the main expedition in June, though in fact they were diverted at the last moment to another task.

The port towns of Devon and Cornwall did not offer much support to the 1585 or later ventures, while Exeter even refused any contribution to the 1586 voyage. But there was to be support in Barnstable and Bideford in North Devon, especially from shipowners who had a prior record of piracy (or, rather, privateering from June 1585 onward, if only Spanish or Portuguese ships were robbed, since war had begun). The primary influence there was Grenville, whose extensive lands (after he had sold Buckland Abbey, near Plymouth, to Drake) were in that area. London merchants, with very few exceptions, remained detached from the expeditions. They were primarily concerned with restoring or safeguarding their existing trades, especially that in unfinished cloth.

A vital question is how much did it cost for the 1585 expedition to set out. We have no precise figures, but when Kenneth Andrews was writing on privateering, he worked out various schedules of costs that, if he is correct, give us some basis on which to calculate.[10] Using his figures, the cost of fitting out the seven vessels that set out in April 1585 for a six-months' transatlantic voyage, which is roughly what the expedition amounted to, would be about £4,000, a good part of which would be covered by the value of the ships (all of which, except one pinnace, came back) and their guns (apart from those left on Roanoke Island). What is very difficult to add up is how much was spent on the pay and equipment of the colonists for their stay of what was estimated to be about nine months, including the initial capital cost of erecting and supplying the fort and housing. We may guess that some two hundred would-be colonists were on board when the ships left England and that the number was almost halved by those marooned on Jamaica by Raymond[11] and those who did not wish to stay when they got there, which brought the number who stayed down to 108. We should probably think of something like £20 each for two hundred, which would make provision for basic rations for nine months about £4,000, even if a good proportion of the stores were destroyed when the *Tiger* grounded on Ocracoke. We might guess that £1,000 to £1,500 would cover the fixed cost of setting up the colony after their arrival. The fifteen gentlemen who stayed would presumably pay for their own keep. That would make a total of at least £5,500, though this is very much a guess. We might say that £7,000 was an absolute maximum. These are tiny figures in relation to today's prices, but they represent as much as one million dollars in contemporary costs. In addition, the *Golden Royal* (and another ship) was supposed to sail in June with additional stores and colonists (we can only faintly guess how many, perhaps another one hundred), but it never sailed to Roanoke.[12] There was also the abortive supply attempt, in which during the summer of 1586 a ship went out, discovered that the colonists had left, and returned. This might have cost Raleigh another £1,000 to £1,500. We do not know whether Drake was rewarded for bringing back the one hundred colonists in July 1586. Probably he brought them gratis. I give these guesses not to dazzle you with numbers but to provide a few clues to the financial effort required to set out the venture and to sustain it.

The returns from the 1585 voyage are better, if not fully, documented. Grenville captured a Spanish vessel, the *Santa Maria de San Vincente*, which had fallen behind the convoyed *flota* to the north of Bermuda and brought it as a prize to Plymouth. It was a matter of chance that by that time war had broken out between England and Spain, rendering the vessel a legitimate prize. The Spanish said that it was worth some £47,000; Grenville said £14,000. The Spanish account is circumstantial, and we may consider as much as £40,000 possible.[13] The crew all made themselves rich, and so did Grenville, even if customs duties and the lord admiral's tenth had to be met and the *Tiger* repaired and returned to the queen. How much Raleigh got is unclear, but perhaps it was as much as £10,000—more than enough to pay his costs and give him a sizable profit. Grenville kept the *Santa Maria de San Vincente* and renamed it *The Virgin God Save Her*. Two smaller prizes, of which we hear nothing, were also taken in the Caribbean.

A further complication occurred. The *Golden Royal*, under Bernard Drake and Amias Preston, was supposed (with another ship), as has been noted, to bring out more colonists and supplies in June.[14] Instead, the queen ordered the captain and crew of the *Golden Royal*, in that month, to sail to Newfoundland and capture or destroy as many Spanish fishing boats as they could in revenge for English ships seized in Spain in May. We may ignore the fishing vessels taken (they were in fact Portuguese, not Spanish), but in Newfoundland Drake and Preston joined up with George Raymond, who had commanded the *Red Lion* in Grenville's squadron but had gone ahead. It was probably he who had in 1585 marooned some colonists on Jamaica (on the excuse that he lacked supplies) to be mopped up by the Spanish and then dumped the rest on Croatoan Island before Grenville arrived. He sailed on to Newfoundland and began to attack the Portuguese fishing vessels there before the *Golden Royal* arrived. On the way back, Raymond sailed southeastward and captured no fewer than four Portuguese ships laden with sugar from Brazil, worth at least £9,000. When he got back, Drake and Preston tried unsuccessfully to get a fair division of the spoils, but Raleigh is said to have seized one vessel as a prize and to have gotten some £3,000 from it. Raleigh did well from this venture too. Walsingham and other investors must have at the very least gotten their investment back and probably made a profit.

This must have pleased Walsingham, but he got less good news from his men who came home with Grenville in the autumn of 1585 and told him that the Outer Banks did not provide any secure anchorage for ships and that only small vessels could enter the sounds around Roanoke Island. He cooled off for a time from Virginia and concentrated on helping privateers to raid the Caribbean. Indeed, it is clear that some of the privateer captains in the 1585 expedition were more interested in privateering than in establishing a permanent colony. Raymond was one example, but the very success of Grenville in taking a valuable prize diverted attention from the original emphasis on American settlement. Even if Raleigh eventually profited by his venture of 1585, by the time Francis Drake brought his men home in July 1586 he must have been deeply disappointed.

Grenville's relief expedition, if it was seriously intended as such, was ready only in late June or July 1586, and even then its precise objective is not clear.[15] Grenville's Spanish prize, *The Virgin God Save Her*, and his ship *Peter*, with Raleigh's *Roebuck*, were joined by three former pirate ships—*Pelican*, *Prudence*, and *Jesus* of Barnstable—and by several smaller vessels. But was Grenville bringing out additional colonists? The three hundred men with whom he was credited could mostly have been for fighting and for prize crews. He carried supplies for the colony, but my opinion is that he intended only to add additional soldiers to guard against Spanish attacks. His main purpose in making his outward voyage was to seize whatever foreign vessels he could and rob indiscriminately, his first robberies being from French and Dutch ships (for which he was subsequently penalized), and his enterprising voyage directly westward from Madeira was influenced by similar objectives. This was what led him to arrive too late to help the colonists, even if Drake had not already removed them, as they would have probably been starving by the time he arrived. His futilely leaving a handful of soldiers behind was, I think, an attempt to maintain a hold on Roanoke Island and maintain the honor of the settlement: they were too few. The Spanish prize with a cargo of hides he took at Terceira on his way home at least helped to pay his costs, but no balance sheet can be estimated. He was not ready to make a further expedition in 1587, although he had begun to make plans for a major one in 1588. This brings to an end the first phase of the Virginia enterprise. It showed that settlement was probable and not too expensive but that a larger or different objective must dominate future plans.

Thus we should probably revise accepted views on the subsequent projects and experiments of 1587-1590 and look at them instead as parts of a coherent plan for an English-controlled area extending from Pamlico Sound to Chesapeake Bay, which, in turn, would provide a springboard for the development of a series of English colonies in mainland North America, as indeed Virginia was eventually to become. Such a plan would build on the explorations and surveys of 1585-1586 and use them as a first stage in the process. If this be so, the 1587-1590 activities would involve four separate enterprises closely linked together.

It would, first of all, involve entrusting Manteo with responsibility for control of Native American relations around the sounds, using Roanoke Island as the base from which he could get English support when he needed it. Roanoke Island would then be retained as a continuing English outpost, not abandoned as we have hitherto thought had been intended. After all, even if it had been found unsuitable for a permanent colony of settlement, it had provided an excellent base for the essential preliminary exploration and potential exploitation of the surrounding area. Harriot was, in 1587 and 1588, extolling it as a center from which deerskins could be traded in quantity, as well as furs, pearls, and other things, while it could produce valuable cedar, plant fibers, and sassafras (and other medicinal plants), which would justify exploitation.[16] More important, it could provide a base on which minerals could be assembled and processed. The value of potential copper, silver, and bog iron deposits to English industry, together with timber to exploit them, was assuredly important, since so much energy had already been employed in English mining development. Ivor Noël Hume has exposed the mineral work, especially on copper, by Harriot and Ganz in 1585. Harriot also stressed the unrivaled resources of the sounds to support a fishery, which was graphically illustrated by White's drawings of so many species. We should, I think, seriously consider that in 1587 and later, Roanoke Island was considered worth retaining, but as a trading post and not primarily as a colony of settlement.

On the other hand, the only explored area in which friendly Native Americans together with open land for English settlement was to be found was south of Chesapeake Bay, where the exploring party had wintered in 1585-1586. An English community could take root there, it was thought, without friction with the current occupants. Such a community was clearly the main objective of the 1587 expedition and the reason for assembling families of colonists.[17] But that in itself would not be sufficient. The discovery of a deepwater entry into the interior (Chesapeake Bay) provided, for the first time, the opportunity to establish a strong naval base in North America. Such a base could be located on the southern shore of the bay, and it would serve a number of purposes. Primarily, it would enable the English to resist any Spanish attempt to destroy the English hold on the area; secondarily, it would let them assault and rob the Spanish homeward-bound fleet, thus providing a profitable means of supporting the other ventures and making money for the investors as well; and finally, it could protect the infant colony immediately to its south and, if necessary, assist the trading base on Roanoke Island. As a result, the English would hold a substantial segment of the North American coast and could eventually penetrate up or down the coast or into the interior as, indeed, the Jamestown colony was to do in different circumstances between 1607 and 1609.

If we turn back from speculation on such a longer-term plan, which might be achieved in two or three years at most, to what was actually done, we face much obscurity that cannot, indeed, entirely be lifted. But, again, we ought to question accepted views and begin by considering the colonists whom Raleigh trusted to establish the first settlement of English families planning to reside permanently in North America. We are well aware of a nominal framework, the grant in 1587 of the City of Ralegh to John White, his assistants and associates; the grant to the leaders of the association of armorial bearings confirming their status to develop a substantial English community status in the New World; and Raleigh's personal gift of £100 for what we would regard as social purposes.[18] We have not answered why White, a prominent member of one of the more prestigious craft guilds, the Company of Painter Stainers, should have been able to gather around him so many people—as many as two hundred in the preparatory stages but little more than half that when he set out on what he expected to be his first, founding, expedition in 1587. Why, we may ask, however promising the inducements that White and Harriot could offer, would a substantial group of people, members of a middle-ranking group, neither poor nor rich, leave their settled lives in southeastern England to take such a gamble?[19] It seems inevitable that they had some collective and probably ideological bond to tie them together in this enterprise. Participation by such a group would suggest that the ultimate inspirer of the enterprise was Walsingham, rather than White, and that Walsingham somehow found the very substantial sum, beyond what the voyagers could raise by selling their homes, land, and other assets, to set them on their way reasonably well equipped. I am suggesting that they, like Walsingham, were Calvinists—"of the religion," as Walsingham wrote to a Huguenot friend. They might, indeed, be loyal members of the Church of England but more Protestant than the Establishment of the Church. They need not be regarded as Pilgrims such as those of 1620 or even the rather radical reformists of the Massachusetts Bay Company when it was formed, but they were anxious all the same to move as a group so as to carry with them the type of religious observance that the Elizabethan puritans (with a small *p*), disliked by Hakluyt yet so well represented in the House of Commons, professed. Such a bond of right-thinking (from their perspective) would enable White to gather them round him from the City of London and its surrounding counties; it would give them the unity of purpose and determination to take the immense risks of launching out as colonists in North America.

If Walsingham was the enterprise's driving spirit, the choice of Simon Fernandez as the commander of the expedition—Fernandez certainly behaved as such, if we can trust White's narrative so far—was intelligible, since Fernandez was Walsingham's man.

Walsingham had saved him in 1577 from hanging as a pirate. Fernandez, though, was far from being a loyal servant to his master once he got to sea and was primarily set on robbery there. The long struggle between him and White in the Caribbean concerned involving the ships in privateering there and led to White's being unable to obtain such fresh food, plants, and, above all, domestic animals as the 1585 expedition had obtained. These deficiencies weakened the expedition, perhaps fatally, from the start.

It is necessary to look again at what happened when the expedition got to Roanoke Island. White's decision to call there was not necessarily only to see if Grenville's little garrison was intact but to decide what men should be left to form the trading post and so lay the foundations of one part of the larger program.[20] White's bitter reaction when Fernandez would go no further would then have been caused primarily by the problem of getting the colonists and their bulky household gear up to their intended settlement site south of Chesapeake Bay. At the same time, the tired colonists would find temporary shelter there in the cottages of 1585.[21] Then, if they used their pinnace effectively, they could transport themselves by stages to the site "50 miles into the main" for which they were about to leave when White unwillingly sailed back in the fly-boat, that crippled and foodless ship, and arrived in London in mid-November to obtain the additional supplies they would shortly need. Most especially, he would bring out whatever livestock he could to set them going as small-holding farmers, using Native American plants, it is true, as well as English ones to get themselves established. They would depend for a time on the bounty of the Chesapeakes, who had so impressed White and Harriot during their stay with them. If this reconstruction is correct, then the carriage of the settlers would have taken two, or more probably three, sailings of the pinnace from Roanoke Island to the nearest point (up the Elizabeth River) to the site of the intended settlement.

The party left on the island, after finding the 1586 garrison gone, would turn slowly to consider the task of preparing the site for the trading post. We can assume that during the winter they lived in the old cottages while preparing timber, a slow task, for the strong defenses needed to secure the post from attack. In the spring they could turn to creating the palisaded enclosure that White found in 1590—"the place very strongly enclosed with a high palisado of great trees, with cortynes and flankers very fort-like."[22] By June they would be able to take down the existing cottages, knock down the older defenses, and be ready to lay the foundations of the trading post. But all this activity came rapidly to an end. There is a possible point to take into account. As Grenville's men were gone, White would have to supply men (perhaps twenty) to work on the trading post. This would cut the eighty-three men left to something over sixty, and so weaken the Chesapeake colony. This may explain White's desperation to get back to England so as to bring reinforcements out as early in 1588 as possible.

The reason why the party left on Roanoke Island departed in such a panic, leaving bulky iron cannons and White's lightly buried chests behind, has provoked much questioning, but the almost certain answer has been staring us in the face for some considerable time. Since the early summer of 1585, the Spanish in Santo Domingo had been aware that the English were settling on the North American coast—on the Chesapeake Bay, they suspected. Drake brought news to Lane in June 1586 that the Spanish were preparing an expedition to search for and destroy the colony.[23] In 1587 Pedro Menéndez Marqués, governor of Florida, sailed as far as the mouth of Chesapeake Bay but was blown back from the entry.[24] Finally, in the early summer of 1588 a small bark under Vicente Gonzalez, with thirty men, sailed into the bay and made a remarkable reconnaissance of it without finding any trace of the English. Early in July, on its return voyage, the vessel, coasting the Carolina Outer Banks, found an entry (probably the one Lane named Trinity Bay) nearly opposite the entry to Albemarle Sound and, sailing south, discovered on Roanoke Island a small *varadero*. The word normally means a shipyard and has been translated as a slipway, but, in fact, here it means a smaller harbor or cove. It was at the northeast end of Roanoke Island and was marked by a projecting point of land, which has long eroded completely. This was the landing and departing place for the colonists. The Spanish sent a party ashore and found some barrel-wells and, crucially, "other debris indicating that a considerable number of people had been there."[25] The "other debris," clearly, was rubbish left by the Chesapeake colonists as they departed the island. Many years later Juan Menéndez Marqués, who was on board, was asked why when they later found the wells they did not go in search of the colony. He answered vaguely that they did not do so because he believed that the English colony was located some ten leagues from the northern opening into the harbour.[26] The real reason was that Gonzales did not have the force to risk confronting an unknown number of Englishmen. But it now must be clear that men preparing the site for the trading post had seen, but had not been seen by, the Spanish. This would explain why they evacuated the island so hurriedly and retreated to Croatoan to be with Manteo, leaving clear signs that indicated where White (expected at any time) would find them—before the Spanish would return, they surely hoped. The reasons why White was unable to do so are only too well known, but what remains mysterious is why in 1590 the enclosure, so carefully built, had evidently remained deserted for three years.[27] We would expect the men to have revisited the island and, not finding any Spanish there, to have gone ahead with erecting the trading post. They must have concluded either that the Spanish were there or that White had been lost at sea and so had been unable to get to Croatoan to revictual them. Perhaps they then reverted to the earlier plan. It is possible, of course, that the pinnace had not returned from its final voyage to the Chesapeake. Yet to row from Croatoan (if they stayed at Croatoan) was not impossible, since they had already done it once in the opposite direction.

One last speculation seems legitimate to make about the men who left Roanoke Island so precipitously in 1588. If fifteen or twenty men got to Croatoan, they could be fed and cared for, but only for a short time. In 1587 Manteo had told White that his people had only a small cultivable area available to them on Croatoan.[28] This meant that they could not sustain newcomers for any length of time. If this were so, and the men felt unable to go back to Roanoke Island, their only alternative was to move to the mainland, ingratiate themselves with the Secotan, and settle in some way in the area visited only once before—by the Grenville reconnaissance in July 1585. And if the men settled with the Secotan, and if the men, now cut off from Roanoke by distance, could have intermingled with their neighbors, as we are told the "Lost Colonists" did with the Chesapeakes, then perhaps—and it is a long shot—these events ultimately helped to create the Lumbee legend on which so much has been written in recent years. But the Lumbees' alleged partial descent from the "Lost Colonists" has never been credibly argued.

In November 1587 White must have been too exhausted to get to work for some time. He found the country alert to the threat from Spain and cheered by the successful raid on Cadiz, in which Raleigh took part. Walsingham, Raleigh, and Grenville were all involved in defensive plans to counter a possible Spanish attack, and White must have found it difficult to concentrate their attention on his urgent problem. It was not money that would have held him back, but the difficulty of getting a small vessel out of the English Channel in adverse weather conditions. There was, too, another obstacle: most maritime activity of a semi-official sort was concentrated on privateering in the Caribbean, and privateers would not take women and children on such a voyage and would not be willing to divert their energies to visit Roanoke Island.[29] Raleigh and Grenville, in spite of other commitments, were anxious to put the coping-stone on the four-stage plan, namely to establish a strong fortress and naval base on Chesapeake Bay that could be used to attack the treasure fleet and, perhaps, divert some Spanish concern away from the planned attack on England. Their preparations were slowly taking shape at Bideford and Barnstable, to which White's colonists would have to travel with their baggage and stores and where supplies might not be easy to assemble. White had to wait, with such colonists as made the long and difficult journey from London, until the escorting squadron was ready to sail. It says much for Grenville that he, with Raleigh's help, was able to get this squadron ready by March 1588, even though to White it must have seemed a long delay. The little fleet of six or more vessels was ready to set out when all privateering was suspended so as to assemble as large a defending force as possible, and on March 31 the squadron was ordered to join the western fleet, which was mobilizing at Plymouth.[30]

White's powerful plea and Walsingham's help alone enabled two small pinnaces to be assigned to him to bring some help to the colonists in the form of foodstuffs and probably tools and other equipment, along with fifteen additional colonists. The cost of transport would have been paid by Grenville and Raleigh, but unfortunately command of the pinnaces was placed in the hands of old allies of Grenville's with a record of piracy and privateering behind them. That decision led to the pinnaces attempting to rob any vessel they met with and actually being robbed themselves, which barely allowed White (wounded) and his distressed would-be colonists to return alive to England; they were fortunate to do so.[31] This meant that there was no link between

England and either the Roanoke trading-post party or the Chesapeake-sited colony, supposing it had been established, while the breakdown at Roanoke Island already traced had taken place, leaving the two parties of English people separated without means of contact, as there surely would have been had the pinnace still been operative. How long it took White to recover from his wounds we cannot tell. We must assume that almost all the intending colonists abandoned the idea of sailing to America.

After the Armada had come and gone and the threat to English integrity had been removed, for the time being at least, it became possible to set in motion a revival of the original enterprise. We should keep in mind that this revival developed on the assumption that the elements of the American enterprise were still in place—the trading post and the Chesapeake colony, with means of maintaining contact between them. This led to the agreement by which Raleigh enlarged the original City of Ralegh organization and empowered it to revive and expand the earlier plans.[32] The enterprise took shape in the famous agreement of March 7, 1589, in which the original grantees of 1587 were joined by two additional elements. A small addition was that of three men— Richard Hakluyt, Thomas Hood, and Richard Wright—who could bring their expertise to bear on the problems of navigation and colonization. Much more significant, though, was the addition of representatives of the Twelve Great London Companies, which had hitherto taken no part in the American enterprise. They were led by Thomas Smith (we cannot be sure if it was the father, who was to die in 1591, or the son, who was to be associated with an array of overseas enterprises from 1599 onward) and William Sanderson, who had backed John Davis in his Northwest Passage voyages in the 1580s and had already involved himself as Raleigh's business associate. The remaining men were new to overseas venturing, so far as we know, but were associated with many important London companies. This group could mobilize the substantial capital that long-term colonization needed if it was to have a chance of success on the lines set out by Hakluyt in 1584. It might seem that Hakluyt had at least convinced the great City of London merchants that America, in the long run, would prove a profitable investment.

Theoretically, there seemed no reason why such a strong and financially viable group should not have gotten an expedition to sea by, say, May 1589. In practice, serious obstacles put off any activity almost indefinitely. On the one hand, for several years the Privy Council was unwilling to permit overseas expeditions for fear of the renewal of the Spanish threat. When they were permitted, permission was confined to those that were directly anti-Spanish, principally those involved in privateering in the Caribbean, whereas the Roanoke venture was not, in modern terms, cost-effective. In 1589 the situation was little better, and by then even the privateering business had become concentrated in the hands of a few entrepreneurs who sent out most of the vessels under their own auspices. The syndicate proved strong enough to get one of these men, John Watts, who was about to send out three ships, to enter into a bond to bring men and supplies (if not women and children) to Roanoke Island, or perhaps the

Chesapeake, on the ships' return voyage from the Caribbean. Watts also consented to permit a vessel equipped by the syndicate to join the squadron in the Caribbean. But when it came to the point, Abraham Cocke, captain of the "admiral" of the squadron, even though some guns may already have been stowed in the hold, refused to take anyone except White himself on board, and time, it appeared, did not permit attempts to enforce the bond for £3,000 on Watts. Nonetheless, the *Moonlight*, a small vessel of only eighty tons, was laden with supplies for the colonists and duly joined the privateers and their three prizes off Cape Tiburon. The ship was involved in various actions with them until Cocke kept to the undertaking and duly brought the vessels, with the *Moonlight* in company, to the Outer Banks.

The sequence of events there is too well known to require repetition,[33] but the loss of Captain Edward Spicer and most of his crew in a boat accident crippled White's venture. In any event, White found only the outer palisade of the trading post intact and the interior long deserted, though with the indication that the men who should have been there were at Croatoan with Manteo. Cocke was clearly unwilling to spend time waiting for calm water in the sounds or to risk his vessels near Cape Hatteras, or indeed to search Chesapeake Bay for the settlers. (White could not be sure of their precise location and had depended on the Roanoke Island party to direct him.) Cocke cruelly allowed the *Moonlight* to sail homeward with White in spite of its inadequate crew, which was weakened further by an accident on board; consequently, White barely got to Ireland alive and must have appeared a broken and forlorn figure on his eventual return to London. News of the desertion of the Roanoke post convinced the syndicate that further expenditure upon Virginia involved throwing good money after bad; they offered no help to White. Discarded, he gave up the struggle and retired to Ireland for the rest of his life, since no trace was ever found of him subsequently. The Roanoke voyages fizzled out as a failed business venture, offering no hope of continuity or profit in the shorter run at least.

No single reason explains why the American colonization sequence stopped during the years 1590-1602. It is true that these were years of economic stringency, with heavy war expenditure and failing commerce, though small-scale activity revived very hesitantly at the very end of the century and in the opening years of the new one. The stoppage had much to do with the continued development of profitable privateering, mainly in the Caribbean, which partly replaced traditional external commerce. But it had much to do also with personalities and the absence of their influence and money from the pre-colonizing scene. Walsingham died in 1590, a major loss; Grenville, in 1591. Raleigh was in disgrace between 1592 and 1595 and turned to a potentially more profitable source of quick profit—gold—in Guiana. Drake, too, was in disgrace between 1589 and perhaps 1593 or 1594. The London merchants of the 1589 syndicate were finding it hard to keep up profitable trade (though there was money to be made from war and privateering). Raleigh, on the assumption that the "Lost Colony" survived (which it did), retained his monopoly over English enterprises in North

America down to the end of Queen Elizabeth's reign and for a few months longer, so that competition without his approval was impossible, though it is most unlikely that any group could have raised the resources to revive a major project for North American colonization even with his permission—though he did tolerate, unwillingly, a small expedition to North Virginia (New England) in 1602.

The basic factor was that Elizabethan England, at peace or war, lacked the resources to finance and maintain a sizable colony that could show no profits for some years and yet would need the fresh injection of capital every year. But the example of the 1589 syndicate, the faithfulness of Richard Hakluyt to the colonizing idea, aided by his emphasis on experiments of the 1580s in his *Principall Navigations* (1589) and his *Principall Navigations* in its three volumes (1589-1600), kept the record of English American ventures in the minds of influential readers and helped to provide a springboard for the new and large-scale enterprise of the Virginia Company from 1606. This is to state the case for American colonization as a purely commercial process, linked with the rising imperialism that was to make such strides in the colonization of Ireland after 1603. There was still room for the small-scale colony of family-linked groups, such as the Chesapeake "Lost Colonists" or, later on, the Pilgrims, which did not seriously threaten Native American society. Commercial colonization was to carry with it the seeds of destruction for the indigenous society, and this was to hamper the settlement of Virginia in its early years and then to result in the progressive ruin of that native society once commercial objectives and, ultimately, mass colonization took hold. There was no possibility of this happening in the 1580s or 1590s.

NOTES

1. See especially Thomas H. B. Symons, ed., *Meta Incognita: A Discourse of Discovery: Martin Frobisher's Arctic Expeditions, 1576-1578*, 2 vols. (Hull: Quebec: Canadian Museum of Civilization, 1999).

2. In his *Principall Navigations* (1589) and, with some variations in content, in his *Principall Navigations* (1598-1600).

3. See David Beers Quinn, *The Voyages and Colonising Enterprises of Sir Humphrey Gilbert*, Hakluyt Society Second Series, Nos. 83-84 (London: Hakluyt Society, 1940).

4. David Beers Quinn, ed., *The Roanoke Voyages, 1584-1590: Documents to Illustrate the English Voyages to North America Under the Patent Granted to Walter Raleigh in 1584*, 2 vols., Hakluyt Society Second Series, No. 104 (London: Hakluyt Society, 1955; reprint, New York: Dover, 1991), contains almost all such documents as survive. A few small items later discovered appear in David Beers Quinn, Alison M. Quinn, and Susan Hillier, eds., *New American World: A Documentary History of North America to 1612*, 5 vols. (New York: Arno Press, 1979).

5. Quinn, *Roanoke Voyages*, 1:122-129.

6. Quinn, *Roanoke Voyages*, 1:124.

7. William Arthur Shaw, *The Knights of England: A Complete Record from the Earliest Time to the Present Day of the Knights of All the Orders of Chivalry in England, Scotland, and Ireland, and of Knights Bachelors*, 2 vols. (London: Sherratt and Hughes, 1906; reprint, Baltimore: Genealogical Publishing Company, 1971), 1:83; Quinn, *Roanoke Voyages*, 1:148-156.

8. Quinn, *Roanoke Voyages*, 1:91-115, 127, esp. 113.

9. Quinn, *Roanoke Voyages*, 1:127-129.

10. This may be somewhat of an understatement.

11. Irene A. Wright, ed., *Further English Voyages to Spanish Americas, 1583-1594*, Hakluyt Society Second Series, No. 12 (London: Hakluyt Society, 1951), 94-99.

12. Quinn, *Roanoke Voyages*, 1:172-174, 234-242.

13. Quinn, *Roanoke Voyages*, 1:220-226, esp. 220 n. 1; Wright, *Further English Voyages*, 97-99.

14. Quinn, *Roanoke Voyages*, 1:172-174, 234-242.

15. Our documentation of this voyage (Quinn, *Roanoke Voyages*, 2:477-488) remains seriously defective.

16. See Harriot's 1588 *A Briefe and True Report*, almost certainly written in the early months of 1587 and circulated in manuscript. It is edited in Quinn, *Roanoke Voyages*, 1:317-387.

17. David Beers Quinn, *Set Fair for Roanoke: Voyages and Settlements, 1584-1606* (Chapel Hill: University of North Carolina Press, 1985), 241-252.

18. Quinn, *Set Fair*, 259-264; Quinn, *Roanoke Voyages*, 2:506-512, 522-543.

19. lebame houston's work in the London Guildhall has brought the White family into clearer focus for the first time; William S. Powell, "Who Were the Roanoke Colonists?" in *Raleigh and Quinn: The Explorer and His Boswell*, ed. H. G. Jones (Chapel Hill: North Caroliniana Society and the North Carolina Collection, 1987) continued to provide information on probable, possible, and, in a few cases, certain identifications of the colonists.

20. It is clear that White wished at Roanoke Island to confer with Grenville's fifteen men (and in the view expressed here to leave a party to erect a trading post), not to remove them, as has been assumed hitherto (Quinn, *Roanoke Voyages*, 2:523-535; Quinn, *Set Fair*, 273-294).

21. Quinn, *Roanoke Voyages*, 2:613.

22. Quinn, *Roanoke Voyages*, 2:614.

23. Quinn, *Set Fair*, 134.

24. Quinn, *Roanoke Voyages*, 2:803.

25. Quinn, *Roanoke Voyages*, 2:811.

26. Quinn, *Roanoke Voyages*, 2:812.

27. Quinn, *Roanoke Voyages*, 2:614-615.

28. Quinn, *Roanoke Voyages*, 2:526.

29. See K. R. Andrews's incisive and critical analysis of privateering in Joyce Youings, ed., *Raleigh in Exeter, 1985: Privateering and Colonisation in the Reign of Elizabeth I* (Exeter, U.K.: University of Exeter, 1985).

30. Quinn, *Roanoke Voyages*, 2:560-563.

31. Quinn, *Roanoke Voyages*, 2:562-569.

32. Quinn, *Roanoke Voyages*, 2:569-576. lebame houston's close analysis of the careers of the persons named in the document throws much light on their varied interests. See also Quinn, *Set Fair*, 311-314, and *Roanoke Voyages*, 2:544.

33. The detail on the voyage is taken up in Quinn, *Roanoke Voyages*, 2:579-716.

Roanoke and Jamestowne:
Supplying England's First American Colonies

Thomas E. Davidson

In 1585, 1587, and again in 1607, Englishmen attempted to establish colonies along the Atlantic coast of North America near the mouth of the Chesapeake Bay. The first two of those colonial ventures at Roanoke Island failed, while the English colony established in 1607 at Jamestown Island in Virginia survived and ultimately prospered. The different fates of the Roanoke and Jamestown colonies were determined not by the ability, judgment, or courage of the colonists themselves but rather by economic and political decisions made by the English backers of the colonies. It is not going too far to say that Raleigh's colonies failed and the Jamestown colony endured because the English investors in the latter enterprise were better able to deal with the practical problems of resupplying their colony.

One absolutely critical factor in the colonization process that all would-be English colonial developers failed to appreciate was just how much continuing support New World settlements needed if they were to survive. Both the investors in Raleigh's projects and the investors in the Virginia Company of London, which founded Jamestown, apparently thought in terms of making a single initial outlay of funds that would be recouped relatively quickly. The assumption was that any future investment in a colony could be funded by profits from that colony.[1] The promoters of those enterprises certainly never raised as a possibility the idea that a New World colony might remain an economic liability for years, requiring repeated expenditures but yielding profits slowly if at all.[2]

This lack of appreciation for the true cost of overseas colonial ventures and for the long-term nature of the investment that they required resulted in part from the fact that the principal figures in the earliest English colonization efforts tended to be courtiers rather than merchants.[3] Even within the English commercial and financial communities, however, knowledge of conditions in the world outside Europe was quite limited, and no real basis existed for accurately assessing the cost of a New World colony. The latter part of the sixteenth century saw a dramatic expansion of England's long-distance seaborne trade, but as for actual colonization the only successful attempt before Jamestown was in Northern Ireland. The establishment of permanent settlements in nearby Ireland required a different kind of financing, organization, and logistical support than did the creation of the transatlantic colonies.[4] It was only by trial and error that England eventually learned how to plant colonies overseas successfully, and this hard-won experience came too late to help the settlers at Roanoke.

By the time of the Roanoke voyages, Spain already had been a colonial power in the New World for nearly a century. Spain, too, had to go through a period of experimentation before devising workable strategies for setting up new colonies in the Americas, but because of a whole range of cultural and geopolitical factors the Spanish colonial experience was of limited relevance to the English colonial ventures. In fact,

Spain's presence in the New World added to the problems of other would-be colonizers, since Catholic Spain had no intention of sharing the New World's wealth with foreign latecomers, especially Protestant Englishmen. An important factor in English colonial planning, therefore, always had to be the possibility of Spanish attack on any settlements in the New World established under the English flag. The unhappy fate of the French colony at Fort Caroline demonstrated how effective Spain could be at protecting its New World sphere of influence.[5]

Before the Roanoke voyages, direct English contact with the New World was limited in the main to trading and privateering expeditions directed toward the Spanish colonies in the West Indies and fishing voyages that had as their destination the fishing grounds off the coast of Newfoundland. When it came to the practical organization and equipping of the early colonial expeditions, it seems clear that the English primarily drew on their West Indian privateering experience. This is hardly surprising in the case of the Roanoke settlements, given Sir Walter Raleigh's background and financial interests. The 1585 Roanoke voyage appears to have been as much a privateering expedition as a colonial venture, and the privateering model considerably influenced the planning of the early Jamestown voyages as well.[6] This is true even though the Virginia Company never evidenced much interest in privateering during the earliest phase of the Jamestown colony's existence.

There were good practical reasons why a colonial expedition should resemble a privateering expedition. During the sixteenth and early seventeenth centuries, English warships were designed and built no differently than were English merchant vessels intended for long overseas voyages.[7] Privateers left England expecting to fight on sea and land, and would-be colonizers needed to be prepared to do the same, so the military requirements of the two sorts of expeditions were analogous. Moreover, privateers sailing to the West Indies had to be fitted out and equipped in such a fashion that they did not need to enter a port for several months at a time, and this was true of vessels sent to colonize new lands in America as well. Finally, both privateering ventures and colonial ventures entailed transporting large numbers of people who had to be supplied with all the necessities of life for six months to a year—a formidable task, given the technological limitations of the day. Because of their hull design, late-sixteenth- and early-seventeenth-century English ships did not transport bulk cargoes efficiently,[8] and on long voyages ships crowded with soldiers or colonists often ran short of essential supplies, especially food.

The ships used in early English colonial ventures rarely exceeded 200 tons in size and most commonly ranged from 30 to 150 tons.[9] When they set out for the Americas, captain and crews of these small vessels had to anticipate a round-trip voyage of at least six months, and for the first leg of the voyage the ships had to transport large numbers of passengers in addition to the crew, as well as the food that the crew and passengers would eat on the voyage out, the food and supplies the colonists would need once they arrived, and the food that the crew would eat on the voyage home. If anything went wrong, if the outward voyage took four or even five months instead of the anticipated three, or if a significant quantity of the stored provisions on board was lost or spoiled, there was no assured way to make up the supply deficit from New World sources. Privateers might anticipate seizing supplies from Spanish ships or settlements, but colonists' options were more limited, especially once the ships that brought them to the Americas had sailed home again.

One way to lessen the risk of supply shortages was to keep the ratio of passengers to cargo capacity on the ships as low as possible, but following this principle would have made colonial ventures even more expensive than they were already. By and large the English backers of New World colonies chose to be optimists and to allocate as many passengers to each ship as possible. During the 1585 Roanoke voyage, the 160-ton vessel *Tyger* carried one passenger for every ton of cargo capacity, while the ships that supplied the Jamestown colony typically carried one passenger for every 1.75 tons of capacity.[10] These passenger-to-tonnage ratios are even higher than the manning ratios for the English warships that fought the Spanish Armada, and they are substantially higher than the one mariner or soldier per 2.4 tons of shipping that Drake and Hawkins allocated during their 1595-1596 expedition against the Spanish colonies in the Caribbean.[11]

In the late sixteenth century, English mariners used two routes to reach the eastern coast of North America. The most popular of these was the southern route, which essentially duplicated the course that most Spanish ships took to the New World. English ships sailed down the English Channel or the Bristol Channel past Land's End and then headed almost due south to the Canary Islands. From the Canaries the ships proceeded westward to American waters, generally making their first New World landfall somewhere in the Lesser Antilles. Then the English vessels sailed along the north coasts of Hispaniola and Cuba to the Straits of Florida and from there paralleled the coast of Florida and Georgia until they reached their destination.

For the English the southern route remained the preferred course to North America for decades and was the one initially employed by both the Roanoke and the Jamestown colonial expeditions. The course has several advantages: it used prevailing winds and currents, numerous landfalls made it relatively easy to navigate, and it offered the possibility to renew fresh food supplies at the islands along the way. The main disadvantage of the southern route was its length: If all went well, a ship could cover its more than six thousand miles in eight weeks or fewer, but a three-month voyage was more likely. With bad luck that voyage could extend to four months or even longer. Fresh food was available intermittently along the way, but the preserved food stocks that the colonists would need at the end of the voyage could not be replaced during these island stopovers. The longer southern voyage and the hot climate of the West Indies always risked depletion and spoilage of those critical supplies.

The sixteenth-century alternative to the southern route was a shorter northern passage pioneered by the fishermen of several European nations. That route involved sailing westward from England to Newfoundland, then south along the North American coast. The northern alternative was quicker than the southern if everything went well, but weather conditions in the North Atlantic made sailing it quite dangerous in the winter months. Even in the spring and summer, ships could experience long delays if they encountered unfavorable winds—a frequent occurrence, since the prevailing winds associated with the Gulf Stream blew eastward. The northern route was used mainly by ships on their return voyage from America, since vessels sailing back to England could take advantage of the generally clockwise flow of winds and currents in the Atlantic.

Discovered in the early seventeenth century was a third route to North America, which involved sailing southwest from England past the Azores to Bermuda and then on to the mouth of the Chesapeake Bay. The so-called "Course of ye Somer Islands" was discovered by accident when in 1609 a Virginia Company supply ship headed for Jamestown was blown off course and wrecked on the previously undiscovered island of Bermuda.[12] The Virginia Company of London took advantage of that misfortune by establishing a second New World colony on Bermuda, and thereafter Virginia Company ships sometimes sailed to Virginia by way of the Bermuda colony.

Officials of the Virginia Company in England very quickly become unhappy with the long southern route to Virginia, and they sponsored a voyage of exploration for a shorter variant of that route as early as 1609.[13] On the other hand, those who actually lived in Virginia generally disliked the northern route via Newfoundland. In 1620 John Pory, a Virginia Company official living at Jamestown, argued that the northern passage was the worst route because bad weather often meant long passages, spoiled supplies, and high death rates among the passengers. Additionally, he pointed out that the best time to sail via the northern route was in the spring, which meant that the vessels did not reach Virginia until summer. Colonists who arrived in Virginia during the summer months suffered more sickness and came too late to help "eyther by plantinge, settinge, howinge, clearinge ground, or bylding" for that year.[14]

By the 1620s some Virginia Company officials in England had become strong advocates of the northern route because per capita it was cheaper. Colonists and supplies could be sent to Virginia aboard ships that would be going to Newfoundland anyway, which saved the company the expense of hiring an entire vessel for the sole purpose of transporting goods and supplies to the Jamestown colony.[15] There is no evidence of that practice during the first decade of Jamestown's existence, however. The southern route was the lifeline of the colony during its critical early years. The middle route via Bermuda was of less importance and appears to have been used primarily on those occasions when company vessels could bring colonists to both Bermuda and Virginia on the same voyage.[16]

One considerable advantage that vessels using the southern route to supply the Jamestown colony had over the ships involved in the Roanoke ventures was that Spain and England were officially at peace during the earliest years of Virginia's settlement. In order to maintain the peace, commanders of Virginia Company supply ships were instructed not to antagonize the Spanish colonial authorities by landing on "any of the Kinge of Spaines his Dominions . . . without the leave or licence of the governor of such place."[17] This conciliatory policy did not always work, and sometimes Virginia-bound ships were attacked when they ventured near Spain's New World possessions.[18] By and large, though, vessels heading to Virginia by the southern route could anticipate a peaceful voyage through the West Indies that would include opportunities to trade and to restock their vessels with fresh food.

Whatever route was chosen, it seems clear from the Virginia Company records that the longer ships were at sea, the higher the death toll among the passengers. Oddly enough, the first Jamestown voyage in 1607 was one of the safest and healthiest on record, given its long duration. Even though the *Susan Constant*, the *Godspeed*, and the *Discovery* took more than four months to reach Virginia, only one among the 105 passengers aboard the three ships died. A decade later, voyages during which no one died were still unusual enough to merit special notice by company officials.[19] A "sore voyage," by contrast, might result in the deaths of 10 percent or more of all passengers.[20] In 1619 the ship *Jonathan* lost twenty-five of its two hundred passengers on the voyage over, and still more died after reaching Virginia.[21] Almost all of the colonists who came aboard a ship called the *Furtherance* died as a result of being fed "corrupt Vittles" while sailing to Virginia.[22] Passengers aboard Virginia Company supply ships complained of "mustie bread, the reliques of former Vioages, and stinckinge beere" and of being "half starved for want of vittles."[23]

As has been previously noted, the overcrowding of ships on colonial voyages was routine, and overcrowded conditions certainly contributed to the high on-board death rate. Disease went hand-in-hand with poor diet on those tightly packed vessels. When Lady Wyatt, the wife of Gov. Sir Francis Wyatt, traveled to Virginia in 1623, she sailed on a vessel that was so crowded that she had "not so much as a cabin free to my selfe." She described her ship as "so pestered with people and goods that we were so full of infection that after a while we saw little but throwing folkes overboard."[24] Deaths resulting from a bad voyage often continued even after a vessel reached Virginia, since colonists weakened by disease and hunger could not cope with the stresses everyone faced when they confronted the unfamiliar climate and epidemiology of the New World for the first time.

Supply ships had to deliver not just colonists to the Americas but also tools, weapons, clothing and equipment of all sorts, livestock, and enough food to support the colonists until they could become self-sufficient. Unfortunately, we don't know what the organizers of the Roanoke ventures deemed necessary supplies for their colonists. No itemized supply lists for the 1585 and 1587 voyages have survived. We don't have such information for the 1607 Jamestown voyage either, but a considerable number of later ships' lading lists and accounts of goods purchased for the Jamestown colony have been preserved in the records of the Virginia Company of London. Those records are available in the published *Records of the Virginia Company*, edited by Susan Kingsbury, and in *The Ferrar Papers, 1590-1790*, edited by David Ransome.

The Virginia Company of London was a joint-stock company whose key organizers were London-based merchants.[25] It was created by royal charter in 1606 and survived until 1624, when Virginia became a royal colony. As a profit-making enterprise, the Virginia Company failed abjectly. Despite the huge amounts of money that the company raised and spent, the Jamestown colony never produced enough to pay the stockholders a meaningful return on their investment. Nevertheless, the company did manage to keep the colony alive until the development of tobacco production gave Virginia an economic basis for survival.

Soon after Jamestown was established in 1607, the Virginia Company discovered that the only way to keep the colony going was to resupply it regularly with literally everything, especially food and new colonists to take the place of those who died. From 1607 to 1624, a year never passed without the company's organizing one or more resupply voyages. In at least one instance, a resupply expedition arrived just in time to halt the total abandonment of the colony.[26] Seventeen years after the initial 1607 settlement of Jamestown, the Virginia colonists still depended upon the company to provide even basic foodstuffs.[27] The Virginia Company's original vision of a colony both self-sufficient in the necessities of life and capable of producing valuable goods for export must have seemed as far away as ever.

Years of experience in resupplying Jamestown should have taught the Virginia Company what was required to give a new colonist a reasonable chance for survival in Virginia, but for reasons of cost the company consistently chose to offer colonists only a bare minimum of provisions upon their initial arrival. By 1612 the company had established a rule of thumb that every colonist should be left in Virginia with at least enough preserved food for a six-month period.[28] By 1620 official company policy had been changed to allow for "victuall for one whole yeare," but that standard does not appear to have been met with any consistency.[29] Colonists continued to be sent out with provisions for just six months.[30] In a 1624 published list of recommended supplies for colonists going to Virginia, John Smith wrote that each person needed "Victuall for a whole year," but the Virginia Company usually was not that generous.[31] The company clearly hoped that after six months a colonist would be producing either his own food or some commodity for export valuable enough to cover the cost of additional imported food.

The company's provisions for Virginia colonists hardly amounted to an adequate diet. The colonists received substantial quantities of wheat meal or biscuit, supplemented by small amounts of oatmeal, peas, butter, oil, and vinegar. A 1620 Virginia Company document probably written by company official John Ferrar provides a table for calculating the quantities of food men should receive in Virginia.[32] Per capita, those provisions amounted to one pound of meal and slightly less than two quarts of cider a day. Everything else was allocated in minuscule quantities. Every group of five men was to receive each week a pound and a half of butter, two pounds of cheese, two quarts of oatmeal, one pint of oil, and slightly less than one pint of vinegar. The same 1620 document notes that for two days a week the men were to eat "such victualls as the Countrie doth yeald."[33]

The cider mentioned above may have been for "newcomers" only, to help them through their first months in the colony.[34] Lading lists for vessels bound for Virginia with supplies for those already settled in the colony did not customarily include cider or any other beverages except for small quantities of wine, sack, aqua vitae, whiskey, and "strong" or "hot" waters. Wines and liquors did not come over in sufficient quantities to have been part of the general issue of provisions, so they probably were intended either to be sold or to become part of the personal stores of the colony's leaders.[35] Non-company ships in particular brought small quantities of spices, sweetmeats, garlic, olives, almonds, raisins, sugar, and beef suet.[36] As in the case of the alcoholic beverages, it is likely that these more expensive supplies were for private use by the colony's elite.

The food that the company allocated to the Virginia colonists clearly was insufficient in variety as well as quantity. Particularly noticeable is the absence of any meat from this diet. The same 1620 document that enumerates the rations for men in Virginia also lists the food that these same men should receive on the voyage to the colony. The shipboard food included substantial quantities of beef, pork, and dried fish.[37] The only one of those commodities mentioned as being sent in any quantity to the colonists in Virginia is fish, and that happened only intermittently.[38] The Virginia Company did not wish to pay for the more expensive protein-rich foods that were a normal part of the diet at sea and took the position that if the colonists wanted to eat meat on shore, then they should raise it, catch it, or shoot it for themselves. Beef, bacon, and "anie eating meate" were among the items most commonly requested by Virginia colonists in their letters to England.[39] If the colonists received such items, however, it was from private sources and not from the company.

In addition to provisions, colonists received clothing, "beddinge and necessaries for houshold," and "implements both for labour and defence."[40] The company seems to have been most scrupulous about providing implements for defense. John Smith's list of suggested supplies and equipment for colonists includes a sword and musket for every man and a complete armor for every second man in the party.[41] A 1619-1620 Virginia muster list notes that there were 670 able-bodied men in Virginia, and the arms available in the colony for these men consisted of 686 "snaphaunces and matchlocks," 516 swords, and 284 "armours complete."[42] The Virginia colonists may have been scantily supplied with everything else, but they did have the wherewithal to defend themselves.

Another Virginia Company document demonstrates that the company-supplied "armours complete" were light pikeman's armors consisting of "a helmet, a breast plate, a back plate, two tassets and a gorget."[43] In 1619 the company paid seventeen shillings for each such suit of armor that it purchased, which is precisely the price that John Smith quoted for armor in 1624.[44] As with most company-supplied hardware, these light pikeman's armors were cheap, mass-produced items. Archaeology provides confirmation of the Virginia Company's preference for light plate armor, since this kind has been found on excavated company-period sites in Virginia.[45]

The Virginia Company's relative generosity when it came to supplying arms and armor did not extend to other categories of goods. The range of household equipment sent to Virginia was extremely limited. The company provided a set of basic cooking utensils consisting of an iron pot, kettle, frying pan, and gridiron with "turnery ware," or wooden plates and bowls, to use for food consumption. For sleeping, there was a "flock bed and bolster, a blanket and covering" for each man.[46] The company did not give colonists tables, chairs, bed frames, chests, lighting devices, or anything else that would now be considered furniture. The clothing that was supplied usually consisted of two cassocks and breeches, three shirts, two or three pairs of stockings, two or three pairs of shoes, a waistcoat or doublet, and a cap.[47] The tools that colonists received varied in number and kind but always included those mainstays of the Chesapeake agricultural economy: the ax and the hoe. Felling axes and broad and narrow hoes were by far the most common types of tools sent.[48]

All in all, it cost the Virginia Company about £20 to equip and send each colonist to Virginia. Passage to Virginia cost approximately £6, arms and armor cost £3 to £4, clothing cost £3 to £4, six months' worth of provisions for use in Virginia cost about £3, tools and household equipment cost £2 to £3, and freight charges for the equipment and supplies amounted to £1 to £2.[49] The shipowner was responsible for providing food for the colonists while they were at sea, so that cost was built into the cost of passage to Virginia. The estimated outlay for provisioning one person at sea was £1 per month, which is twice what the Virginia Company paid to feed that same person when he got to Virginia.[50]

In addition to paying for the colonists' passage, the company also had to pay the cost of freighting supplies and equipment to Virginia. Carrying freight to Virginia normally cost three pounds per ton, and the personal supplies and equipment of each colonist took up about a half-ton of the ship's capacity.[51] Over and above that, the company also had to ship new supplies for its colonists already in Virginia. Costs for items that could not be packed into barrels and stowed in the ship's hold exceeded the three-pound-per-ton rate.[52] Transporting livestock was very expensive: freight charges for shipping a cow to Virginia amounted to ten pounds.[53] Cattle appear to have been sent to Virginia in ships that were specially fitted out for that purpose, since vessels that carried cattle transported few or no passengers.[54]

For the most part the company did not own the vessels that transported its people and goods to Virginia. It preferred either to pay a shipowner a flat rate to carry a specified quantity of colonists and supplies to Virginia or to hire an entire vessel for a monthly or per voyage fee.[55] Both of those arrangements had disadvantages. If the Virginia Company simply paid a shipowner to carry people and supplies to Virginia, the shipowner probably anticipated engaging in other profit-making activities while he was in the New World. Sometimes the arrival of goods and colonists in Virginia could be delayed because the ship carrying them became involved in other commercial enterprises along the way.[56]

On the other hand, hiring a vessel outright had its own problems. Since a greater tonnage of shipping was needed to take people and goods to Virginia than was needed to transport goods back to England from Virginia, ships frequently returned to England empty. In effect the company had to hire a ship for a six- to nine-month round trip when it only needed it for the first three months of the outward voyage. Even if a cargo for England could be found in Virginia, it might take weeks or months to assemble, and all the while the costs of hiring and operating the ship continued to mount.[57] The Virginia Company never found a satisfactory solution to that problem.

The company organized supply voyages on an ad hoc basis. It held general meetings or "courts" every quarter, wherein the decision to send a ship or ships to Virginia was made. The task of making practical arrangements for the voyage was then given to one of the company's sixteen standing committees.[58] The committee bought the supplies, assembled the colonists, and hired a ship for that specific voyage only. There was a provision in the company rules that all purchases for the voyage had to be negotiated by at least two committee members working together, presumably to avoid the possibility of collusion with the suppliers.[59]

All sorts of administrative problems arose because of this piecemeal approach to supplying the Virginia colony, particularly since the membership of the company was deeply divided on a wide range of policy questions. Given the cumbersome structure of the Virginia Company of London and the amount of internal feuding that went on, it is surprising that it accomplished as much as it did on the resupply front. During the first twelve years of its history, the Virginia Company spent more than 70,000 pounds to keep the Virginia colony going, a large investment of capital by early-seventeenth-century standards.[60] By 1619 eight or more supply ships a year were being dispatched to Jamestown, and in 1621 a total of twenty-one company and private supply vessels reached the colony.[61]

Even so, the colonists in Virginia always seemed to be unhappy with the company's supply efforts. Typical complaints were that the food and other supplies were insufficient and of poor quality, that too many new colonists arrived each year to be housed and fed adequately, and that supply vessels arrived at the wrong time of the year.[62] The company was certainly aware of these complaints but for the most part chose to ignore them. The dominant philosophy within the Virginia Company was that rapid growth was the key to the colony's success. That philosophy translated into an operational goal of transporting as many colonists as quickly and cheaply as possible to Virginia. That practice in turn meant vessels crowded with people (rather than supplies) arriving at Jamestown on a schedule dictated by the cost and availability of shipping (rather than the needs of the colony). The result so far as Virginia was concerned was a continual scarcity of practically everything and a very high death rate among recent immigrants, who arrived poorly prepared to deal with the realities of life in the New World.

It is easy to see in hindsight that the Virginia Company would have had more success at Jamestown if it had chosen a policy of slower, better-planned growth. A smaller number of more carefully selected, better-equipped colonists could have accomplished more in the new land over time. The people who created the Virginia Company, though, had no way of knowing that when the settlement process began in 1607. Thanks to the earlier Roanoke ventures, the founders of Jamestown knew many of the problems that might face a New World colony over the short term, but the Roanoke settlements failed too quickly to reveal the long-term supply problems that a North American colony inevitably encountered. It is fortunate that the company's investors did not know what was in store for them, since if they had known they probably would not have put their money into that particular colonial venture in the first place.

The ultimate success of the Jamestown settlement is a tribute to the stubborn optimism of the Virginia Company of London and its investors, who for seventeen years threw good money after bad and kept the supply ships coming. Jamestown also benefited from the fact that England and Spain were not at war during the colony's earliest years, when the southern route through the West Indies was the most practical way known to reach Virginia. For those reasons, enough supplies always got through to sustain the colony. Finally, after years of trying, the Virginia colonists did manage to justify their existence by growing tobacco for England and then for the world. That economic breakthrough came too late to benefit the company's investors, however, who received nothing for their money but the satisfaction of having helped create England's first successful New World colony.

NOTES

1. A 1608 letter from Capt. John Smith to the Treasurer and Council of the Virginia Company effectively demonstrates how unrealistic the company's expectations for the newly established Jamestown colony were. The company wanted enough exports to defray the costs of future supply voyages immediately, while Smith pointed out the many reasons why this was impossible (Philip L. Barbour, ed., *The Jamestown Voyages Under the First Charter, 1606-1609: Documents Relating to the Foundation of Jamestown and the History of the Jamestown Colony Up to the Departure of Captain John Smith, Last President of the Council in Virginia Under the First Charter, Early in October 1609*, 2 vols., Hakluyt Society Second Series, Nos. 136-137 [Cambridge: Cambridge University Press, 1969], 1:241-245).

2. John L. Humber, *Backgrounds and Preparations for the Roanoke Voyages, 1584-1590* (Raleigh: America's Four Hundredth Anniversary Committee, North Carolina Department of Cultural Resources, 1986), 68-69.

3. Carole Shammas, "English Commercial Development and American Colonization, 1560-1620," in *The Westward Enterprise: English Activities in Ireland, the Atlantic, and America, 1480-1650*, ed. K. R. Andrews, N. P. Canny, and P. E. H. Hair (Liverpool: Liverpool University Press, 1978; reprint, Detroit: Wayne State University Press, 1979), 153.

4. See Karl S. Bottigheimer, "Kingdom and Colony: Ireland and the Westward Enterprise, 1536-1660," in Andrews, Canny, and Hair, *The Westward Enterprise*, for the differences between the Irish and American colonial experiences.

5. David Beers Quinn, *Explorers and Colonies: America, 1500-1625* (London: Hambeldon Press, 1980), 272.

6. Some prominent former privateers were among the original patentees of the Virginia Company, but most of them were associated with the northern branch of the company, which wished to establish a colony in New England (Barbour, *Jamestown Voyages*, 1:16).

7. Ralph Davis, *English Merchant Shipping and the Anglo-Dutch Rivalry in the Seventeenth Century* (London: National Maritime Museum, 1975), 10.

8. Davis, *English Merchant Shipping*, 10.

9. Humber, *Backgrounds and Preparations*, 93; Philip L. Barbour, ed., *The Complete Works of Captain John Smith (1580-1631)*, 3 vols. (Chapel Hill: Institute of Early American History and Culture and the University of North Carolina Press, 1986), 2:137.

10. Humber, *Backgrounds and Preparations*, 33; Susan Myra Kingsbury, ed., *The Records of the Virginia Company of London*, 4 vols. (Washington: Government Printing Office, 1906-1935), 3:115, 239, 639.

11. Kenneth R. Andrews, ed., *The Last Voyage of Drake and Hawkin*, Hakluyt Society Second Series, No. 142 (Cambridge: Cambridge University Press, 1972), 44.

12. Barbour, *Complete Works of Captain John Smith*, 2:348.

13. Barbour, *Jamestown Voyages*, 2:275. On this voyage Samuel Argall pioneered a new, short southern route that involved sailing southwest from England to a point some distance west of the Canaries and then sailing to the West Indies.

14. Kingsbury, *Records of the Virginia Company*, 3:301.

15. Kingsbury, *Records of the Virginia Company*, 1:257, 269.

16. David Ransome, ed., *The Ferrar Papers, 1590-1790* (East Ardsley, U.K.: Microfilm Academic Publishers, 1992), roll 1, item 209; Kingsbury, *Records of the Virginia Company*, 3:145.

17. Barbour, *Jamestown Voyages*, 2:262.

18. Barbour, *Complete Works of Captain John Smith*, 2:270-272.

19. Kingsbury, *Records of the Virginia Company*, 3:245.

20. Kingsbury, *Records of the Virginia Company*, 1:229.

21. Kingsbury, *Records of the Virginia Company*, 3:301.

22. Kingsbury, *Records of the Virginia Company*, 4:144.

23. Kingsbury, *Records of the Virginia Company*, 4:233, 451.

24. Kingsbury, *Records of the Virginia Company*, 4:232.

25. Barbour, *Jamestown Voyages*, 1:20.

26. Barbour, *Complete Works of Captain John Smith*, 1:276.

27. Kingsbury, *Records of the Virginia Company*, 4:538.

28. Ransome, *Ferrar Papers*, roll 1, item 32.

29. Kingsbury, *Records of the Virginia Company*, 3:314.

30. Kingsbury, *Records of the Virginia Company*, 3:456.

31. Barbour, *Complete Works of Captain John Smith*, 2:321-322.

32. Ransome, *Ferrar Papers*, roll 1, item 210.

33. Ransome, *Ferrar Papers*, roll 1, item 210.

34. Kingsbury, *Records of the Virginia Company*, 4:451-452.

35. Kingsbury, *Records of the Virginia Company*, 3:96, 260, 691.

36. Kingsbury, *Records of the Virginia Company*, 3:178-189, 4:220, 278-283.

37. Ransome, *Ferrar Papers*, roll 1, item 210.

38. Kingsbury, *Records of the Virginia Company*, 4:253.

39. Kingsbury, *Records of the Virginia Company*, 4:41, 60, 233, 235.

40. Ransome, *Ferrar Papers*, roll 1, item 85.

41. Barbour, *Complete Works of Captain John Smith*, 2:322.

42. Ransome, *Ferrar Papers*, roll 1, item 159.

43. Ransome, *Ferrar Papers*, roll 1, item 110.

44. Barbour, *Complete Works of Captain John Smith*, 2:322.

45. Ivor Noël Hume, *Martin's Hundred: The Discovery of a Lost Colonial Virginia Settlement* (New York: Knopf, 1982), 200-202, 206; Alain Charles Outlaw, *Governor's Land: Archaeology of Early Seventeenth-Century Virginia Settlements* (Charlottesville: University Press of Virginia, 1990), 57.

46. The household implements generally supplied by the Virginia Company typically match the items recommended by Smith in 1624 (Barbour, *Complete Works of Captain John Smith*, 2:321-322; Ransome, *Ferrar Papers*, roll 1, item 137; Kingsbury, *Records of the Virginia Company*, 3:96).

47. Kingsbury, *Records of the Virginia Company*, 3:95; Ransome, *Ferrar Papers*, roll 1, item 137.

48. Ransome, *Ferrar Papers*, roll 1, item 212.

49. Kingsbury, *Records of the Virginia Company*, 4:227-228; Ransome, *Ferrar Papers*, roll 1, item 137.

50. Ransome, *Ferrar Papers*, roll 1, item 209.

51. Ransome, *Ferrar Papers*, roll 3, item 492; Kingsbury, *Records of the Virginia Company*, 3:261. "Ton" in this context is a measurement of the volume supplies took up within a ship's hold rather than the weight of those supplies.

52. Kingsbury, *Records of the Virginia Company*, 3:501.

53. Kingsbury, *Records of the Virginia Company*, 1:257, 3:260.

54. Kingsbury, *Records of the Virginia Company*, 3:115, 240.

55. Kingsbury, *Records of the Virginia Company*, 3:465; Ransome, *Ferrar Papers*, roll 1, item 210.

56. Kingsbury, *Records of the Virginia Company*, 4:127, 469.

57. Kingsbury, *Records of the Virginia Company*, 1:269, 3:481.

58. Kingsbury, *Records of the Virginia Company*, 3:350.

59. Kingsbury, *Records of the Virginia Company*, 3:351.

60. Kingsbury, *Records of the Virginia Company*, 4:183.

61. Kingsbury, *Records of the Virginia Company*, 3:639.

62. Kingsbury, *Records of the Virginia Company*, 3:78, 226, 263, 4:154, 175, 263.

ACKNOWLEDGMENT

I would like to acknowledge the important contribution made by Genevieve L. Holterman to this paper. While an intern at the Jamestown Settlement Museum, Ms. Holterman prepared a computerized database that includes all of the references to supplies for the Jamestown colony contained in the published records of the Virginia Company.

Talcott Williams, "Pinky" Harrington, and Other Searchers for the "Lost Colony"

Bennie C. Keel

Fort Raleigh National Historic Site was established to commemorate the first British attempt to settle in the New World. Every schoolchild has heard something of Virginia Dare, the first English child born in North America, who with more than a hundred other British colonists disappeared from history. Relatively few people know, however, that the "Lost Colony" was the last of three sixteenth-century British expeditions to use Roanoke Island as a base of operations.

In June 1585 Sir Richard Grenville (Sir Walter Raleigh's cousin) established the first colony, with Ralph Lane as governor. John White, Thomas Hariot, and Joachim Ganz were important men among the first colonists. Sir Francis Drake rescued Lane's colony and returned to England in early June 1586. Grenville's supply ships arrived within a few days of Lane's departure. Grenville left fifteen men with two years' worth of supplies to hold the country until a new colonizing force could be sent over. Those men, attacked by hostile Indians, fled the island in a small boat. They were never heard of again. The third colony, headed by John White, arrived at Roanoke Island near the end of June 1587. Members of that group had not intended to settle on Roanoke but rather to pick up the men left by Grenville, get their land legs, and then sail to the Chesapeake Bay to establish their estates. White returned to England for more colonists and supplies but did not return until 1590. He found the colony deserted and the word "CROATOAN" carved upon a tree.[1]

Explorers from the Jamestown colony visited Roanoke Island in 1608 and 1609 in search of the colonists. In 1653 the local Indian chief showed another Jamestown group the remains of the fort. In 1701 John Lawson visited the site, where he saw the ruins of Lane's fort, as well as some English coins, a brass gun, a powder horn, and iron barrel staves and hoops.[2] The historian Benson John Lossing states that traces of the fort's ruins were still visible in the mid-nineteenth century.[3] Union soldiers pot-hunted the fort during the Civil War and apparently recovered colonial materials.[4] Edward C. Bruce provided the first detailed description of the fort ruins in 1860.[5] These periodic visits kept the location of the Cittie of Ralegh in communal knowledge from the colonial period through the Civil War and up to 1895.

Talcot Williams conducted the first archaeological investigations at the fort in 1895.[6] Williams was a descendant of Robert and Elizabeth Williams, who arrived in Massachusetts in 1637. In January 1849 the American Board of Commissioners for Foreign Missions sent Talcott's father, a Presbyterian missionary, and his mother to Mosul in eastern Turkey. Talcott was born there on July 20 of the same year, received his early education in the mission school, and visited a number of archaeological sites with his father, who assembled archaeological collections and sent them back to the

United States. Talcott remembered vividly his visit to Nineveh, at which Sir Austen Henry Layard had left the trenches open from his investigations in 1845. The Williams family returned to America in 1857 after the death of Talcott's mother. Talcott and his younger sister and brother were left in the hands of his Aunt Sophie. His father and stepmother, who had met and married within three weeks, returned to the States in 1859 to reunite with the children and take them back to the Near East.

Three years later the children moved back to America because their father was concerned about their education and needed a replacement for his second wife, who had died at the first of the year. They would be raised and educated by relatives. "Turkey" Williams, as his chums at Philips Academy knew him, published his first paper as a senior, then enrolled at Amherst College in 1869. Although by age nine he had read the Bible from cover to cover, and by age twelve had read all twenty-one volumes of the *Encyclopædia Britannica*, he was no more than an adequate scholar, graduating in the middle of his class (twenty-sixth of fifty-two). Ten weeks after graduation he began a lifelong career as a journalist, reporting first for the *New York World* and later for the *New York Sun* as the paper's Washington correspondent. After a stint on the editorial staff of the *Springfield Republican Independent*, he joined the *Philadelphia Press* in 1881. He remained with the newspaper until 1912, when he became the director of Columbia University's School of Journalism, which had been established by a gift of Joseph Pulitzer.

Williams published hundreds of articles (not only in the papers for which he worked but also in scholarly journals and magazines) and was recognized as an outstanding newsman throughout his career. A popular speaker, he gave numerous commencement addresses. Always, it seems, he was a mixture of contradictions—supporting the advancement of American blacks, the eradication of tuberculosis, and aid to museums and arts but staunchly opposing women's suffrage.

During his time at the *Philadelphia Press*, he undertook at least four archaeological expeditions. In 1887 he visited the Outer Banks, where he dug in at least three Native American sites and mapped Fort Raleigh. In 1889, with the support of the Smithsonian Institution, he visited Morocco, where he excavated in a cave, collecting "prehistoric flints." He also assembled an ethnographic collection of contemporary Moroccan musical instruments, clothing, and old manuscripts. Interestingly, the Smithsonian provided him with field equipment and instructions, as well as some funding. He returned to Morocco in 1897, collecting this time for the University of Pennsylvania Museum. In November 1891 he vacationed in Piedmont North Carolina, where he collected a number of ceramic vessels from Jugtown potters, some of which he donated to the Smithsonian.

It is interesting to speculate how Williams's 1895 excavations at Fort Raleigh came about. On his return to Philadelphia from his 1887 vacation on Albemarle Sound, he stopped in Baltimore to visit Dr. Herbert B. Adams, secretary of the American Historical Association. Adams apparently became quite excited that the remains of the

Fig. 3. Location of excavations at Fort Raleigh by Talcott Williams in 1895.

fort could still be seen and hatched a plan to buy the fort. The Roanoke Colony Memorial Association, created for that purpose, acquired the property in 1894. One wonders whether Williams returned to the fort at the association's behest or on his own initiative. In any event, he received permission from the new owners and returned to the fort in November 1895.

Though he opened thirteen small trenches, even as he avoided digging in the slopes of the embankment, Williams recovered only a small amount of material related to the fort's colonial occupation (Figure 3). Nevertheless, his observations in his 1896 report remain useful to consider. First, he was concerned that the space within the fort embankment seemed too small to accommodate the number of colonists. He also noted the lack of material related to the sixteenth-century occupation. Finally, he reported "a black ashy layer" at the base of which he found a smattering of European and Native American artifacts. Within a few months after completing his fieldwork, Williams published his findings in the *Annual Report of the American Historical Association for 1896*. The markers he placed to outline the fort would serve as a plan for the reconstruction of a conjectural "frontier-type" fort by the state of North Carolina in the 1930s. In 1950 and 1991 excavators found evidence of that ill-conceived reconstruction.

After Williams had concluded his work, archaeological investigation of the site did not resume until southeastern archaeologist A. R. Kelly conducted a small, inconclusive survey at what was to become Fort Raleigh National Historic Site and the surrounding area, and wrote a report in 1938 for the National Park Service. In 1947 Jean Carl "Pinky" Harrington, acknowledged by many as the father of American historic archaeology, began the next archaeological investigation of the area. Harrington's entry into archaeology came as a second career. Graduating from the University of Michigan in 1924 with a degree in architectural engineering, Harrington pursued that profession until the job market crashed in the Great Depression. He then decided to enroll in graduate study in archaeology at the University of Chicago, from which he received his master's degree in 1935. His interest in archaeology probably stemmed from his senior project with the School for American Research, which involved making architectural drawings of Spanish missions under the direction of an archaeologist. In 1936 the National Park Service recruited him to take over the excavations at Jamestown, where open warfare had broken out between the architects and the archaeologists. While Park Service managers had hoped that the project could be improved by the presence of an archaeologist with architectural credentials, Harrington made it a roaring success. He later excavated at Fort Necessity, Fort Frederica, and other National Park sites, including, of course, Fort Raleigh. After retiring from the Park Service, he and his wife Virginia excavated for four seasons at Nauvoo, Illinois, for the Church of Jesus Christ of Latter-Day Saints and later on Constitution Island at West Point, New York.[7]

In 1947 Harrington initiated archaeological investigations at Fort Raleigh for the National Park Service that would last several years and be written up in several reports and publications.[8] He aimed in 1947 to authenticate the site and to provide planning data for a larger-scale project, which he conducted over the next two years. During the course of his work, he recorded twelve of the thirteen trenches dug by Williams in 1895.[9] In the spring of 1948 he obtained evidence about the shape and construction of the fort. By the autumn of 1950 he had completed this initial phase of his investigations. During the summer of 1953, he dug in the area about to be developed as the Elizabethan Garden.[10] His final investigation, just west of the fort at the outwork, took place in 1965. Harrington's efforts between 1947 and 1963 produced a plan of the sixteenth-century occupancies (Figure 4). Harrington concluded that the ditch was the remains of Lane's fort (1585-1586) and that the outwork had served as a temporary defensive work antedating the fort. His collection contained sixteenth-century European material, sixteenth-century Native American pottery, a very small number of earlier Indian relics, and small amounts of recent material.[11]

During 1982 and 1983, John E. Ehrenhard of the Southeast Archaeological Center (SEAC) of the National Park Service conducted soil resistivity and magnetometer surveys based on conjectural similarities between the "outwork" and structures at Wolstenholme in Virginia, first suggested by Phil Evans, park historian at Fort Raleigh National Historic Site. Ehrenhard's surveys located a number of anomalies, many of which were examined by block excavation, as noted in several reports Ehrenhard and his colleagues wrote between 1982 and 1984 (Figure 5). National Park Service archaeologist Jack Walker carried out additional work in 1984 at an anomaly thought to be a bastion of a Wolstenholme-type fortification.[12] Although none of these investigations led to the identification of either the "habitation area" or additional fortifications, they did produce information important to understanding the archaeological nature of Fort Raleigh National Historic Site.

In 1991 Ivor Noël Hume of the Virginia Company Foundation, with assistance from SEAC, initiated archaeological investigations within and to the west of the fort. That work has substantially altered our understanding of the fort and outwork.[13] Early in the current round of archaeological investigations, Noël Hume and I discussed the meaning of the Native American artifacts that Harrington and others had recovered from the site over the preceding fifty years. Were these remains of the former village occupied by Wingina's people, material given or traded to the colonists, remains of an earlier aboriginal occupation, materials discarded by Indians who reoccupied the site after the departure of the colonists, or a combination of such possibilities? I immediately enlisted the expertise of David S. Phelps of East Carolina University in re-analyzing the Indian collection. By the spring of 1994 we had gone through the available collections.

Native American material with acceptable contextual provenance came from Harrington, Ehrenhard, and Noël Hume's work, along with some Colington sherds recovered by me. Harrington's excavations of "Lane's Old Fort," the Elizabethan Gardens, and the "Outwork" brought the total sherd count to 782. Distribution studies show that 93 percent of the ceramics were recovered from the fort and outwork areas. Of these items, 76 percent were from the outwork and 24 percent from the fort. Some 77 percent of the sherds recovered from the fort can be attributed to vessels Harrington illustrates as "complete" pots. More than 99 percent of the ceramics belong to the contemporary Colington and Cashie series. The resident Algonkian Roanoke potters produced the shell-tempered Colington ware, while the Cashie specimens represent trade from the interior Tuscarora peoples. The ratio of

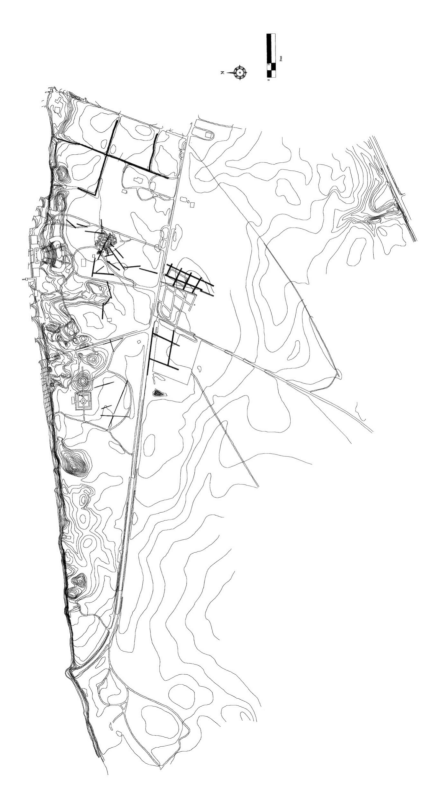

Fig. 4. Location of excavations by J. C. Harrington on Roanoke Island, 1947-1963.

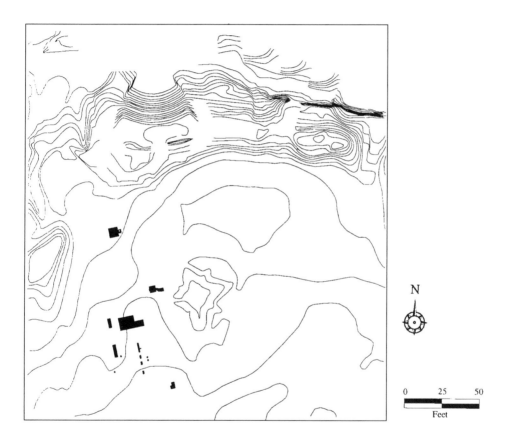

Fig. 5. Location of excavations on Roanoke Island by John E. Ehrenhard and Jack Walker, 1982-1985.

Colington sherds to Cashie sherds is almost 7-to-1. Needless to say, the small number of vessels of Colington and Cashie ceramics could have been easily consumed by Hariot's and Ganz's scientific experiments.

We have concluded that Native Americans never occupied the fort/outwork and surrounding area. With the exception of the ceramics, there is virtually nothing related to even a temporary campsite, let alone a village. Aside from the sparse artifact assemblage, no aboriginal features (hearths, structures, or shell middens) have been encountered. Lane's 1585 colony obtained the North American pottery by trade with or as gifts from the Indians. The extent of this traffic indicates that Lane's group had either no expertise or no desire to make pottery. Just as they depended upon the Roanokes for food, they used some elements of the Native Americans' technology.

During the 1990s, SEAC archaeologists undertook several projects described below (Figure 6), as did David Phelps. Likewise, the Virginia Company Foundation (led by Ivor Noël Hume, Nicholas Luccketti, and William Kelso)—working under an Archaeological Resource Protection permit and with assistance from the Fort Raleigh National Historic Site and SEAC—excavated at the site on various occasions between 1991 and 1995. The Association for the Preservation of Virginia Antiquities continued that research effort at the end of 1996 directed by Luccketti and Kelso.

National Park Service archaeologist Susan Hammersten in 1990 dug a number of shovel tests along the corridor for installation of buried telephone lines between the maintenance yard and park housing. When she recovered only modern material, she discarded the artifacts.[14] That same year I excavated five one-meter-by-one-meter units at the site of the electrical utilities building west of the headquarters building but encountered no buried sixteenth-century gray sand horizon. All of the material recovered was modern.[15] In June 1991 I monitored the installation of a new sewage treatment facility for the Waterside Theatre. Three Colington simple stamped sherds were recovered from the gray sand zone between the septic tanks.[16] National Park Service archaeologist Douglas Potter monitored the installation of an 840-foot telephone cable in July and August 1991. In his report he mentioned that some fragments of brick unearthed resembled those found in the "outwork." Potter noted that this project crossed the old highway bed.[17] Later that year he shovel-tested the area that contained the "new" visitor center rest rooms. The stratigraphy is apparently similar to that in the vicinity of the electrical facilities building, i.e., *no* buried sixteenth-century gray sand layer. Potter recovered only modern materials.[18] In 1992 Ken Wild, another National Park Service archaeologist, monitored the installation of a manhole, sewer line, and drain. The excavations revealed no prehistoric or historic cultural materials or features.

In 1993 National Park Service archaeologist Daniel Penton and David Phelps excavated fourteen 5-foot-by-5-foot units immediately north of the northwest corner of the visitor center so that a drain could be installed. The buried sixteenth-century gray sand horizon was not present. With the possible exception of a lead sprue and a

Fig. 6. Location of excavations on Roanoke Island by Southeast Archaeological Center archaeologists, 1990-1997.

Fig. 7. Location of excavations on Roanoke Island, 1985-1997.

single cut nail, the remainder of the collection dated to the twentieth century.[19] In the fall of 1993, I tested in the maintenance yard to clear the area for the installation of an above-ground fuel facility. The area had been totally disturbed from previous construction and grading work. No artifacts were recovered.[20]

In September 1995 David Phelps and I excavated three 5-foot-by-5-foot test units immediately north of the headquarters building to clear the route for the utilities lines to the new visitor center rest rooms. Materials recovered from those units was of modern vintage; in fact, the majority of it was composed of items related to the construction of the headquarters and visitor center buildings in the 1960s. We also tested along the roads from a junction box, just north of the park maintenance building, to the Elizabethan Gardens maintenance shop. Except for four creamware sherds, which reaffirm a late-eighteenth- to early-nineteenth-century occupation of the northern part of Roanoke Island, the sparse amount of material recovered was modern.[21]

In September 1997 I excavated three 5-foot-by-5-foot test units in the impact zone of the Waterside Theatre renovation. Gray sand (the sixteenth-century soil horizon) was encountered at a depth of 3.55 feet in Test Unit 1. But no cultural material was recovered. Only an 1852 U.S. three-cent coin, from Test Unit 3, antedates this century. The vast majority of the collection does not predate the construction of the Waterside Theatre.[22]

Observations

The small projects described above provide some interesting though negative data in respect to the sixteenth-century settlement of Roanoke Island. Not one item from this period or earlier has been recovered, except for the three Native American Colington series sherds from the sewage treatment facility west of the Waterside Theatre. These projects establish broad-scale boundaries for the buried sixteenth-century gray sand horizon. We know that it is present north of the fort but vanishes somewhere to the south between the fort and the visitor center. It does not exist east, west, or south of the visitor center. These projects provide little data for the later (seventeenth-, eighteenth-, and nineteenth-century) occupations. The vast majority of the materials recovered from these projects date to the mid-twentieth century.

Both Talcott Williams and Jean Harrington believed that the fort was constructed by Ralph Lane's colony, but both had some misgivings. Williams was concerned that the earthwork was too small to protect the number of settlers in Lane's group. Harrington was likewise concerned about the size of the earthwork, as well as its location. John Ehrenhard and Ivor Noël Hume have posited that the fort was an element of a much larger fortification similar to the facility at Wolstenholme Towne, but subsequent fieldwork has not supported that hypothesis. Noël Hume also suggested that the fort was not built by the sixteenth-century colonists but was in fact a mid-eighteenth-century earthwork put up for the defense of Edenton shipping.[23] Neither archaeological evidence nor colonial documents support that proffer, as I noted in a 1993 letter to him.[24] The evidence presently available implies that a late-sixteenth-century English occupation occurred before the erection of the earthwork—e.g., Harrington recovered European material from the original topsoil beneath the parapet and in the parapet fill. It is possible that White's colony built the earthen fort, but the more likely builders are the contingent of fifteen soldiers Sir Richard Grenville ordered in June 1586 to remain and hold the queen's claim. The location and size of the fort are more appropriate to a detachment and mission of that size than to either of the colonies attempted by Sir Walter Raleigh.

A century of digging has yet to locate the Cittie of Ralegh (Figure 7). Where might it be? Some say that the dashing waters of Albemarle Sound have eroded it away completely. This hypothesis needs testing. Several investigators have suggested that the living area, now destroyed, of the sixteenth-century colonies may have been located east of the fort, in the Waterside Theatre parking lot. However, Harrington investigated there and found absolutely nothing. Others have suggested that the colony was situated several miles to the south, in the vicinity of Shallowbag Bay. The real answer is that we do not know where the remains of these domestic settlements are situated. But we plan additional investigations that will continue well into the new millennium.

NOTES

1. David Beers Quinn, *Set Fair for Roanoke: Voyages and Settlements, 1584-1606* (Chapel Hill: University of North Carolina Press, 1985), 327.

2. John Lawson, *A New Voyage to Carolina*, ed. Hugh Talmage Lefler (Chapel Hill: University of North Carolina Press, 1967), 68-69.

3. Benson John Lossing, *The Pictorial Field-Book of the Revolution*, 2 vols. (New York: Harper and Brothers, 1860), 244.

4. Talcott Williams, "The Surroundings and Site of Raleigh's Colony," in *Annual Report of the American Historical Association for 1895* (Washington: Government Printing Office, 1896), 58.

5. Edward C. Bruce, "Lounging in the Footprints of the Pioneers," *Harper's New Monthly Magazine* 20 (May 1860): 733-735.

6. The following sketch of this man is based primarily on Elizabeth Dunbar, *Talcott Williams: Gentleman of the Fourth Estate* (Brooklyn, N.Y.: R. E. Simpson and Son, 1936).

7. A good overview of Harrington's life and career is George L. Miller, "Memorial: J. C. Harrington, 1901-1998," *Historical Archaeology* 28 (1994): 30-38.

8. Among Harrington's publications on his excavations at Fort Raleigh are "Plain Stamped, Shell Tempered Pottery from North Carolina," *American Antiquity* 13 (January 1948): 251-252; "Archeological Explorations at Fort Raleigh National Historic Site," *North Carolina Historical Review* 26 (April 1949): 127-149; "Historic Relic Found: An Old Iron Sickle from Fort Raleigh, North Carolina," *Iron Worker* 15 (summer 1951): 12-15; *Search for the Cittie of Ralegh: Archeological Excavations at Fort Raleigh National Historic Site, North Carolina*, Archaeological Research Series, No. 6 (Washington: National Park Service, U.S. Department of the Interior, 1962); and *An Outwork at Fort*

Raleigh: Further Archeological Excavations at Fort Raleigh National Historic Site, North Carolina (Philadelphia: Eastern National Parks and Monuments Association, 1966).

9. Harrington, *Search for the Cittie of Ralegh*, fig. 13.

10. Harrington, *Search for the Cittie of Ralegh*, 35.

11. Harrington, *An Outwork at Fort Raleigh*.

12. J. W. Walker and A. H. Cooper, *Archeological Testing of Aerial and Soil Resistivity Anomaly Fora a-1, Fort Raleigh National Historic Site, North Carolina* (Tallahassee: Southeast Archeological Center, National Park Service, 1989).

13. See Noël Hume's two reports for the National Park Service, as well as his book *The Virginia Adventure*.

14. Susan Hammersten, *Archeological Survey for Park Housing* (Tallahassee: Southeast Archeological Center, National Park Service, 1990).

15. Bennie C. Keel, *Archeological Clearance for Electrical Facilities Building* (Tallahassee: Southeast Archeological Center, National Park Service, 1990).

16. Bennie C. Keel, *Archeological Monitoring of Installation of Sewer System at Waterside Theater, Fort Raleigh National Historic Site, NC (FORA), May 31-June 19, 1991* (Tallahassee: Southeast Archeological Center, National Park Service, 1991).

17. Douglas Potter, *Archeological Investigations for Telephone Cable Installation* (Tallahassee: Southeast Archeological Center, National Park Service, 1991).

18. Douglas Potter, *Archeological Investigations for Restrooms, Waterside Theater* (Tallahassee: Southeast Archeological Center, National Park Service, 1991).

19. D. T. Penton, *Archeological Investigations for Telephone Cable and Drainage* (Tallahassee: Southeast Archeological Center, National Park Service, 1993).

20. Bennie C. Keel, *Archeological Investigations for a New Fuel Facility* (Tallahassee: Southeast Archeological Center, National Park Service, 1993).

21. Bennie C. Keel, *Archeological Investigations of Utility Lines at Fort Raleigh National Historic Site* (Tallahassee: Southeast Archeological Center, National Park Service, 1996).

22. Bennie C. Keel, *Investigations at Waterside Theater, Fort Raleigh National Monument, Sept. 2-5, 1997* (Tallahassee: Southeast Archeological Center, National Park Service, 1997).

23. Ivor Noël Hume, *The Virginia Adventure: Roanoke to James Towne: An Archaeological and Historical Odyssey* (New York: Knopf, 1994), 86.

24. Bennie C. Keel, Trip report to Ivor Noël Hume, 1993, Southeast Archeological Center, National Park Service, Tallahassee.

Invaded or Traded? Three Models for Explaining the Presence of Iberian Olive Jars at Fort Raleigh and Other British Colonial Sites

John J. Mintz and Thomas E. Beaman Jr.

Iberian olive jars are recognized as the primary shipping containers used by the Spanish colonial empire. Their ubiquitous presence throughout the Caribbean and the Spanish Americas has often been used as an archaeological marker to identify sites that date to the time of the Spanish colonization in the Americas and/or had a sustained Spanish colonial presence. Works by archaeologists John Goggin, Stephen James, and Mitchell Marken have thoroughly detailed the presence, forms, and functions of this utilitarian ceramic type at Spanish colonial sites.

However, archaeologists are beginning to recognize that olive jars have a larger presence in the interconnected global trade networks of the sixteenth, seventeenth, and eighteenth centuries, which often transcended the Spanish colonial empire. These vessels, and presumably the goods contained within them, are now thought to encompass a much larger area of distribution than previously assumed. Fragments and whole vessels are now being recognized on British colonial-period sites in the Americas and the Caribbean. This network of distribution continued into Britain and the North Sea area of northwestern Europe, where olive jars have been recovered in eighteenth-century contexts.[1]

Based on historical documents and archaeological evidence from Brunswick Town, three models have been proposed to explain how olive jars arrived at mainland British colonial ports. The first model considers them material remnants of Spanish occupation. A second involves direct trade by the British colonists with Spanish ships. A third presumes inter-island trading by the Spanish, British, and other colonial powers in the Caribbean. Olive jar sherds have been identified on at least seven other British colonial-period sites in North and South Carolina, including Fort Raleigh, a site that has yielded material evidence of sixteenth-century English settlement (Figure 8). Archaeological evidence from the Fort Raleigh National Historic Site and documented accounts of the early settlements on Roanoke Island provide a unique opportunity to test these three hypotheses at another British colonial site.[2]

Forms and Functions

While the term *olive jar* has been credited to archaeologist W. H. Holmes, one of the first comprehensive studies of olive jars was conducted in the 1950s by John Goggin. Based on forms recovered at terrestrial Spanish colonial sites in the Americas and the Caribbean, Goggin classified olive jars into Early (ca. 1500-ca. 1580), Middle (ca. 1585-ca. 1800), and Late (ca. 1800-ca. 1850) periods (Figure 9). Goggin's seriation study still represents the authoritative chronology of olive jar forms. More recently, archaeologists Stephen James and Mitchell Marken have produced alternative

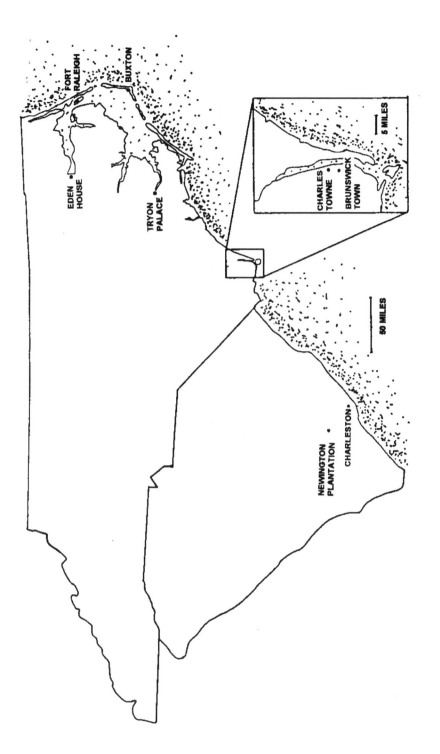

Fig. 8. British colonial-period sites in North and South Carolina at which olive jar sherds have been identified.

categorization systems for olive jars by examining vessels found on Spanish colonial shipwrecks. Though each of these classification systems varies slightly from Goggin's, the vessel forms identified are essentially the same. However, both James and Marken identify a flat-bottom olive jar, a form not noted by Goggin.[3]

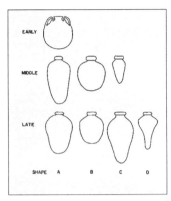

Fig. 9. Representative forms of olive jars from the three periods classified by John Goggin in the 1950s.

Goggin speculated that the majority of olive jars were manufactured in and around Seville. He based this theory on the fact that the majority of ships bound for Spanish colonies in the Americas sailed from Seville. Archaeologist A. Vince confirmed Goggin's Seville hypothesis with a thin-section analysis of several vessels recovered in England. While no other places of manufacture are currently known, archaeologist Charles Fairbanks speculated that if the shipping quantity was a valid criterion, then vessel production must be relatively widespread. The lack of large quantities of ceramic waste materials at suspected sites of manufacture could reveal that imperfect jars commonly entered trade networks with little regard for aesthetics.[4]

The primary use of olive jars in Spanish colonial contexts was as transatlantic and overland shipping containers for a variety of products. The use of ceramic containers for shipping is a Mediterranean tradition dating back thousands of years to Greek and Roman times, but it is not part of the trading traditions of northern Europe. Charles Fairbanks attributed the continuation of the Mediterranean tradition on the Iberian Peninsula from the sixteenth through the nineteenth centuries to the relative scarcity of timber. He suggested that the numerous forests in northern European countries served as abundant natural resources for the manufacture of wooden casks and barrels, which became the primary shipping containers for that region. Spanish shipping records mention beans, chick-peas, lard, olives in brine, olive oil, pitch, soap, tar, vinegar, and wine as commodities transported over sea and land in olive jars. Some of these products have been found intact, sealed in their original containers. Given the primary use of olive jars as shipping containers, the common presence of those vessels at Spanish colonial-period archaeological sites in the Americas and the Caribbean has inspired several archaeologists to term them "the cardboard boxes of the day."[5]

Archaeologists working at Spanish colonial sites have noted two secondary uses for olive jars. First, olive jars found in domestic contexts may have been used for liquid and general storage. Velazquez's 1623 painting *The Waterseller of Seville* (Figure 10) illustrates a handled olive jar used as a container for water. The porous fabric of an unglazed olive jar would cool water by evaporation, a useful property in the warm Caribbean climate. Foodstuffs such as corn, flour, and beans, as well as any number of general items, could have been stored in olive jars as well. The porous body would allow airflow around dry goods, thus retarding mold and mildew. Second, the jars'

Fig. 10. A handled olive jar used as a water container figures prominently in the 1623 painting *The Waterseller of Seville* by Velazquez. (Reproduced courtesy of the Victoria and Albert Picture Library, London.)

durability led to their functional and decorative use in Spanish colonial architecture. Whole vessel forms have been found as part of roof vaults, walls, and gate arches. Fragments were used as roofing tiles and paving materials in floor and patio construction. Intact late-style olive jars served as decorative embellishments on buildings and finials on gateposts.[6]

Invaded or Traded?: Three Hypotheses for Consideration

Unlike the other studies in this volume, the foundation of this investigation does not begin on Roanoke Island in the sixteenth century but at Brunswick Town, an eighteenth-century port town on the Cape Fear River in southeastern North Carolina. During the eighteenth century, Brunswick Town was one of the British colonial empire's most valuable ports for exporting naval stores and a major center for importing consumer goods into the Cape Fear region. Archaeological excavations at Brunswick Town conducted by E. Lawrence Lee and Stanley A. South from 1958 until 1968 yielded olive jar fragments from six of the twenty-two excavated ruins within the town. If olive jars containing consumer goods were brought to Brunswick Town, those commodities would eventually be exhausted, leaving empty vessels. As with the presence of olive jars at Spanish colonial sites, the discovery of these vessels primarily in domestic contexts suggests they were recycled into storage containers.[7]

The anomalous presence of olive jars at Brunswick Town and other British colonial settlements and ports invites a question: how did these Iberian coarse-ware forms appear in English-controlled ports on mainland North America? The information contained in state records, travelers' accounts, period newspapers, and the Port Brunswick Shipping Register suggest three hypotheses to account for the presence of olive jars at Brunswick Town.[8] Stanley South attributed that presence to a 1748 Spanish attack. As detailed in the October 24, 1748, issue of the *South Carolina Gazette*, Spanish privateers sailed up the Cape Fear River and captured Brunswick Town. The residents of the city initially fled, then regrouped and returned three days later. In the skirmish to retake the city, one of the Spanish ships, the *Fortuna*, sank in the Cape Fear River off Brunswick Town. The *South Carolina Gazette* noted that the townspeople salvaged various goods from the *Fortuna*. Some were sold to support the construction of St. Philips Church, while others were kept for personal use. Any olive jars retrieved from the *Fortuna* probably were recycled into domestic use at that time.[9]

A second hypothesis suggests that olive jars may have reached Brunswick Town through direct trade with Spanish ships. The eighteenth-century British Parliament attempted to regulate, and in some cases prohibit, trade between British merchants and other colonial powers. Provincial law and trade regulations varied from colony to colony. In some ports, parliamentary and provincial regulations were only loosely enforced and sometimes virtually ignored. The import register for Port Brunswick confirms lax enforcement of trade regulations. Several ships that originated from such Spanish colonies as Florida and Hispaniola are reported to have docked at Brunswick Town. Even if those ships carried no commodities or cargo, they may have borne olive jars that were traded informally to dock workers or town residents.[10]

A third hypothesis proposes that these coarse earthenware forms entered the British colonial trade network through inter-island trade in the Caribbean. Spanish ships trading at British ports, British ships trading at Spanish ports, or another country's ships trading at both Spanish and British colonial ports could easily have exchanged goods shipped in olive jars. The jars could have then entered British ports in North America aboard British ships. The Port Brunswick Shipping Register kept by William Dry reveals that in the years 1774 and 1775 more than half the vessels entering the Cape Fear River originated at Caribbean ports, while only about a third came from Britain, and less than one-seventh from northern ports in colonial America.

Olive Jars from Fort Raleigh

The first English attempt to colonize mainland North America occurred on Roanoke Island in 1585. The second such attempt, in 1587, resulted in the mysterious disappearance of the colonists who were left on the island. Beginning with Talcott Williams's excavations in the autumn of 1895, archaeological explorations for the elusive settlement at the site of Fort Raleigh National Historic Site have been conducted for more than a century without success. Those numerous investigations have yielded only a small number of Elizabethan-period artifacts, including a total of twenty-seven Iberian olive jar fragments.

Excavations at the site of the reconstructed earthen fort by J. C. Harrington between 1947 and 1953 yielded twenty-two fragments. Nineteen of those sherds were recovered from the interior of the fort, three from the fort ditch. The fragments were determined to have originated as a single vessel. Harrington surmised that an olive jar was broken during the construction of the fort. The tightly defined sixteenth-century context of these sherds provided John Goggin with the earliest appearance of his "Middle Period" style of olive jars.[11]

Joint archaeological investigations by the Virginia Company Foundation and the Association for the Preservation of Virginia Antiquities in 1994 and 1995 near the northern boundary of Fort Raleigh National Historic Site yielded five additional unglazed Middle Period-style sherds, but the jar form remained indeterminate. It is possible, though doubtful, that those body sherds were from the vessel identified by Harrington. The spatial distribution of the two collections suggests that they represent two different vessels, though all of the sherds are of Middle Period style and likely date to the brief sixteenth-century settlements.[12]

Evaluating the Three Hypotheses

The first hypothesis to consider is that olive jars are present in context with other Elizabethan-period artifacts found at Fort Raleigh as a result of a temporary or lengthy Spanish occupation at the site. From the sixteenth-century settlement on Roanoke Island onward, many residents of colonial North and South Carolina lived in fear of Spanish privateer and pirate attacks on British settlements, such as those at Ocracoke in 1741; at Beaufort, North Carolina, in 1747; and at Brunswick Town in 1748. Other than Brunswick Town, none of the British colonial sites or settlements at which olive jars have been recovered in North and South Carolina is known to have been the focus of Spanish attack, much less a sustained occupation. Moreover, the absence of a cross, a sign of distress proposed to the Roanoke Island colonists by John White before his departure, and the presence of the carved message "CROATOAN" suggest that the colonists were not the victims of a Spanish attack.[13] This hypothesis does not appear to explain validly the presence of olive jars at Fort Raleigh.

The second hypothesis, whereby direct trade with the Spanish brought Iberian ceramics into British colonial ports and settlement, is a relatively unexplored issue. However, material evidence of trading by the Spanish with English colonies, a practice forbidden under both Spain's and England's mercantilist economic policies, has been observed by archaeologists at sixteenth-, seventeenth-, and eighteenth-century Spanish sites. Given the absence of documentary support, direct trade by the Spanish at any English port or settlement is difficult if not impossible to detect. Moreover, since no Spanish presence at or near Roanoke Island in the sixteenth century is known, this hypothesis does not convincingly explain the presence of olive jars at Fort Raleigh.

The third hypothesis, that of inter-island Caribbean trade, best accounts for the arrival of olive jars at Roanoke Island in the sixteenth century. Unlike Charleston or Brunswick Town, Fort Raleigh and other small settlements lacked resources to attract foreign commercial traders. The very brief existence of the sixteenth-century Roanoke settlements likewise supports the possibility that olive jars (and the commodities they contained) arrived with the colonists.

Olive Jars from Croatoan?

John White recorded in his narrative that when he returned to Roanoke in August 1590 he found a deserted fort without houses and a number of broken chests whose damage he attributed to Indians from Dasamongwepeuk. The only clues to where the colonists may have gone were the letters "CRO" carved on a tree near the beach and the word "CROATOAN" carved on a tree inside the fort's entrance. From those carvings and the absence of a distress mark, White concluded that the English colonists were safely at the Native American village of Croatoan. The notion, never confirmed, that the colonists departed for Croatoan has persisted in popular thought for more than four centuries, and their fate remains one of North Carolina's oldest mysteries.

Naturally this notion has also found its way into archaeological research, though archaeology has the potential to offer more tangible evidence than does popular lore. Two olive jar fragments have been recovered from 31Dr1, a large site near Buxton on Hatteras Island believed to be the village of Croatoan. Harry Davis of the North Carolina Museum of Natural History and his protégé Joffre L. Coe recovered the first fragment in 1938. Davis and Coe collected prehistoric and early European artifacts from an eroded bank and placed one 5-foot-by-5-foot test unit in a shell midden. The specific context in which the olive jar fragment was recovered is not known. During recent investigations at the southern end of the site in 1997 and 1998, David S. Phelps of East Carolina University recovered the second fragment, along with other prehistoric and historic artifacts, in a stratigraphic context that could date to the time either of the Roanoke Colony or of later European settlement on Hatteras Island.[14]

It is not yet known whether these two olive jar fragments and other European artifacts recovered near Buxton are material remnants of the resettled colony, goods that were traded to local Native Americans by the Roanoke colonists, or artifacts scavenged from the Roanoke site by Native Americans following the abandonment of the settlement. Olive jar fragments found in context with other Elizabethan-period artifacts certainly offer the possibility that they originated from the Roanoke colony. It is also possible that these and other European artifacts recovered at the site near Buxton are related to the later seventeenth- and eighteenth-century European settlement of Hatteras Island and interaction with the local Native Americans at that time. Further archaeological research may offer more insight into the origin of the two fragments and the other European artifacts found near Buxton.

Conclusions

The presence of olive jar fragments from the short-lived sixteenth-century settlements on Roanoke Island has provided an opportunity to test three hypotheses on how Iberian olive jars reached British colonial settlements and ports. The first two hypotheses, involving interaction with the Spanish, are not likely, given the colonies' brief durations and the absence of other evidence of Spanish attack or occupation. The most satisfactory hypothesis is that the olive jars recovered from Fort Raleigh National Historic Site arrived with the sixteenth-century English colonists as a result of inter-island trade in the Caribbean.

Historical documents likewise support inter-island Caribbean trade as the most probable explanation for the presence of the olive jars. While en route to "Virginia" in 1585, English ships attempted to trade for supplies at Puerto Rico and Hispaniola. The abortive attempt at Puerto Rico was followed by friendly commercial exchanges at Puerto Plata on Hispaniola, where the English acquired both livestock and trade goods and collected fruit and vegetable samples in hopes that they would grow in the new colony. Though Spanish colonists were not supposed to trade with other foreign powers, some towns on Hispaniola situated outside the main trade routes, such as Puerto Real, possess well-documented histories and archaeological evidence of illicit trade practices. While it is not known what comestibles the olive jars at Fort Raleigh originally contained, it is very probable they were acquired at this time.[15]

While that exchange may seem an insignificant trading occurrence, its timing and location are important factors when considering the Caribbean in 1584. Political tensions between Britain and Spain were very high in Europe four years before the British navy defeated the Spanish Armada in 1588. The fact that material evidence of ongoing trade between these two nations exists signifies that ports in the Caribbean were perhaps affected less by the immediate political actions of their mother nations than by a long-standing history of, and substantial profit from, illicit trade.

NOTES

1. John G. Hurst, David S. Neal, and H. J. E. van Beuningen, *Rotterdam Papers VI: Pottery Produced and Traded in North-West Europe, 1350-1650* (Rotterdam: Museum Boymans-van Beuingen, 1986), 66.

2. See in particular Thomas Beaman Jr. and John J. Mintz, "Iberian Olive Jars at Brunswick Town and Other British Colonial Sites: Three Models for Consideration," *Southeastern Archaeology* 17 (summer 1998).

3. W. H. Holmes, *Aboriginal Pottery of the Eastern United States*, Bureau of American Ethnology Annual Report No. 20 (Washington: Government Printing Office, 1903), 129; John Goggin, *The Spanish Olive Jar: An Introductory Study*, Yale University Publications in Anthropology, No. 62 (New Haven: Yale University Press, 1960); Stephen R. James Jr., "A Reassessment of the Chronological and Typological Framework of the Spanish Olive Jar," *Historical Archaeology* 22 (1988) (hereafter cited as "Reassessment of the Spanish Olive Jar"); Mitchell W. Marken, *Pottery from Spanish Shipwrecks, 1500-1800* (Gainesville: University Press of Florida, 1994).

4. Goggin, *Spanish Olive Jar*, 5; A. Vince, "Medieval and Post-Medieval Spanish Pottery from the City of London," in *Current Research in Ceramics: Thin Section Studies*, ed. I. Freestone, Catherine Johns, and T. Potter, British Museum Occasional Papers, No. 32 (London: British Museum, 1982), 135-144; Charles H. Fairbanks, "The Cultural Tradition of Spanish Ceramics," in *Ceramics in America*, ed. Ian M. G. Quimby (Charlottesville: University Press of Virginia, 1973), 144; Marken, *Pottery from Spanish Shipwrecks*, 48.

5. Fairbanks, "Cultural Tradition of Spanish Ceramics," 143; James, "Reassessment of the Spanish Olive Jar," 43; Charles R. Ewen and Maurice W. Williams, "Puerto Real: Archaeology of an Early Spanish Town," in *First Encounters: Spanish Explorations in the Caribbean and the United States, 1492-1570*, ed. Jerald T. Milanich and Susan Milbrath, Ripley P. Bullen Monographs in Anthropology and History, No. 9 (Gainesville: Florida Museum of Natural History, 1980), 71.

6. Goggin, *Spanish Olive Jar*, 6-7; Kathleen Deagan, *Artifacts of the Spanish Colonies of Florida and the Caribbean, 1500-1800* (Washington: Smithsonian Institution Press, 1987), 32; Marken, *Pottery from Spanish Shipwrecks*, 42.

7. John J. Mintz and Thomas Beaman Jr., "Invaded or Traded? Olive Jars and Oil Jars from Brunswick Town," *North Carolina Archaeology* 46 (October 1997): 35-50. For a history of the Brunswick Town excavations, see Thomas E. Beaman Jr. et al., "Archaeological History and Historical Archaeology: Revisiting the Excavations at Brunswick Town, 1958-1969," *North Carolina Archaeology* 47 (October 1998): 1-33.

8. Beaman and Mintz, "Iberian Olive Jars at Brunswick Town."

9. Stanley A. South, *Colonial Brunswick, 1726-1776* (N.p., 1960), 32; Walter Clark, ed., *The State Records of North Carolina*, 16 vols. (11-26) (Raleigh: State of North Carolina, 1896-1906), 23:535-537; William L. Saunders, ed., *The Colonial Records of North Carolina*, 10 vols. (Raleigh: State of North Carolina, 1886-1890), 4:891-892.

10. See the Port Brunswick Shipping Register, 1767-1775, kept by William Dry, Collector of Customs for Port Brunswick, in Treasurer's and Comptroller's Papers, State Archives.

11. Jean Carl Harrington, *Search for the Cittie of Ralegh: Archaeological Excavations at Fort Raleigh National Historic Site, North Carolina*, Archaeological Research Series, No. 6 (Washington: National Park Service, U.S. Department of the Interior, 1962), 22; Goggin, *Spanish Olive Jar*, 24.

12. Nicholas M. Luccketti, *Fort Raleigh Archaeological Project: 1994-1995 Survey Report* (Jamestown: Virginia Company Foundation and the Association for the Preservation of Virginia Antiquities, 1996), 21.

13. John White, "John White's Narrative of the 1590 Voyage to Virginia," ed. David Beers Quinn, in *The Roanoke Voyages, 1584-1590: Documents to Illustrate the English Voyages to North America Under the Patent Granted to Walter Raleigh in 1584*, 2 vols., Hakluyt Society Second Series, No. 104 (London: Hakluyt Society, 1955), 2:613-616.

14. Field notes and correspondence related to Davis and Coe's exploration of 31Dr1 are on file at the Research Laboratories of Archaeology, University of North Carolina at Chapel Hill. Information on David S. Phelps's investigation of 31Dr1 comes from a January 21, 1999, talk to the Coastal Plain Chapter of the North Carolina Archaeological Society and from personal communication.

15. Quinn, *Roanoke Voyages,* 1:159-163. Archaeological data on illegal trading practices at Puerto Real and other Spanish colonial sites comes from Russell K. Skowronek, "Empire and Ceramics: The Changing Role of Illicit Trade in Spanish America," *Historical Archaeology* 26 (1992): 109-118, and Charles R. Ewen, *From Spaniard to Creole: The Archaeology of Cultural Formation at Puerto Real, Haiti* (Tuscaloosa: University of Alabama Press, 1991).

ACKNOWLEDGMENTS

Dr. Billy L. Oliver, Dr. David S. Phelps, and Dr. Vincas P. Steponaitis provided access to artifacts from and information on the excavations at 31Dr1 (the Buxton site), for which we are most grateful. Special thanks go to Dr. Linda F. Carnes-McNaughton and Stephen R. Claggett for commenting on drafts of this study. We also wish to acknowledge the Victoria and Albert Picture Library in London for permitting us to reproduce an image of *The Waterseller of Seville* from its collection.

Gift Exchange and the Ossomocomuck Balance of Power: Explaining Carolina Algonquian Socioeconomic Aberrations at Contact[1]

Seth Mallios

Introduction

Native tribes of the Carolina sounds during the 1580s maintained separate identities and frequently antagonized each other; their different reactions to gift-exchange violations by the English repeatedly aligned more with deliberate attempts at gaining and preserving power and status within Ossomocomuck territory than with specific colonist transgressions. An analysis based on the intersection of anthropological models of exchange and contemporaneous historical records regarding European settlement at Ajacan, Roanoke, and Jamestown reveals that colonists violated native economic rules at all three locales. The Roanoke case is exceptional, however, because the natives, instead of merely abandoning dependent settlers or launching violent attacks in response to European affronts, often manipulated the colonists as tools in their intracultural disputes. Economic offenses were avenged, but with careful consideration of the social and political implications for the area's indigenous groups.

This study establishes three points. First, late-sixteenth- and early-seventeenth-century Chesapeake and Carolina Algonquians followed a gift economy. Second, exchange violations that fomented intercultural hostilities at Ajacan and Jamestown did not cause parallel hostility at Roanoke. Third, Roanoke tribes ignored and deflected certain English transgressions, focusing more on strengthening their position in the overall native balance of power than on correcting or avenging errors in reciprocity. In order to substantiate these claims, the discussion presented here touches briefly on additional issues as well: defining and contrasting models of gift- and commodity-exchange systems, exploring the origin and transformations of the ethnic slur "Indian giver," explaining similar sequences of exchange and violence at Ajacan and Jamestown, presenting an exchange-based narrative on the dynamic intercultural events of the 1580s in the Carolina sounds, and noting an overall pattern of interaction at all three locales. The Roanoke example is essential to the broad analysis of contact-period relations because, unlike Ajacan and Jamestown, it includes situations in which natives perceived exchange violations as secondary and somewhat peripheral to intricate political alliances. Although economics and politics are inseparable components of a larger and multidimensional cultural whole, analyses of this sort provide insights into Algonquian social priorities.

Gift- and Commodity-Exchange Models

Intercultural exchange practices play a vital role in any contact-period study of the Chesapeake and Carolinas because European survival at Ajacan, Roanoke, and Jamestown depended almost exclusively on gifts from and trade with the indigenous population. Of the many scholars who have studied exchange, none figures more prominently in this work than the anthropologist Marcel Mauss. On the basis of extensive description from existing ethnographies, Mauss, in his 1925 publication *The Gift*, developed a theory on gift-exchange systems. Mauss built his ethnological model on strikingly similar cross-cultural social and economic elements from contemporaneous societies in Polynesia, Melanesia, and the American Northwest, as well as past Roman, Hindu, Germanic, Celtic, and Chinese civilizations.

The back-and-forth giving of goods guides a gift-exchange system. The transactions appear as unconditional and unsolicited offerings. Mauss asserted that although these propositions assume the semblance of "something for nothing" and maintain a "voluntary form," the gift is, quite to the contrary, "strictly compulsory."[2] Paradoxically, there is nothing free about the seemingly free gift and nothing altruistic or disinterested about the giver. Participants in the gift economy must satisfy three obligations: they have to give, receive, and reciprocate.[3] A member of the gift-exchange system who fails to fulfill any of the three general gift duties loses social status: "[T]o lose one's prestige is to lose one's soul."[4]

Those in a gift economy attempt to gain status by giving and to avoid the social reduction that results from denying or not making offerings. Since debt and status are gained at the expense of others, those who participate in a gift economy emphasize "who owes" instead of "what is owed."[5] With the utility of the dealt goods being secondary to the connection formed between exchange partners by the reciprocal offerings, gifts become powerful tools to create and manipulate interpersonal relationships. Positioning in the social hierarchy controls to whom one gives gifts and from whom one receives gifts. High-rank individuals exchange high-rank gifts because not only can they repay them but these gifts and these gift partners also reaffirm their dominant hegemonic position.[6] Likewise, low-rank individuals, incapable of giving or receiving high-rank gifts, must exchange low-rank gifts. These transactions produce exchange partnerships, hierarchically based intra- and intergroup connections.

In societies in which gift-giving dominates, individuals refuse to restrict the movement of any particular type of goods. They give, accept, and reciprocate everything. Other factors that reinforce the self-starting, self-perpetuating, and self-intensifying nature of the gift system include individuals' hastening to give first in order to secure immediate debt, and the passing of inalienable goods that are believed to contain the spirit of the giver.[7] The unlimited transference of gifts and debts creates groups that are "permanently allied" and "perpetually interdependent."[8] This combination of permanence and perpetuity further emphasizes the close relationship between the people involved in the gift exchange and de-emphasizes the actual goods being transacted. The folklorist Henry Glassie, when simultaneously discussing interpersonal relations and the concept of history, summarized, "I make a gift. You accept. Therefore, we are."[9] Likewise, the literary theorist Lewis Hyde concluded in his analysis of exchange that "Gifts bespeak relationship."[10]

Successful gift-giving forms interpersonal bonds between individuals, but unsuccessful offerings often result in hostilities. Expanding on Marcel Mauss's beliefs that accepting a present forms an alliance between exchange partners, the anthropologist Claude Levi-Strauss posited a causal link between exchange and hostility. He wrote, in specific reference to the native Nambikwaras of western Brazil and in general of gift societies, "Wars are the result of unsuccessful transactions."[11] Unsuccessful transactions that strain or sever the gift-based links between exchange partners, such as failing to give, accept, or reciprocate adequately, undermine the gift economy. Exchanges dependent on amicable interpersonal relations cease with the removal of a gift-exchange partner. Likewise, hostile actions toward one's transaction associate violate the gift system and disrupt the alliance. Theft, abduction, murder, and other antagonistic activities between those bonded by previous gift-giving dissolve the accord as well. Engaging and privileging the rivals of one's transaction associates also upset the supposed permanent alliance and perpetual interdependence of those connected by gift offerings. With status frequently gained through mutually beneficial exchanges, transactions with social competitors of one's exchange partners diminish the former alliance and ensure its dissolution. Since those in a gift economy esteem the act of giving over the actual object given, the details of the individual adversarial acts are secondary to the overall destruction of the alliance. Without immediate reparations, the infraction obliterates ties between exchange partners.

Diametrically opposed to a gift economy, an ideal commodity-exchange system is guided by principles of private ownership and the accumulation of goods. Whereas individuals in a gift system attempt to acquire debt and obligation from each other, those in a commodity exchange desire immediate access to and acquisition of material wealth.[12] The *economic* relationship between goods of like and equated exchange values is the only significant consideration. The *personal* relationship between individuals engaging in the transaction is de-emphasized.[13] The transactors are "reciprocally independent," and their relationship is only a momentary alliance, conceived to terminate upon the conclusion of the exchange.[14] The closeness of the relationship between commodity-exchanging individuals and their respective inter- and intragroup status does not necessarily fluctuate with or reflect the closure of each purchase. Like buying a soda from a vending machine in modern Western society, the actual objects that are transferred in each exchange—the money and the drink—and their equated value dwarf the identity, status, and relationship of and between the transactors—the customer and the machine, or its owner.

Chesapeake and Carolina Algonquian Economies

Contemporaneous historical records indicate that Chesapeake and Carolina Algonquians, when engaging European settlers, followed a gift economy. This assessment is based on the general form of the transactions the natives initiated, the like status of those involved, their prioritizing the acquisition of debt over wealth, the emphasis the indigenous population placed on the bond between exchange partners, and Algonquian accusations of insufficient European return gifts. Of course, gift- and commodity-exchange systems do not mutually exclude each other. Gift-giving frequently exists in commodity economies, and sale and trade repeatedly occur in gift-based systems. Nevertheless, one type of exchange overshadows others, permeating nearly every aspect of the group's "total social phenomenon."[15] Although the indigenous population of the Chesapeake and Carolinas at contact engaged in some intercultural commodity transactions, historical documents indicate that gift exchange dominated native society.

Well over three-quarters of the documented exchanges initiated by the natives at Ajacan, Roanoke, and Jamestown were gifts, classified on the basis of the something-for-nothing form of the exchange and the like status of the individuals involved. Chief Powhatan, the *Mamanatowick*, or paramount chief, of the thirty-one somewhat unified tribes that made up the native Chesapeake chiefdom, explained certain exchange rules to English colonist John Smith in January 1608. Captain Smith reported that transactions with the native leader had to follow a specific sequence and form. He wrote: "we [the English] freely should give [to] him, and then he liberally would requite us."[16] Furthermore, Chief Powhatan proclaimed that he did not "agree to trade," "did scorne to sell," and "despise[d] the nature of a Merchant."[17] So long as the English and Powhatans maintained an alliance, Chief Powhatan largely dismissed commodity-based transactions as a means of exchange. He labeled gifts and countergifts as "agreeable" forms of exchange, intimating that trade was disagreeable.[18]

Smith appreciated the nuances of the Algonquian gift-exchange system, telling Chief Powhatan, "By the gifts you bestow on us [colonists], you gain more than by trade."[19] Powhatan's gifts had placed the English in debt to the *Mamanatowick*, and it appeared to Smith that the Algonquian leader would accumulate more wealth, status, and power through European reciprocation and payment of that debt than he would through trading commodities. In complimenting Chief Powhatan for successfully following, using, and reaping the rewards of the native gift economy, Smith demonstrated an awareness of the Algonquians' distinct exchange system. The English captain also described his own success in the intercultural gift economy, boasting that "he had received contribution from 35 native kings."[20] According to gift-economy norms of bonds between exchange partners of similar status, having been regaled by many native leaders reflected Smith's elite social position in the eyes of the Algonquians. Smith likely acquired a knowledge of non-Western socioeconomic practices during his captivity in Turkey, years before his travels to the New World. In addition, his 1607-1608 stint as Jamestown's Cape Merchant, a position that required him to oversee the movement of any goods into or out of the colony, "manag[e] all things abroad," and keep "an account of all that [was] received, or delivered," certainly strengthened his understanding of Algonquian exchange tendencies and norms.[21]

Other Jamestown settlers noted key economic differences between Europeans and natives. Colonist Gabriel Archer, likely focusing on the immediate debt that resulted from Algonquian gift-giving as opposed to both anticipated reciprocation and the importance of securing interpersonal bonds, criticized the Powhatans in 1607 for having "no respect for profitt."[22] Archer's ethnocentric and myopic observation indirectly showcases dissimilar English and indigenous cultural rules regarding status, wealth, and acquisition and foreshadows an economic catalyst for subsequent conflict.

During the initial exploration of Roanoke Island in 1584 by the English explorers Philip Amadas and Arthur Barlowe, Roanoac interim chief Granganimeo made explicit the indigenous practice of exclusive gift-giving between those of elite status. Amadas and Barlowe offered gifts to the Algonquian leader, which he immediately accepted. They then attempted to present additional goods to other, lesser-ranking, natives, but Granganimeo interceded and physically intercepted the offerings. The chief declared that "the rest [of the natives] were but his servants and followers" and, thus, "all things ought to be delivered to him."[23] In fact, only elite natives—marked by their adornment with the preeminent spiritual good, copper—were allowed to exchange with the English in the presence of Granganimeo.[24] Two-and-one-half decades later, Chief Powhatan reaffirmed this link between status and gift-giving, declaring to Captain Smith, "if your king [England's James I] has sent me presents, then I am also a king."[25]

Linguistic Metamorphosis of "Indian Giver"

Over the past four centuries, the definition of the phrase "Indian giver" has undergone a meaningful transformation. Thomas Hutchinson, a colonial Massachusetts politician and author of *The History of the Colony and Province of Massachusetts Bay,* first printed the term in 1764, defining an "Indian gift" as "a proverbial expression signifying a present for which an equivalent return is expected."[26] The belief that each gift warrants reciprocation corresponds with Marcel Mauss's explanations of the obligation to reciprocate in a gift economy. Furthermore, Hutchinson's description of "Indian giver" as "proverbial" or "well-known because commonly referred to" supports the belief that by the eighteenth century the phrase linking Native Americans and that behavioral trait was "already an old saying."[27] Nearly one hundred years later, John R. Bartlett defined *Indian giver* in the 1860 edition of his *Dictionary of Americanisms* in the following context: "When an Indian gives any thing, he expects to receive an equivalent, or to have his gift returned."[28] This historical explanation matches with nuances of Mauss's model. An individual participating in a gift economy who has an item offered to him has two alternatives: he may either accept the gift—and the

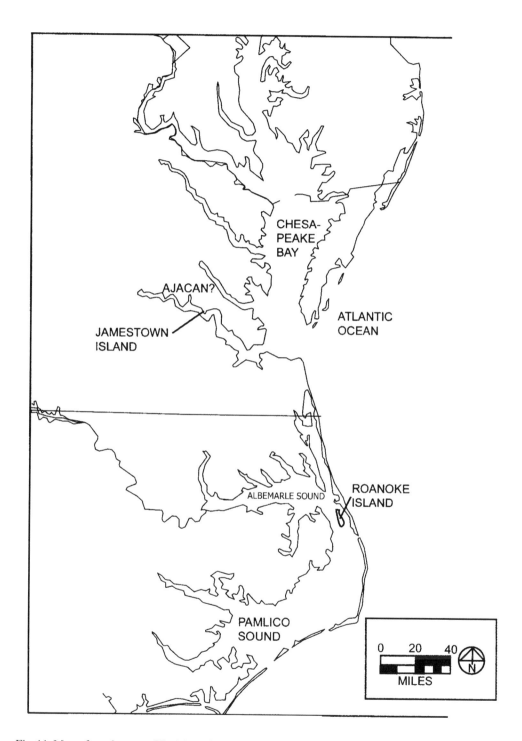

Fig. 11. Map of southeastern Virginia and northeastern North Carolina showing location of Jamestown Island and Ajacan.

alliance—and reciprocate, or he may refuse the gift and reject the interpersonal bond. Accepting the gift without making a return offering—in effect simultaneously embracing and denying one's exchange partner—would be ambiguous and undoubtedly confusing for the initial giver.

By the turn of the twentieth century, "Indian giver" referred to someone who had given something and then regretted the offering.[29] Presently it is a derisive saying that describes an individual who makes offerings and then takes them back. Overall, the meaning of "Indian giver" has changed over time through three different forms: natives who made offerings and expected return goods, natives who regretted offerings they had made, and natives who gave goods and then took these offerings back. The gradual linguistic transformation parallels actual European violations of native gift systems and indigenous responses to those transgressions. Contemporaneous historical records of the Chesapeake and Carolinas at contact include examples of natives making offerings and expecting reciprocity, then regretting the offerings and attempting to take them back once Europeans failed to reciprocate within a given time period. Natives acted as "Indian givers"—according to the modern definition—only *after* settlers accepted gifts without offering compensation or countergifts. The modern slur "Indian giver" is a warped interpretation of historic and likely prehistoric indigenous exchange practices. Its cultural and historical contexts reveal the phrase's initial and intended accuracy and subsequent semantic metamorphosis.

Exchange and Violence at Ajacan and Jamestown

European economic violations of native gift systems fomented violence at Ajacan in the 1570s and Jamestown in the early 1600s (Figure 11). Jesuit Father Vice Provincial Juan Baptista de Segura, guided by a Chesapeake Algonquian neophyte named Don Luis and hoping to convert the native's kin and countrymen through the construction, maintenance, and operation of a mission, led a team of inexperienced and unarmed clerics into the Chesapeake Bay in the fall of 1570. Segura, wary of failing ecclesiastical ventures throughout Spain's *La Florida* territory, prevented jaded missionaries from enticing or being enticed by soldiers to mutiny by excluding both from his retinue. When the European ship anchored and the crew came ashore on September 10, the local indigenous population celebrated the return of Don Luis to his former home at Ajacan. Amicable relations between the two groups flourished for weeks, perhaps months, before the neophyte and his Algonquian followers abandoned the missionaries. The clerics survived the winter months by trading iron hatchets to a neighboring tribe for corn. Only when Segura sent a team of Jesuits offering forgiveness to the neophyte for his desertion and asking him to return to Ajacan did Don Luis and a handful of other natives embark upon a series of violent attacks on the missionaries. They slew the messenger-clerics on February 4 and 5, 1571, then, a few days later, during a second surprise attack, decapitated the remaining ecclesiastics, except for one young Spanish boy.

Traditional explanations for the Algonquian violence center on Don Luis's singular personal motivations—revenge for initial abduction, torn loyalties, embarrassment for the abandonment, and so on.[30] Hypotheses that suggest Don Luis intended to kill the Jesuits all along are undone by the initial amicability between the two groups at Ajacan, which lasted anywhere from two to twelve weeks. If Don Luis intended to avenge past European atrocities, then why did he secure benevolent relations during the first month in the Chesapeake? Theories that spotlight a single catalyst for the Algonquian hostility unjustifiably suggest that one action caused three distinct native responses: initial abandonment, months of avoidance, and ultimate lethal assaults. In addition, none of these explanations answers why Don Luis abandoned the Jesuits and then waited to be contacted by the missionaries before eliminating them. What happened between the desertion and the attacks that so upset the Algonquians?

An exchange-based investigation of these matters reveals that differential economic transgressions of the native gift system by the Spanish Jesuits immediately preceded the hostile Algonquian acts. Distinct economic errors resulted in different punishments—abandonment and death. Simply put, according to rules of the native gift economy, the missionaries made two mistakes in the 1570s. First, the clerics did not compensate the indigenous population for numerous gifts of food and labor during their initial few weeks at Ajacan. Father Segura, in an effort to prevent the natives from spiritual contamination, prohibited nonreligious exchange with the Algonquians whom the missionaries intended to proselytize.[31] The Jesuits' failure to reciprocate to the natives, a symbolic denial of intercultural alliance, alienated their former exchange partners. As a result, Don Luis and the Ajacan natives deserted the missionaries. According to the rules of Chesapeake Algonquian society, the slight did not merit direct violent retribution.

The second Jesuit economic error had more severe repercussions. Between the desertion and the attack, the clerics traded iron hatchets—prestige goods in the indigenous world—to a village of neighboring natives, who happened to be the social rivals of the former Ajacan locals. Since both Algonquian groups participated in the same competitive tribute system, the Jesuits inadvertently privileged one native group at the expense of the other. Father Segura allowed the trades because the missionaries did not immediately intend to convert the neighboring tribes. Failing to compensate the Ajacan locals and then rewarding their rivals with prestige goods socially diminished Don Luis and his followers. Years later at Jamestown, Capt. John Smith noted that Algonquians "make warrs . . . principally for revendge, so vindictiue they be, to be made derision of, and to be insulted."[32] As soon as the missionaries informed the Ajacan locals of their recent trades, the natives annihilated the clerics.

Don Luis and his native followers murdered the missionaries in a most symbolic way. Historic Algonquian warfare across eastern North America was much more than mere violence. In the words of anthropologist Frederic Gleach, it was "undertaken to right a wrong, to correct improper actions; it was a means of restoring justice and teaching proper behavior."[33] There were two surprise native attacks on the Spanish Chesapeake missionaries in 1571. Moments before each assault, the Algonquians made false gift offerings to the unarmed and outnumbered clerics. They baited the Jesuits with duplicitous presents—promises to provide food and build a church—and then struck. Furthermore, the natives attacked their victims with the same iron hatchets that the missionaries had refused to give them initially as reciprocation for food. As punishment for violating the indigenous gift exchange, Ajacan Algonquians lured the clerics close with reciprocal deceit, then slaughtered them in a most meaningful manner.

Whereas traditional explanations of native violence perpetrated on Father Segura and his brethren propose one catalyst for two very different Algonquian actions, an analysis that appreciates the nuances of gift exchange and social competition within a collective tribute system is able to allot two distinct indigenous motives for the bifarious behavior of the Ajacan natives. Failure to reciprocate provoked abandonment; engaging one's social rivals after failing to reciprocate resulted in immediate and deadly retribution. Distinct indigenous punishments corresponded with individual European socioeconomic crimes. When exchange violations merited violence, the natives killed in symbolic fashion. In fact, historical records include many descriptions of Algonquians attacking in meaningful ways: slaying colonists who repeatedly pilfered food and stuffing the mouths of the deceased with bread, murdering settlers who stole land and filling the mouths of the corpses with dirt, and assaulting Europeans with Western tools of encroachment and destruction—hatchets, hoes, muskets, and so on.[34]

At Jamestown Island in 1607 the English failed to reciprocate the Paspaheghs—geographically the closest tribe in the Powhatan chiefdom to the new European settlement—on four separate occasions during the first weeks of colonization (Figure 12). Wowinchopunk, the *weroance*, or local leader, of the Paspaheghs, gave the settlers food, the land on which the colonists would build James Fort, and other goods, but the English made no return offerings. The natives grew frustrated, at one point even attempting unsuccessfully to steal reciprocity. A Paspahegh warrior took an iron hatchet from the English camp following the series of native offerings, but a colonist snatched it back in a confrontation that nearly erupted into violence. As a result, the Paspaheghs temporarily kept their distance from the settlers. The English then repeatedly offered gifts to the Weanocks, a neighboring tribe with whom the Paspaheghs regularly battled. During the same time, the English responded to Pamunkey, Arrohattoc, Kecoughtan, and Appamattoc presents with lavish reciprocation. Immediately following English trade with enemies and social rivals of the Paspaheghs, Wowinchopunk and his followers championed a multitribal attack on the colonists at James Fort. Overall, exchange transgressions by the Europeans—be they failures to give, accept, or reciprocate property; launching hostilities at or removing elite exchange partners; or repeatedly inundating native society with trade goods—immediately preceded nearly every intercultural assault at Jamestown during the colony's first five years.

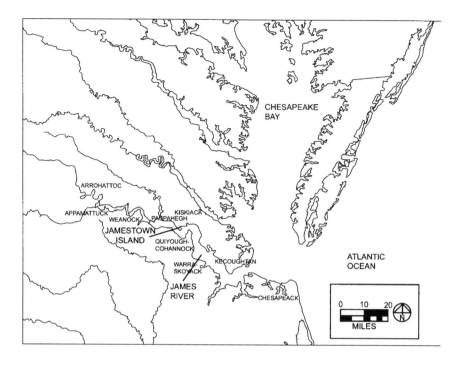

Fig. 12. Map of southeastern Virginia locating Powhatan tribes along the James River in 1607.

The Roanoke Case Study

Intercultural relations between the English and the indigenous population of the Carolina sounds during the 1580s did not follow the same pattern of repeated European exchange transgressions, often followed by abandonment or violent reaction, that occurred elsewhere. Some economic violations were ignored, and others paradoxically resulted in stronger overall relations between natives and non-natives. The same types of exchange transgressions that provoked Don Luis and his Ajacan followers to annihilate the Chesapeake Jesuits in 1571 and that led the Paspaheghs to spearhead a nearly successful multitribal attempt at destroying James Fort in 1607 produced entirely different Algonquian reactions in and around Roanoke Island at contact. When the English burned the Algonquian village of Aquascococke over a disputed stolen silver cup, *the Secotans did nothing.* When the settlers failed to compensate the Roanoacs for numerous gifts, *the Roanoacs encouraged them to find other trade partners.* And, when the colonists initiated hostilities with the Chawanoacs and refused multiple offerings, *the Chawanoacs promptly presented themselves and an additional tribe to the English as servants of Queen Elizabeth I.* These apparent socioeconomic aberrations raise a question: why did Ossomocomuck tribes respond to economic violations differently than Algonquians in the Chesapeake?

Appreciating the nuances of the overall indigenous balance of power in the Carolina sounds adds a new analytical dimension to inter- and intracultural relations and provides an answer to this query. The six tribes and seven thousand native inhabitants that resided in Ossomocomuck territory during the late sixteenth century formed no cohesive, static, or stable alliance and repeatedly battled one another for social supremacy (Figure 13). The Chawanoacs, led by Chief Menatonon, sustained the largest and most powerful tribe in the area, with more than twenty-five hundred inhabitants.[35] Nearly as formidable were separate tribes of Roanoacs and Secotans, whose territories were divided by the Alligator River. Arthur Barlowe noted that in the early to mid-1580s the Roanoacs and Secotans "maintain[ed] a deadly and terrible war" with each other.[36] In addition, the Roanoacs informed the English in 1584 that their *weroance*, Chief Wingina, had been recently "shotte in two places through the bodye, and once cleane through the thigh" during a Secotan attack.[37]

Alone, the three Carolina sounds Algonquian reactions to European economic transgressions mentioned above seem peculiar. But when properly contextualized within intracultural political struggles of the time, they do not appear to deviate from native norms. At Aquascococke in July 1585, Sir Richard Grenville and the crew of the *Tyger* visited a series of Secotan villages, in which the indigenous population entertained them. Grenville noticed that a silver cup was missing from his crew's possessions and demanded its immediate return from the natives. A journal from an anonymous individual aboard the *Tyger* reported that the Secotan Aquascocockians promised to locate and hand over the allegedly stolen item. When they did not produce the cup, Grenville and his men "burnt, and spoyled their corne, and Towne."[38] Immediately afterward, the English leader guided his vessel and men out of Secotan territory to Roanoke Island, where they reunited with the rest of the colonists. The Secotans took no immediate action to avenge the loss of their village.

Although contemporaneous historical records do not include enough details to substantiate whether the silver cup incident conclusively parallels the May 1607 English/Paspahegh iron hatchet dispute mentioned earlier—perceived by colonists as theft and natives as owed reciprocation—this analysis focuses on the lack of prompt Secotan retribution for Aquascococke's destruction and the subsequent amicability between the settlers and the Roanoacs. In order for the Secotans to avenge the loss of their burned village, they would have been forced to venture into Roanoac territory, an unlikely event, considering the frequent hostilities between the two tribes during this time. Having established their settlement on Roanoke Island provided the colonists with a formidable territorial and political buffer between themselves and the Secotans— the Roanoacs. Following the line of reasoning that an enemy of an enemy would be a friend, it is not surprising that relations between the English and the Roanoacs

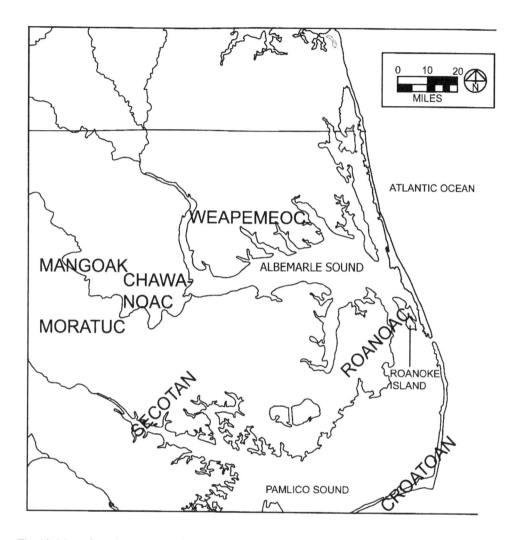

Fig. 13. Map of northeastern North Carolina showing the tribes of Ossomocomuck territory in 1585.

flourished following Grenville's violent dispute with the Secotans. Hostility between the English and Secotans likely pleased the Roanoacs and solidified their alliance with the colonists.

Relations between the Roanoacs and the English began to deteriorate during the winter of 1585-1586. The noted Roanoke historian David Beers Quinn attributed the decline in intercultural amicability to three factors: (1) European maladies; (2) settler demands on the limited native food surplus; and (3) the colonists' "imperialist, conquering mentality."[39] In terms of intercultural exchange obligations and transgressions, these factors translate to: (1) the removal (death by disease) of elite exchange partners; (2) inequitable exchanges; and (3) failures to give, accept, and reciprocate property.

Up to this point, the analysis presented here has focused on unfair exchanges and those that ignored native economic norms—the second and third factors listed above. The removal of an elite exchange partner, which eliminates the interpersonal connection essential to gift exchange and alliance-building in the native world, ruptured relations at Roanoke and Jamestown as well. Twice, the death of a Roanoac chief or elder sympathetic to the colonists severed bonds between the English and the local natives and led to immediate indigenous hostility. Granganimeo's demise in the winter of 1585-1586 and Ensenore's passing on April 20, 1586, both preceded native conspiracies against the English. Intercultural amicability at Jamestown two-and-one-half decades later likewise turned to antagonism with the departure of an elite exchange partner. In that case, John Smith's October 1609 return to England for medical attention following a debilitating gunpowder explosion anticipated a series of Powhatan attacks by a matter of days. In all three cases (Granganimeo's, Ensenore's, and John Smith's), the removal of an elite intercultural liaison followed other exchange-system violations. Consequently, their departure not only prevented their easing tension as they had in the past but ignited hostility as well.

Following Granganimeo's death and English failures to give properly, the Carolina sounds Algonquians again reacted in a peculiar manner. Instead of abandoning the English at Roanoke Island or launching a direct attack following the onslaught of disease and unfair exchanges, the Roanoacs baited the colonists into attacking the Chawanoacs under the guise of searching for new exchange partners at Chaunis Temoatan, a territory well inland of the Carolina sounds. Chief Wingina, who had changed his name to Pemisapan following the death of his brother Granganimeo, told Ralph Lane, Fort Raleigh's first governor, that the Chawanoacs intended to attack the English party on their way upriver. The Roanoac *weroance* simultaneously had a message delivered to the Chawanoacs warning of an impending English invasion. Just in case that scheme failed, the Roanoacs attempted to starve the English party on its way back to Roanoke Island by encouraging all native groups in the area to avoid the virulent foreigners at all costs. Chief Pemisapan attempted to rid himself of the settlers and devastate the most powerful indigenous group in the region as well, the Chawanoacs.

Guns blazing, Lane and his men burst into Chawanoac territory and seized Chief Menatonon. They later exchanged the Chawanoac leader for his son Skiko. The Chawanoacs responded to that hostile action and additional slights not with animosity but by embracing and regaling the English. Over the next few weeks, Lane repeatedly refused gifts from the Chawanoacs, failed to make return offerings to them, and forbade the return of the *weroance's* son to his father. Those affronts only strengthened the Chawanoac's apparent amicability and generosity. Moments after the English refused to return Skiko, Chief Menatonon made the settlers a remarkable offer. He declared that both the Chawanoacs and Weapemeocs, whom he indirectly commanded as well, now served England. Governor Lane reported, "Menatonon commanded Okisko, king of Weapemeoc, to yield himself servant to the great

Weroanza [queen] of England . . . and Menatonon let me know that from that time forward he and his successors were to acknowledge her Majesty [Elizabeth I] as their only Sovereign."[40]

While these actions may appear to be those of a man desperate to reacquire his son, a review of Carolina sounds political geography suggests additional factors in Menatonon's decision-making process. By placing themselves and the Weapemeocs under English control, the Chawanoacs succeeded in completely surrounding the Roanoacs with native enemies and friends of the colonists through gift exchange (Figure 14). To the north were the Weapemeocs and Chawanoacs, both English allies and newly proclaimed servants of the queen. To the west were the longtime Roanoac foes the Secotans. And to the east were the Croatoans, who had allied themselves with the English from first contact. The Roanoacs had tried to use both the English and gift-exchange deceit to eliminate the Chawanoacs, and now the Chawanoacs had completely surrounded the Roanoacs with enemies by the same means.

The Roanoacs promptly repaired relations with the Secotans, who likely had been longing for a chance to avenge their torched village, and bribed other tribes—not including the mighty Chawanoacs—with copper to join them in an attack on the English. Chawanoac prince Skiko, much more of a native informant and political aide than a hostage, learned of the planned hostilities and warned the colonists of the coming attack. Lane, never one to wait for conflict, launched a preemptive strike that resulted in the decapitation of Roanoac chief Pemisapan. Ultimately, the Chawanoacs managed to devastate the Roanoacs in the same manner in which the Roanoacs attempted to undermine them—with an English attack. Historian Karen Kupperman concluded that historic Carolina natives in their system of justice emphasized maintaining an equilibrium and retaliating in kind. The Chawanoacs did just that, avenging the previous Roanoac conspiracy in a parallel and symbolic manner, again with the unknowing help of the English.

Conclusion

Economic violations affected intercultural relations at Roanoke, as they had at Ajacan and Jamestown. However, unlike the direct catalytic sequence of settler economic transgression and resultant Algonquian desertion or violence in the historic Chesapeake, additional political considerations significantly altered the reactions of those indigenous to Ossomocomuck territory. Following English transgressions of native socioeconomic rules, the Secotans delayed vengeance while the colonists remained under Roanoac protection, the Roanoacs attempted to lure the settlers and Chawanoacs into annihilating each other, and the Chawanoacs ignored the repeated European affronts, concentrating instead on punishing, provoking, and terrorizing the Roanoacs for their previous treachery. The overall balance of power in the Carolina sounds controlled how and when the natives avenged English exchange transgressions.

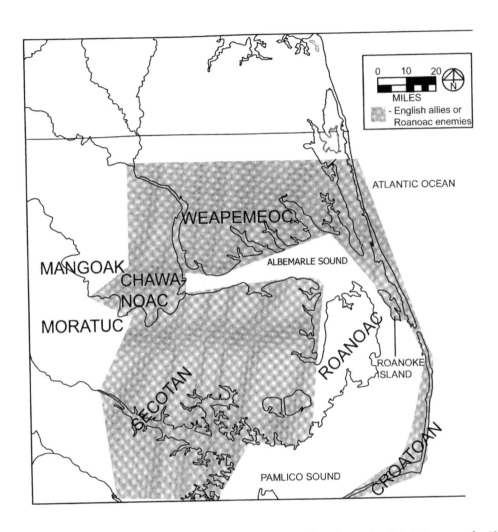

Fig. 14. Map showing the balance of power in Ossomocomuck territory after Chief Menatonon's gifts to the English in 1586.

NOTES

1. This article is extracted from chapter four of Seth Mallios's 1998 University of Virginia doctoral dissertation, "In the Hands of 'Indian Givers': Exchange and Violence at Ajacan, Roanoke, and Jamestown."

2. Marcel Mauss, *The Gift: The Form and Reason for Exchange in Archaic Societies*, trans. W. D. Halls (New York: Norton, 1990), 5; originally published as *Essai sur le Don: Forme et Raison de l'echange dans les Societies Archaiques* (Paris: Press es Universitaires, 1925).

3. Mauss, *The Gift*, 39.

4. Mauss, *The Gift*, 39, 41.

5. Chris Gregory, *Gifts and Commodities* (London: Academic Press, 1982), 19.

6. Gregory, *Gifts and Commodities*, 57.

7. Mauss, *The Gift*, 39-49; Marshall Sahlins, *Stone Age Economics* (Chicago: Aldine-Atherton, 1972), 153.

8. Mauss, *The Gift*, 62.

9. Henry Glassie, *Passing the Time in Balleymenon: Culture and History of an Ulster Community* (Bloomington: Indiana University Press, 1997), 651.

10. Lewis Hyde, *The Gift: Imagination and the Erotic Life of Property* (New York: Random House, 1983), 69.

11. Claude Levi-Strauss, *The Elementary Structures of Kinship* (Boston: Beacon Press, 1969), 67.

12. Gregory, *Gifts and Commodities*, 19.

13. Gregory, *Gifts and Commodities*, 42.

14. Karl Marx, *Capital: A Critique of Political Economy*, 2 vols. Translated by Ben Fowkes and D. Fernbach (New York: Vintage Books, 1977), 1:91.

15. Hyde, *The Gift*, xv, attributed to Mauss.

16. Philip L. Barbour, ed., *The Complete Works of Captain John Smith (1580-1631)*, 3 vols. (Chapel Hill: Institute of Early American History and Culture and the University of North Carolina Press, 1986), 1:71.

17. Barbour, *Complete Works of Captain John Smith*, 1:71.

18. Barbour, *Complete Works of Captain John Smith*, 1:71.

19. Barbour, *Complete Works of Captain John Smith*, 1:249.

20. Barbour, *Complete Works of Captain John Smith*, 1:215.

21. Barbour, *Complete Works of Captain John Smith*, 3:83.

22. Philip L. Barbour, ed., *The Jamestown Voyages Under the First Charter, 1606-1609: Documents Relating to the Foundation of Jamestown and the History of the Jamestown Colony Up to the Departure of Captain John Smith, Last President of the Council of Virginia Under the First Charter, Early in October 1609*, 2 vols., Hakluyt Society Second Series, Nos. 136-137 (Cambridge: Cambridge University Press, 1969), 1:101.

23. David Beers Quinn, *The Roanoke Voyages, 1584-1590: Documents to Illustrate the English Voyages to North America Under the Patent Granted to Walter Raleigh in 1584*, 2 vols., Hakluyt Society Second Series, No. 104 (London: Hakluyt Society, 1955; reprint, New York: Dover, 1991), 1:100-103.

24. Archaeologically, copper is a remarkably reliable barometer of European-Algonquian relations. Its relative quantity at seventeenth-century sites in the Chesapeake can be used to predict the mean date of the specific colonial occupation (Seth Mallios, *Archaeological Investigations at 44JC568, the Reverend Buck Site* [Jamestown, Va.: APVA (Association for the Preservation of Virginia Antiquities), 2000], 60; Mallios, *At the Edge of the Precipice: Frontier Ventures, Jamestown's Hinterland, and the Archaeology of 44JC802* [Jamestown: APVA, 2000], 50; Mallios, *The 1999 Interim Report on the APVA Excavations at Jamestown, Virginia* [Jamestown: APVA, 2000], 20.)

25. Barbour, *Complete Works of Captain John Smith*, 1:236.

26. "Indian," *Oxford English Dictionary*, 2d ed. (1989).

27. "Indian"; Hyde, *The Gift*, 3.

28. "Indian."

29. Charles Earle Funk, *Heavens to Betsy! and Other Curious Sayings* (New York: Harper, 1955), 103.

30. Carl Bridenbaugh, *Jamestown, 1544-1699* (New York: Oxford University Press, 1980), 1033; Charlotte M. Gradie, "The Powhatans in the Context of the Spanish Empire," in *Powhatan Foreign Relations, 1500-1722*, ed. Helen Rountree (Charlottesville: University Press of Virginia, 1993), 167; Helen Rountree, *Pocahontas's People: The Powhatan Indians of Virginia Through Four Centuries* (Norman: University of Oklahoma Press, 1990), 17.

31. Clifford M. Lewis and Albert J. Loomie, *The Spanish Jesuit Mission in Virginia, 1570-1572* (Chapel Hill: University of North Carolina Press, 1953), 43; Mary W. Helms, *Ulysses' Sail: An Ethnographic Odyssey of Power, Knowledge, and Geographical Distance* (Princeton, N.J.: Princeton University Press, 1988), 224-225.

32. Barbour, *Complete Works of Captain John Smith*, 1:165.

33. Frederic Gleach, *Powhatan's World and Colonial Virginia: A Conflict of Cultures* (Lincoln: University of Nebraska Press, 1997), 51.

34. Gleach, *Powhatan's World and Colonial Virginia*, 51.

35. Karen O. Kupperman, *Roanoke: The Abandoned Colony* (Totowa, N.J.: Rowman and Allanheld, 1984), 75.

36. Quinn, *Roanoke Voyages*, 1:101.

37. Quinn, *Roanoke Voyages*, 1:101.

38. Quinn, *Roanoke Voyages*, 1:191.

39. David Beers Quinn, *Set Fair for Roanoke: Voyages and Settlements, 1584-1606* (Chapel Hill: University of North Carolina Press, 1985), 237.

40. Quinn, *Roanoke Voyages*, 1:279.

The Roanoke Sagas: Lane's Fort and Port Ferdinando

Fred Willard and Barbara Midgette, with E. Thomson Shields Jr.

Introduction

The Outer Banks of North Carolina constitute a geographic feature known throughout the world. These islands, among the first mapped and studied areas in North America, continue to be researched at present. Understanding ocean currents, sand movements, and the dynamics related to this attenuated sand ribbon and its environs remains a major challenge at this time. The same dynamics of the shifting Outer Banks that challenge modern geologists also challenge those researching archaeological sites connected with the 1580s English voyages to the area. Although solutions to the mysteries surrounding the Roanoke sagas and the lost 1587 John White colony have been sought for more than four hundred years, a great deal of misinterpretation and confusion has hampered these investigations. A study of maps, geography, and geology reveals that the search for archaeological sites related to these Elizabethan explorers might need to expand a little farther south and east from Roanoke Island to the Outer Banks.

Roanoke Island, in particular the Fort Raleigh area, has attracted most of the historic and archaeological study related to the 1580s English expeditions. While the town associated with John White's colony has never been found, artifacts do connect the Fort Raleigh Roanoke Island site with the 1580s Roanoke voyages.[1] Most recently, Ivor Noël Hume proposed that a sixteenth-century "science center," a site for conducting metallurgical testing, was located in the vicinity of the reconstructed fort at the north end of Roanoke Island.[2] In addition to the work on Roanoke Island, attention has moved to Hatteras Island on the Outer Banks with work on the Croatan Project by Dr. David Phelps, director of East Carolina University's Office of Coastal Archaeology.

The research to be discussed here likewise centers on the Outer Banks, but farther north, near the Bodie Island Lighthouse. We suggest a new site for possible archaeological exploration, based upon a new hypothesis that places the historically reported Ralph Lane fort of 1585 at Ferdinando Inlet and places that inlet near Bodie Island Lighthouse rather than on Roanoke Island.

Forts have long been a central feature in research connected with the 1580s Roanoke expeditions. Starting with the 1585-1586 colonization attempt led by Ralph Lane, these expeditions erected forts on at least four sites: two in Puerto Rico, one at Port Ferdinando, and at least one on Roanoke Island. These forts remain mysterious. For example, the location and size of the fort that archaeologist J. C. Harrington reconstructed in the early 1950s on Roanoke Island tend to refute the possibility of its being the fort Ralph Lane built in 1585.[3]

One of the major issues concerns the forts' locations. At present, most researchers assume that the still unlocated fort Lane says was at Port Ferdinando—the site for entry from the Atlantic Ocean to the English's Roanoke Island settlements—was actually built on Roanoke Island, probably in the vicinity of the present-day town of Manteo. A reexamination of the evidence suggests, however, that the fort for Port Ferdinando was located not on Roanoke Island but along the Outer Banks in the vicinity of Bodie Island Lighthouse.

Lane first mentions Port Ferdinando in his letter of August 12, 1585, "To ye Right honorable Sir Frances Wallsingham, Knight": "Thys other called ye FerdyNando hathe a barre also but at xij foote vppon the same at hyghe water: and ye barre very shorte, beyng within iij, iiij, and v, fathom water: Soo as thys Porte at ye poynte of ye lande beyng fortefyed with a skonse, yt ys not to be enterdde by all ye force yt Spayne canne make, wee hauynge ye fauure of God."[4] Slightly modernized, Lane's letter states: "This other [inlet] called Ferdinando has a bar also but at 12 foot upon the same at high water [i.e., at high tide]; and the bar [is] very short being within 3, 4, and 5 fathoms of water. So as this port at the point of land is fortified with a sconce [i.e., a fort], it is not to be entered by all the force that Spain can make, we having the favor of God." In other words, Lane says that Port Ferdinando is the deepest and best inlet and the safest anchorage found. Lane further states that he has built a fortification so well that all of the force of Spain cannot enter. Historian David B. Quinn assumes that this fort was never built on the barrier islands but, rather, that only on Roanoke Island was a fort built and that the restored fort now known as Fort Raleigh is the one (or part of the one) referred to in this and other letters signed by Lane as being from "the new fort in Virginia."[5]

Our present study of the Roanoke expeditions points to a new venue for research involving the location of a relic inlet that may be the remains of the one discovered and named by Simon Fernandez in 1584. The physical position of this site and the activities that took place there have attracted little prior interest or research.[6]

Background

Maps are important research materials because they give us geographic information through time about space, i.e., the locations of old sites and boundaries and the claims of ownership people may have made on land and water. Historians have studied maps drawn by European explorers from 1529 to 1775 in the hope of understanding how the Outer Banks of North Carolina were first visited and mapped (see Table 1). Cape Hatteras (later aptly named the "Graveyard of the Atlantic") must have presented huge obstacles and major hazards to early explorers, since they gave the feature various names and mapped it as early as 1529.

But these maps also give researchers misinformation. For example, in 1524 Giovanni da Verrazzano mistook the Carolina sounds for the Sea to Cathay, and his brother Gerolamo da Verrazzano repeated the mistake on his map of 1529.[7] The error persisted on several maps over at least the next seventy years, including those by Münster (1540), the anonymous cartographer of the Harleian World Map (ca. 1547), John Dee (ca. 1582), Michael Lok (1582), and John White (1585).[8] Many maps misnamed or confused the Outer Banks of North Carolina with the Chesapeake Bay, called the *Bahía de Santa Maria* at the time. An anonymously drawn sketch map from the 1585 Lane expedition made this error. Mapmakers frequently copied the mistakes of earlier cartographers, as the early maps of North Carolina demonstrate: many misplaced and even nonexistent geographic features are mapped and recopied repeatedly, a good example being Cape Kendricks on the Outer Banks. Although placed without being named on a 1590 map engraved by Theodore de Bry based on John White's 1585 watercolor maps,[9] Cape Kendricks subsequently disappeared, washed away by storms. Yet it continued to appear on maps such as that by Nicholas Comberford in 1657, on which it was mistakenly labeled "Cape Hatteras."[10] The misinformation about Cape Kendricks influenced some historians and mapmakers to incorrectly place the village of Croatan, locating it too far south, near the Core Banks, where some historians are still looking for it.[11]

Just as interesting is the fact that some maps contain information not recorded on other maps. This is evident in John White's 1585 chart of eastern North America.[12] This map—or copies of it made by other cartographers—is the only known map that names and shows Port Ferdinando and the small island north of it. Even though White alone records Port Ferdinando cartographically, many of the people involved in the Roanoke expeditions documented the inlet in writing. On July 13, 1584, Capt. Arthur Barlow, Philip Amadas, and their crews performed a ceremony whereby the North American continent was claimed for Sir Walter Raleigh, Queen Elizabeth, and England.[13] Barlow writes that they entered an inlet (named later as Port Ferdinando), rowed ashore, "and cast anker about three harquebushot [three times the distance a small handgun could shoot] within the hauens mouth, on the left hande of the same: . . . we manned our boates, and went to view the lande next adioyning," and took possession of the land in the name of Queen Elizabeth.[14]

To locate Port Ferdinando, one must consider, besides the historical record of maps and documents, the geology of the region. The inlets of the Outer Banks are composites of geomorphic landforms that have remained discernible features for hundreds of years or longer. The three principal depositional sand units affiliated with Outer Banks inlets are the recurved spit-inlet sediments associated with south-migrating inlets, tidal deltas formed on the ocean and sound sides of an inlet, and the depositions of sand on the upsides of inlets that accumulate at right angles to the shore and form high ridges. These features identify an old, or relic, inlet.[15]

Sand deposits moving southward may eventually force an inlet to close on the ocean side. This closing process can presently be seen at Oregon Inlet, in spite of human attempts to keep it open. As of early 1999, the sand spit at Oregon Inlet had encroached all the way to the high span of the bridge across the inlet. When the bridge was first built, this sand spit was at least a mile from the middle of the inlet, where the high span rises. Therefore, it is not surprising that of the twelve inlets open along the Outer Banks in 1584, only Ocracoke Inlet remains open.[16] When a southward-moving spit closes an inlet, a lagoon results that will eventually seal on the sound side as well. This ponding landform may endure for hundreds, if not thousands, of years.[17]

Tidal flow at an inlet produces an ebb- and flood-tide delta made of shallow-water sediment deposits. On the sound side a flood-tide delta creates a marsh island after the inlet closes. Such an island then becomes attached to the original land as the lagoon forms and then closes to become a pond.[18] The flood-tide delta forms a bulge or node on the sound side. This is the most important and discernible geomorphic marker readily seen on modern maps of the Outer Banks.[19] The energy of large waves causes a diminished ocean-side delta, which becomes flattened and dispersed by wave-action energy. No ocean-side deltas can remain on the Outer Banks.[20]

All three inlet depositional sand deposit markers, when considered in conjunction with John White's original map and other historic maps, can help identify the location of relic inlets that date back to the time of the Roanoke voyages. Specifically, the bulge or node near Port Ferdinando is traceable on almost all these maps up to the present time. Geomorphic landforms of two relic inlets with an island in between are suggested near Bodie Island Lighthouse (Figure 15).

Hypothesis

Our working hypothesis is that Port Ferdinando and its accompanying inlet (which we have called Ferdinando Inlet, having been found by the pilot Simon Fernandez in 1584), where the Roanoke voyagers found an anchorage in a safe harbor, became for the Roanoke expeditions the first and primary entrance to the sounds behind the Outer Banks. This hypothesis also includes the proposition that the Ralph Lane fort location mentioned in most of the historic records is actually on the Outer Banks near the existing Bodie Island Lighthouse. There a defensive fortification and a ship-repair facility were constructed, and wells were dug. There, as well, the Spanish reported finding in 1588 a *varadero*, or shipyard, and *pozos hechos de pipas*, English casks or wells, and other debris indicating that a considerable number of people had been at that location.[21] The site was also used both as an observation post and a campsite.

The evidence for such a site comes in part from a deposition taken from Pedro Díaz Franco in Havana in 1589. Díaz had been captured by Richard Grenville during Grenville's return to England after leaving the Ralph Lane colony on Roanoke Island in 1585. Díaz then served the English as a pilot on two voyages to Roanoke Island, escaping from them on the second voyage—the 1588 attempt to resupply the "Lost Colony." More significant, however, is Díaz's first term as a pilot following his capture: Grenville's 1586 voyage undertaken to resupply the Ralph Lane colony and the only voyage during which Díaz actually reached the Outer Banks near Roanoke Island. The 1586 voyage arrived just weeks after Lane had left for England, taken by Francis Drake; finding no one at the colony, Grenville left fifteen (or perhaps eighteen) men there before returning to England himself. Díaz's deposition was important enough

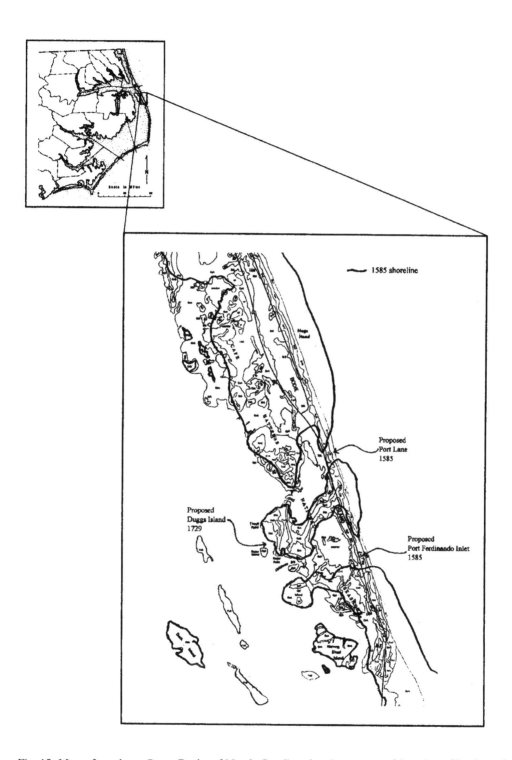

Fig. 15. Map of northern Outer Banks of North Carolina showing suggested location of banks and inlets at the time of the Roanoke voyages.

that it was a source for Luís Hierónimo de Oré, who published his *Relación de los mártires que ha habido en las Provincias de la Florida* sometime between 1614 and 1619.

From Oré's work we discover the limitations of Díaz's observations—the limitations that make his report especially interesting. It seems that Díaz was not allowed to leave the ship. When he was asked why he had not seen the settlement from the ship, "he answered that he was not able to see, since it was ten leagues from the port by the arm above the shore of the northern entrance."[22] Assuming approximately two miles to a Spanish league, the main settlement was some twenty miles from the inlet in which Díaz sat aboard ship. Yet, in his deposition, Díaz reports, "On the island they have a wooden fort of little strength and it is inside by the water."[23] The fort referred to may be that at Ferdinando Inlet rather than at the main settlement, because Díaz is giving a firsthand account; it would have been the only one he could have seen from aboard ship. After all, according to Díaz, "In the said fort he [Grenville] left eighteen men and did not allow the said Pero [*sic*] Diaz to go on shore or enter the fort. The said captain stayed there for fourteen days and left in the said fort four pieces of artillery of cast-iron and supplies for the eighteen men for a year."[24] Díaz's deposition may be the only firsthand account of Ralph Lane's "New Fort in Virginia"—the fort we are suggesting was located at Ferdinando Inlet.

Applying the scientific methods of archaeology to the Bodie Island location may help solve the problem of primary access—that is, whether over time it would have been most likely that ships would have used avenues other than Ferdinando Inlet to reach Roanoke Island. Some histories chronicle Trinity Inlet rather than Ferdinando Inlet as the entryway of choice among the Roanoke colonists, but the idea of Trinity Inlet as the primary access to Roanoke Island has now fallen out of favor. Narratives, published papers, and letters of Richard Grenville, John White, Sir Francis Drake, and Arthur Barlow, as well as Díaz's deposition, all indicate that Ferdinando Inlet was the primary entrance to Roanoke Island in all the Roanoke voyages, providing both passage and anchorage.[25]

Additionally, if remnants of Ferdinando Inlet can be found, some interesting questions may be answered regarding England's early colonial settlements and outposts in the New World. The ceremony of July 13, 1584, described by Captain Barlow would be both historically and archaeologically significant. A year earlier, Sir Humphrey Gilbert had performed a similar ceremony in Newfoundland, where a lead seal engraved with the queen's arms was either erected or buried.[26] When John Smith documented a similar ceremony at the fall line of the James River on May 25, 1607, he wrote: "So vpon one of the Iletts at the mouth of the falls he [Captain Newport] set up a Crosse with this inscription: 'Jacobus Rex 1607' and his own name below, at the erecting here of we prayed for or Kyng and our own prosperous success in the actyon, and proclamyed him Kyng with a great showt."[27]

Summary and Conclusions

If the foregoing hypothesis is correct, corroboration of the existence of Port Ferdinando could be expected from at least three sources. The first is remote aerial imaging or photography. The use of computerized interpolators for feature enhancement is a new and emerging discipline. The second is datable core samplings indicating a historic inlet near the location of the present Bodie Island Lighthouse. The third is finding significant features and artifacts of the Roanoke expeditions such as wells, a ship-repair facility, campsite(s), or a fort used during the Roanoke expeditions. Follow-up confirmation employing archaeology's scientific methods could be undertaken if a promising prospect appears.

Certain problems may make locating an archaeologically significant site at Port Ferdinando difficult, however. Ferdinando Inlet closed sometime between 1775 and 1808 and was sealed by sand-laden storms.[28] Storms have washed away many historical and archaeological sites on the Outer Banks of North Carolina. The greatest threats to these sites continue to be hurricanes, Hatteras low-pressure systems, and northeasters. The power of these meteorological events to obliterate both artifacts and features is incalculable. The Ferdinando Inlet area has endured as many as six inlet openings and a significant loss of ocean beach since the inlet closed.[29]

Still, if Ferdinando Inlet can be scientifically confirmed, it will rival Plymouth Rock and Jamestown in historical importance as the site of one of the earliest English explorations and colonizations in the New World. That early outpost was involved in six ocean crossings: the 1584, 1585, 1587, and 1590 Roanoke expeditions and the two led by Drake and Grenville bearing relief supplies in 1586. Some of the ships involved in those voyages carried hundreds of people, while Drake's fleet alone comprised as many as twenty-five ships and twenty-five hundred people.[30] With so many people on shore, relevant artifacts should be fairly abundant if any undisturbed areas remain. And there is the remote possibility of recovering an artifact from July 13, 1584, placed there by Capt. Arthur Barlow—ideally with a seal or crest of Queen Elizabeth of England proclaiming possession of most of North America.

The search for beginnings goes on. More than four hundred years have passed since Amadas and Barlow performed their ceremony at Ferdinando Inlet. Although storms and successive new inlets may already have destroyed this historic site, it remains an important goal to locate, document, and confirm its location before it is lost forever.

Table 1. Maps of the Outer Banks from the Early Sixteenth to the Late Eighteenth Centuries

The following list of maps includes those that show features relevant to the Roanoke colonization efforts, especially the possible location of Fort Ferdinando and the historical inlets associated with Port Ferdinando. When possible, all maps have been listed with their identification number from the third edition of William P. Cumming's *The Southeast in Early Maps*. If a map is not listed in that volume, its location in Cumming's *Mapping the North Carolina Coast (MNCC)* is given parenthetically.

YEAR	MAPMAKER	MAP NUMBER
1529	Gerolamo da Verrazzano	03
1540	Sebastian Münster	(MNCC, 103)[31]
ca. 1547	Anonymous (Harleian World Map)	(MNCC, 111)
1580	John Dee	(MNCC, 123)
1580	Simon Fernandez, John Dee	4A
1582	John Dee	4B
1582	Michael Lok	(MNCC, 129)
1585	Anonymous (Ralph Lane colonist)	6
1585	John White	7
1585	John White	8
1590	John White, Theodore De Bry	12
1590	John White, Theodore De Bry	13
1606	Gerard Mercator, Jodocus Hondius	26
1608	Pedro de Zuñiga	28
1611	Anonymous (for Alonso de Velasco)	29
1624	John Smith	32
1657	Nicholas Comberford	50, 51
ca. 1672	John Ogilby, James Moxon	70
1682	Joel Gascoyne	92
1733	Edward Moseley	218
1770	John Collet	394
1775	Henry Mouzon	450

NOTES

1. David Stick, *Roanoke Island: The Beginnings of English America* (Chapel Hill: University of North Carolina Press, 1983), 237.

2. Ivor Noël Hume, *The Virginia Adventure: Roanoke to James Towne: An Archaeological and Historical Odyssey* (New York: Knopf, 1994), 89.

3. David Beers Quinn, *Set Fair for Roanoke: Voyages and Settlements, 1584-1606* (Chapel Hill: University of North Carolina Press, 1985), 909; Noël Hume, *Virginia Adventure*, 88-89.

4. David Beers Quinn, ed., *The Roanoke Voyages, 1584-1590: Documents to Illustrate the English Voyages to North America Under the Patent Granted to Walter Raleigh in 1584*, 2 vols., Hakluyt Society Second Series, No. 104 (London: Hakluyt Society, 1955; reprint, New York: Dover, 1991), 1:202. Lane's original spelling and capitalization as recorded by Quinn have been maintained, but the passage's erratic italicization has been removed.

5. Quinn, *Roanoke Voyages*, 1:198, 202 n. 4, 210.

6. One direction for research would be the use of aerial imaging and microwave multispectral imagining. Those technologies could be used to delineate features leading to the possible location not only of Port Ferdinando but also of important Native American villages such as Aquascogoc, Secotan, Tramaskecooc, Pomeiooc, Panauuioc, and Dasemunkepeuc.

7. All maps mentioned are given in Table 1 with citation information.

8. William P. Cumming, *Mapping the North Carolina Coast: Sixteenth-Century Cartography and the Roanoke Voyages* (Raleigh: America's Four Hundredth Anniversary Committee, North Carolina Department of Cultural Resources, 1988), Map 7.

9. Cumming, *Mapping the North Carolina Coast*, Map 12.

10. Quinn, *Roanoke Voyages*, 2:864-865.

11. Stick, *Roanoke Island*, 237; John Joseph Fisher, "Geomorphic Expression of Former Inlets along the Outer Banks of North Carolina" (master's thesis, University of North Carolina at Chapel Hill, 1962), 72.

12. Cumming, *Mapping the North Carolina Coast*, Map 7.

13. Conway Whittle Sams, *The Conquest of Virginia: The First Attempt* (1924; reprint, Spartanburg, S.C.: Reprint Company, 1973), 60-62; Quinn, *Roanoke Voyages*, 1:94-95.

14. Quinn, *Roanoke Voyages*, 1:94.

15. Fisher, "Geomorphic Expression," 15.

16. Fisher, "Geomorphic Expression," Map 46. Some inlets, such as Oregon Inlet, have opened up since 1584.

17. Fisher, "Geomorphic Expression," 32-34.

18. Fisher, "Geomorphic Expression," 14.

19. Fisher, "Geomorphic Expression," 15.

20. Miles O. Hayes, et al., "The Investigation of Form and Processes in the Coastal Zone," in *Coastal Geomorphology*, ed. Donald R. Coates (Binghamton: State University of New York, 1973), 33-37.

21. Quinn, *Set Fair for Roanoke*, 307-309; Quinn, *Roanoke Voyages*, 2:810-811.

22. Luís Hierónimo de Oré, *The Martyrs of Florida (1513-1616)*, trans. Maynard Geiger, Franciscan Studies 18 (New York: Joseph F. Wagner, 1936), 49; originally published as *Relación de los mártyres que ha havido en la Florida* (Madrid [?]: n.p., ca. 1617).

23. Quinn, *Roanoke Voyages*, 2:790.

24. Quinn, *Roanoke Voyages*, 2:791.

25. Quinn, *Roanoke Voyages*, 1:94-95, 106-108, 191-192, 198, 201-204, 2:789-791.

26. Quinn, *Roanoke Voyages*, 1:94 n. 5; Sams, *Conquest of Virginia*, 62.

27. John Smith, *Travels and Works of Captain John Smith, President of Virginia and Admiral of New England, 1580-1631*, ed. Edward Arber, 2 vols. (1910; reprint, New York: Burt Franklin, 1967), 1:46.

28. Fisher, "Geomorphic Expression," 96.

29. Fisher, "Geomorphic Expression," 83-85.

30. Noël Hume, *Virginia Adventure*, 45, 50, 53.

31. Cumming does not include this map of both the Americas in his map list in *The Southeast in Early Maps* (3d ed., revised and enlarged by Louis De Vorsey Jr. [Chapel Hill: University of North Carolina Press, 1998]), but a copy of the map is included as his Color Plate 1.

If It's Not One Thing It's Another:
The Added Challenges of Weather and Climate for the Roanoke Colony

Dennis B. Blanton

Any colonizing effort faces risk, and some elements of it are better calculated than others. Weather surely ranks among the most difficult factors to predict, and the late-sixteenth-century English experience in the New World was hardly sufficient to anticipate well the nature of climatic norms and extremes on what is today's Outer Banks. Certainly the thin barrier strand presently bears a notorious reputation for weather extremes, especially in the form of warm-season hurricanes and cold-season northeasters. Only regular firsthand observation over at least many decades permitted recognition of such dangerous extremes typical of the Roanoke area. And even under the best of circumstances unanticipated challenges can arise.

This paper offers a look at some of the climatic factors that affected early English colonization, especially during the late sixteenth century's several attempts to secure a foothold on present-day coastal North Carolina. Some pieces of this picture are relatively familiar and, as noted, define the reputation of the Outer Banks as the "Graveyard of the Atlantic." Other pieces, such as the effect of severe drought, have emerged recently. Together they remind us that the natural world often matters a great deal in human affairs.

A Startling Reminder

Roanoke-related climate held little interest for me before about two years ago, when I, along with colleagues from the University of Arkansas's Tree Ring Laboratory, found that subject suddenly thrust into our lives. We serendipitously identified evidence of a climatic extreme—a remarkably severe drought—precisely at the time the final Roanoke party arrived in 1587.[1] Our original purpose had been to explore conditions associated with the ultimately successful English colony at Jamestown in 1607. David Stahle and his colleagues, specialists in dendroclimatology, use annual tree-ring patterns of ancient, living bald cypresses to reconstruct past conditions.[2] I had enlisted their help for the Jamestown study and had even formed a hunch that drought might have contributed to that colony's struggles. Indeed, the Arkansas analysis established that a significant drought did coincide with the period 1606-1612 and must have played a role in the now-legendary hardships there.[3]

I recall well our early, excited conversations about the Jamestown finding. Almost as an aside, Stahle called my attention to a major "blip" in the eight-hundred-year-long tree-ring record from southeastern Virginia and northeastern North Carolina. He reported that, statistically speaking, the absolute worst drought of those eight centuries occurred between 1587 and 1589. We were both so taken by the revelations of the

Jamestown record that several days passed before we connected this most severe drought with Roanoke! Suffice it to say that it was a startling realization that drought conditions had handicapped not just one but two of the earliest English colonial settlements. It is a circumstance whose implications now warrant careful consideration.

Understanding Atlantic-Area Climate at the End of the Sixteenth Century

Climate, defined as the long-term patterns of atmospheric conditions of a given area, is a fact of human existence everywhere but generally gets taken for granted—it is among the conditions to which a culture adapts and its members become accustomed. This is not to say that the effects of climate are trivial, since it is essential that human societies adapt over the long run in order to sustain themselves within their environment. Indeed, the adaptive patterns of a society can virtually define its culture, or significant elements of it at least.

English-speaking Europeans were only vaguely familiar with climatic conditions in "Virginia" and could not accurately anticipate how the differences in climate could affect their activities. Even after they arrived, their first impressions of the local environment were not always accurate for a variety of reasons. I summarize below the conditions familiar to the men and women who left England in order to demonstrate how the new Virginia climate challenged them.

Hindsight helps us all, and paleoclimatologists make it their business to look back, determine the nature of past climatic conditions, and apply the knowledge to the present and future. Climate historians have recognized the onset of a cooling period in Europe that extended variably from the twelfth through the mid-nineteenth centuries. This period probably did not, however, feature uniformly lower temperatures but, instead, more frequent intervals of extended cold than at present.[4] Moreover, the episodes of cooling also did not necessarily affect the whole of Europe each time; often they were regional. Detailed reconstruction for England is not yet sufficient to permit certainty about local conditions, but the balance of the European record indicates that those who embarked for Virginia from England in the late sixteenth century were leaving a generally cooler climate and that the periods 1560-1570 and 1590-1610 were among the coolest.[5] The relatively high-frequency periodicity in the records indicates that during this so-called Little Ice Age the climate was more subject to extremes,[6] and Swiss data suggests that the period around 1600 was the height of that trend.[7]

Given the paucity of records, conditions across the Atlantic in eastern North America during the 1580s are even more difficult to measure. The dendroclimatological data reported here is one segment of a long record that can provide a broader view of regional conditions not available before, but, as indicated, they are most pertinent to precipitation reconstruction. Cumulative tree-ring records from all of North America indicate that a prolonged drought plagued the continent in the late sixteenth century.[8] That dry period applies to the Carolinas and Virginia in the 1580s. Ice-core records for northern Canada indicate that conditions there were markedly colder from 1550 to

1620.[9] Well to the south, South American research records a moderate to strong El Niño event between 1589 and 1591.[10] The potential effect of this pattern in present-day North Carolina is somewhat milder and wetter winters and a lower frequency of hurricanes, although the effects of El Niño on the Middle Atlantic region are not yet well understood. As Stahle and others note, both hurricane frequency and the likelihood of drought rise during La Niña years, and such conditions may have prevailed at Roanoke when the English push was under way.[11] Until more thorough reconstructions are available for the eastern United States, these far-flung hemispheric patterns only suggest general conditions.

Specific Factors in the Roanoke Story

Drought at Roanoke

Bald cypress (*Taxodium distichum*) tree rings provide an extraordinary record of past climate for the area of the Roanoke colony. Millennium-old trees not only extend the chronicle well back in time but also translate into an independent, quantifiable gauge of the characteristics of historical climate. It happens that these trees are very sensitive to trends in growing-season precipitation, which each year extends between about April and July, especially when they grow in sedimentary as opposed to peaty substrates. Cores from several living trees are analyzed, and ring measurements are combined into a single, calibrated sequence for the region. By standardizing the ring record, a series of indexes can be applied to the sequence in order to measure relative severity of droughts and other trends.[12]

The tree-ring record for southeastern Virginia and northeastern North Carolina generated by David Stahle and his team at the University of Arkansas was full of surprises. Most notable is the severe downturn in rainfall during the years 1587-1589. Measured statistically, it amounts to the deepest low in the entire eight-hundred-year story of regional precipitation trends (Figure 16).[13] Although it is tricky and sometimes misleading to offer modern analogies for such events, it is reasonably safe to say that this Roanoke-period deficit exceeds anything experienced in the region in the late twentieth century. A drought of this magnitude, though short-lived, would affect human welfare in these pre-modern societies.

Almost always, severe drought most directly affects water supply and food supply. Precious little corroborating evidence can be gleaned from the scant records left from the Roanoke period, but there are occasional suggestions of drought-induced hardship. The clearest comes when John White describes the initial reunion of the English and Indians during July 1587. White relates that the natives immediately expressed concern about their lack of corn: "Some of them [the Indians] came to us, embracing and entertaining us friendly, desiring us not to gather or spoil any of their corn, because they had but little."[14] Establishing the certain and precise meaning of these recorded statements is among the more difficult challenges historians face, but

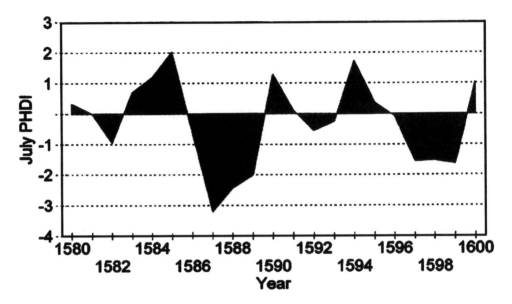

Fig. 16. Graph showing growing season soil moisture in the Roanoke area from 1580 to 1600, derived from tree-ring records and measured by the Palmer Hydrological Drought Index.

one would be remiss to dismiss the local Indians' expressed concern as entirely deceitful or calculating, especially in the light of the new and independent evidence from bald cypress trees.

The water question is more difficult to pin down. Fresh water is perhaps the human requirement least to be taken for granted on the barrier islands. The sandy soils of these thin coastal strands not only drain quickly but have limited reservoirs of potable groundwater accessible to shallow wells. Drinkable surface water was likewise scarce, probably even in the best of times, as John White's 1590 account of an island exploration following the drought period attests: "[N]or had we found any fresh water in all this way to drink. . . . The sailors in our absence had brought their cask ashore for fresh water, so we deferred our going to Roanoke until the next morning, and caused some of them to dig in the sandy hills for fresh water—which we found very sufficient."[15] Suffice it to say that a drought very likely all but erased surface water sources and reduced the volume and quality of shallow wells in the sandy island soils.

The fate of the "Lost Colony" population remains one of the great mysteries of the nation's history. The introduction of drought as a potential factor leading to the demise is warranted now, but it is not sufficient to account for the disappearance singlehandedly. The lack of rainfall probably introduced more stress into a situation already stressful for both the Indians and the English. The apparent food shortfall cited earlier could well translate into competition for a suddenly limited food staple for both groups and, thus, engender conflict as the two sides struggled to control the supply. Water problems would only have exacerbated the quandary. Under another scenario, the colonists may have opted to "go native" and adopt the Indians' traditional survival tactics during times of crop failure.

It is worth noting that tree-ring and other records suggest greater-than-average overall climatic variability during the late sixteenth century, including significant swings in precipitation.[16] One would wonder how, otherwise, each early English colonizing attempt in the Middle Atlantic could have confronted dry conditions. Nor was it only the English who suffered as a result. As noted, compelling evidence suggests that the Spanish settlement at Santa Elena in present-day coastal South Carolina encountered serious drought-induced food shortages.[17]

Hurricanes

The intrepid English struggling to establish a presence at Roanoke perceived impressive storms much more readily than drought, and they left a vivid record of their experiences with them, as would any seafaring people. Historical climatologists refer to hurricanes as extreme events, in this case short-lived but potentially very influential natural phenomena. Even in more recent times, severe storms have sculpted coastal geography on the Outer Banks, creating various landmarks, including Oregon Inlet in 1846.[18]

At present the defined hurricane season for the section of the Atlantic coast occupied by the Outer Banks extends from June to the end of October.[19] Hurricanes occurred in the sixteenth century as they do today, but their frequency and intensity then are less certain. Some storm researchers have suggested that hurricanes are subject to cyclical patterns over periods spanning several decades.[20] The hurricanes that Gilbert, Raleigh, and Drake encountered off Roanoke were among the first to be described, and since 1583 hurricanes documented as tracking near or across the present-day Outer Banks number in the hundreds.[21] During the 1583-1590 English colonization at Roanoke, at least four probable hurricanes were described off the North Carolina coast (Table 2). In the age of exploration, the preferred sailing season overlapped the hurricane season, and sailors and settlers frequently encountered the powerful storms. To travel in warmer weather with favorable winds made the risk worthwhile.

One such apparent hurricane directly affected the course of events at Roanoke. A storm of June 13-16, 1586, as described by Ralph Lane, forced abandonment of the first settlement.[22] Its four-day ferocity is described dramatically as follows: "[T]he storm drove sundry of the fleet to put to sea. . . . The weather was so boisterous and the pinnaces so often aground, that most of all we had . . . were cast overboard by the sailors—the greater number of the fleet being much aggrieved with their long and dangerous abode in that miserable road."[23] This bout with a hurricane facilitated the decision to abandon the initial settlement after about a year rather than stay to await resupply.

Less pivotal but probably no less troublesome were other great "tempests" that hampered colonial progress. Soon after White established a settlement in the summer of 1587, a storm "at northeast" complicated Sir Francis Drake's landings for six days in

Table 2

"Summary of Apparent Hurricanes during the Roanoke Period"

Julian Cal. Date	Gregorian Cal. Date	Storm Effect	Source
June 13-16, 1586	June 23-26, 1586	Forced decision to abandon first settlement after one year	Ludlum, 9; Noël Hume, *Virginia Adventure*, 50-51; Quinn, *Set Fair*, 136-137
Aug. 21-26, 1587	Aug. 31-Sept. 5, 1587	Hampered vessels during White's effort to establish a second settlement	Ludlum, 9
Aug. 1-9, 1590	Aug. 10-19, 1590	Complicated White's searches after a severely delayed return to resupply the 1587 enclave	Ludlum, 9; Quinn, *Set Fair*, 323-324
Aug. 16, 1591	Aug. 26, 1591*	Plagued expedition to Roanoke area	Ludlum, 9

* Four additional storms recorded in the open Atlantic during 1591 damaged or sank both English and Spanish vessels.

August.[24] The streak of bad luck continued when two more storms interfered with White's long overdue resupply trip in August 1590.[25] In a 1593 letter to Hakluyt, White's disappointment and frustration with the last storms are clear: "When we arrived there the season was so unfit and the weather so foul, that we were constrained to forsake that coast, without having seen any of our planters. We lost one of our ship's boats, seven of our chief men, and three of our anchors and cables. Most of our casks with fresh water were left on shore, not possible to be had aboard."[26] The rest of the story is all too familiar.

Lessons to Remember

This examination of climatic conditions at the time of Roanoke colonization cannot solve the "Lost Colony" mystery, nor is it intended to reinterpret the events from a wholly environmentalist standpoint. The aim, rather, has been to introduce these factors in a systematic fashion so that climate can be respected among the many contributing elements of historical analysis. In the present technological age, we are buffered from environmental extremes in ways unimagined before—to the point that it is easy to dismiss climate as a legitimate agent of cultural change, especially during the more recent historical period.

Another purpose has been to demonstrate the usefulness of an explicitly interdisciplinary approach to the study of history. Little of what is presented here could be possible without the benefit of collaboration with natural scientists concerned with climate change. Introducing these factors, I believe, produces a richer, more accurate interpretation of the riveting events surrounding the Roanoke colonies.

NOTES

1. David W. Stahle et al., "The Lost Colony and Jamestown Droughts," *Science* 280 (April 24, 1998): 564-567.

2. David W. Stahle and Malcolm K. Cleaveland, "Reconstruction and Analysis of Spring Rainfall over the Southeastern U.S. for the Past 1000 Years," *Bulletin of the American Meteorological Society* 73 (December 1992): 1947-1961.

3. Stahle et al., "The Lost Colony."

4. Raymond S. Bradley, *Paleoclimatology: Reconstructing Climates of the Quaternary*, 2d ed. (San Diego: Academic Press, 1999), 461-463; Raymond S. Bradley and Phillip D. Jones, "Climate Variations Over the Last 500 Years," in *Climate Since A.D. 1500,* ed. R. S. Bradley and P. D. Jones (London: Routledge, 1995), 658-659.

5. Bradley and Jones, "Climate Variations Over the Last 500 Years," 652, 659.

6. F. Serre-Bachet, J. Guiot, and L. Tessier, "Dendroclimatic Evidence from Southwestern Europe and Northwestern Africa," in *Climate Since A.D. 1500*, ed. R. S. Bradley and P. D. Jones (London: Routledge, 1995), 364.

7. Christian Pfister, "Monthly Temperature and Precipitation in Central Europe from 1525-1979: Quantifying Documentary Evidence on Weather and Its Effects," in *Climate Since A.D. 1500*, ed. R. S. Bradley and P. D. Jones (London: Routledge, 1995), 135.

8. David W. Stahle et al., "Tree Ring Data Document 16th Century Megadrought over North America," *EOS, Transactions of the American Geophysical Union* 81 (2000).

9. R. M. Koerner and D. Fisher, "Acid Snow in the Canadian High Arctic," *Nature* 295 (January 14-20, 1982).

10. W. H. Quinn and V. T. Neal, "The Historical Record of El Niño Events," in *Climate Since A.D. 1500*, ed. R. S. Bradley and P. D. Jones (London: Routledge, 1995), 628.

11. Stahle et al., "Tree Ring Data Document 16th Century Megadrought."

12. Stahle and Cleaveland, "Reconstruction and Analysis of Spring Rainfall"; Stahle et al., "The Lost Colony."

13. Stahle et al., "The Lost Colony."

14. David Beers Quinn, *Set Fair for Roanoke: Voyages and Settlements, 1584-1606* (Chapel Hill: University of North Carolina Press, 1985), 283.

15. lebame houston and Barbara Hird, *Roanoke Revisited: The Story of the Lost Colony, A Modernized Version of Original Documents* (Manteo: Times Printing Co., 1997), 65-66; Quinn, *Set Fair for Roanoke*, 325.

16. Stahle and Cleaveland, "Reconstruction and Analysis of Spring Rainfall"; Bradley and Jones, "Climate Variations Over the Last 500 Years."

17. David G. Anderson, David W. Stahle, and Malcolm K. Cleaveland, "Paleoclimate and the Potential Food Reserves of Mississipian Societies: A Case Study from the Savannah River Valley," *American Antiquity* 60 (April 1995): 258-286.

18. Orrin H. Pilkey et al., *The North Carolina Shore and Its Barrier Islands: Restless Ribbons of Sand* (Durham: Duke University Press, 1998), 121.

19. Pilkey et al., *North Carolina Shore*, 20-21.

20. Jack Williams, *The Weather Book*, 2d ed. (New York: Vintage Books, 1997), 159-161.

21. David M. Ludlum, *Early American Hurricanes, 1492-1870* (Boston: American Meteorological Society, 1963); Pilkey et al., *The North Carolina Shore*, 24-25.

22. Ludlum, *Early American Hurricanes*, 9; Quinn, *Set Fair for Roanoke*, 137; Ivor Noël Hume, *The Virginia Adventure: Roanoke to James Towne: An Archaeological and Historical Odyssey* (New York: Knopf, 1994), 50-51.

23. houston and Hird, *Roanoke Revisited*, 35-36.

24. Ludlum, *Early American Hurricanes*, 9.

25. Ludlum, *Early American Hurricanes*, 9; Quinn, *Set Fair for Roanoke*, 324.

26. houston and Hird, *Roanoke Revisited*, 78; Quinn, *Set Fair for Roanoke*, 330.

Strangers in a Strange Land: Patterns of European Colonization in the New World

Charles R. Ewen

Introduction

The preceding chapters in this volume run the full gamut of the Roanoke colonization experience and attempt to solve, or at least speculate about, some of the mysteries associated with the "Lost Colony." These diverse contributions show that many routes lead to understanding the Roanoke colonies and that each approach, be it folklore or literature or history or archaeology, can help to reach that goal.

As a historical archaeologist, I get to dabble in more than one approach to knowing but am always after the "truth" of what happened in the past. My post-modernist colleague and coeditor, Tom Shields, on the other hand, jokes with me that as an English professor he is less concerned with the truth, so long as it's a good story! I have always thought that the best stories usually are the true ones. With the papers in this volume we have both: the truth (at least as we understand it) and several good stories.

I would like to conclude this book with a look ahead toward the stories yet to come, specifically the stories we can tell once the historical gaps have been filled when we find all the lost colonies and determine what happened to them. What kind of questions do we ask then? Or is the story over? A reexamination of the processes of colonization in the New World, looking beyond the shores of Roanoke Island, will illustrate what kind of new questions answering the old questions will inspire.

The Colonial Experience

Europe had little colonial experience prior to Christopher Columbus's voyages of discovery to the New World. Its nations had spent most of their time squabbling over their holdings within Europe itself or in North Africa and the Near East. It wasn't until the fifteenth century that many European powers even knew of other lands, let alone entertained notions of conquest and colonization.

Spain was one of the first European powers to look outside the known world for colonial purposes. It had planted a small colony in the Canary Islands by the end of the fifteenth century, but that limited experience beyond its borders hardly prepared it for colonizing its discoveries in the New World. Yet, even before the full extent of its discoveries was realized, Spain rushed to solidify its claims by establishing colonies. Columbus, Spain's point-man in the New World, proved to be a better explorer than colonizer, and the Spanish crown quickly relieved him of any real administrative responsibility. A string of successors of varying abilities followed, and the early colonial experience was turbulent. After this shaky start during the last decade of the fifteenth century, the Spaniards quickly rebounded and had overrun the Caribbean by 1550. *La Florida* (Spain's name for what would become the southeastern United States), however, would prove an even greater challenge.

Following the abortive colonial attempts of Juan Ponce de Leon (1521), Lucas Vazquez de Ayllón (1526), Pánfilo de Narvaéz (1528), and Hernando de Soto (1539), Spain decided that North America was not worth its immediate attention and focused its efforts on areas in which gold and silver rewarded those endeavors. French intrusions on their domain at Charlesfort (Jean Ribault in Port Royal Sound in South Carolina) in 1562 and then at Fort Caroline (Rene de Laudonnière on the St. John's River in Florida) in 1564 caused Spain to reconsider the strategic importance of *la Florida*. Pedro Menéndez de Avilés, governor and captain general of *la Florida*, responded by massacring the French and establishing colonies at Saint Augustine (in present-day Florida) in 1565 and Santa Elena (on present-day Parris Island, South Carolina) in 1566.

But what of the English? For most of the sixteenth century, England settled for trying to pirate the wealth that Spain was extracting from its New World colonies. Though the English might have preferred to go to the source of the gold and silver, Spain's grip on the Caribbean was sufficient during the sixteenth century to make England look elsewhere for establishing a foothold in the New World. The ill-fated first colony at Fort Raleigh in 1585 represents England's initial bid to challenge Spain in *la Florida*.

Roanoke Colonization

I will not recount here the story of Sir Walter Raleigh's repeated attempts to establish a colony in Virginia. Nor will I recapitulate the repeated attempts of archaeologists to find solid evidence of that venture. What I would like to discuss is what we should be looking for and why it is important.

At the 1987 annual conference of the Society for Historic Archaeology, a plenary session gathered the leading scholars in the field to discuss the "questions that count" in historical archaeology. What sorts of questions should we be asking of the archaeological record? Some immediately obvious questions arose, such as "Where did Columbus first make landfall?" but many less obvious but possibly even more important questions quickly followed, among them "What were the long-term biological consequences of that landfall?" Similar questions could be asked about the Roanoke colonies.

Questions that Count

The first question that archaeologists have asked and continue to ask is "Where was the fort?" Well, there is a modest earthwork at the Fort Raleigh National Monument that the National Park Service presents as a likely candidate for the original site of Fort Raleigh. Recent archaeological interpretation has called this choice into question, however.[1] Is this Ralph Lane's fort? Is it Richard Grenville's 1585 fort? Is it a sixteenth-century fort at all, or perhaps an earthwork built more than one hundred years later? If these earthworks do not date to the sixteenth century, where should we look? It has been suggested that the original fort was lost to the sound's encroaching water, but perhaps the fort might still be found, as was the fort at Jamestowne, which was likewise considered lost to erosion.

The next obvious question, and one that has more to say about the colonists, is "Where is the accompanying settlement?" That is, where did the people who built the fort live? The prevailing wisdom has been to find the fort first, and the settlement must then be nearby. The extensive archaeological work around the earthworks at the Fort Raleigh National Monument (see the essay by Bennie C. Keel in this volume) has yet to turn up any solidly residential artifacts beyond some scattered sixteenth-century material.

The final big question is "Where did the 'Lost Colony' go?" This designation is ironic, since the sites of all three colonies—both those on Roanoke Island and the place where the third colony relocated—are lost. Paradoxically, the "lost" colony site may be relocated first, since it commands the most attention.

Questions That Will Count

These are all important questions that must be answered before any further research can be conducted. Nonetheless, we should be ready with a research design that is built around the "questions that will count" when these important sites are finally pinpointed.

A guiding research question that immediately springs to mind would be "Why did the colony fail?" Several hypotheses can be tested. Conventional wisdom has it that the colonists were too poorly supplied and inexperienced to sustain a colony. Another hypothesis, perhaps affiliated, holds that bad relations with the local Indians made settlement impossible. A recent hypothesis based on newly acquired dendrochronological data suggests that the English were trying to found a colony during the worst drought in eight hundred years on the Carolina coast (see the essay by Dennis B. Blanton in this volume). Thus, nature, rather than ineptitude, caused the crops to fail, and the resulting competition for scarce resources precipitated the conflict between the European colonists and the Indians.

Investigations into the failure of the Roanoke colony must consider the English strategy for survival. How did the colonists try to adapt to their new environment? This question is not as obvious as it might seem and has been the object of my own research, though in a different region of the New World.[2]

Patterns of Colonization

To examine patterns of colonization, one must weigh the range of possibilities available to the colonist. This is not to say that you ask "What would I do if I were a sixteenth-century English colonist?" You are not, and it is important to keep that in mind. It has been said that "common sense" is neither. Our actions in different situations are often culturally determined. This phenomenon explains why businessmen wear coats and ties in the summer when it would make more "sense" to wear something cooler. Instead, the question should be "What are the range of possible cultural responses when confronted with a new environment?" After identifying the possible responses, the next step is to determine how they compare with the documentary and archaeological evidence.

The first response to a new colonial endeavor might be to re-create your country of origin. After all, this is the only experience from which you can draw. At least initially, though, this was simply impossible, given the logistics of the time. How do you pack for such an adventure, especially when you know that the next supply boat is at least a year away? Some changes to the colonists' pattern of living occurred even before they departed for the New World. Decisions had to be made as to what supplies to take and what skills the colonists chosen had to possess. The personal preferences and idiosyncrasies of the colonists themselves were magnified in the select group that left Mother England. The Founder Effect, which holds that the genetic characteristics of the initial colonists determine those of the descendents, well accepted in biological evolution, applies to cultural formation as well.

The opposite response is to reject your own culture and "go native." After all, wouldn't that make sense, since the Indians had been living there for centuries and probably understood the best way to adapt to the environment? Such a response is not borne out in the documentary record and points up the fallacy of "common sense." It would make sense to shed bulky clothing in the hot and humid Coastal Plain or to forgo the clumsy arquebus in favor of the more efficient bow and arrow, but there is no record of that having happened anywhere in colonial America. Far from it, as only captives seemed to "go native," and this was not necessarily by choice.

No, clearly the response to the new colonial environment is a compromise on the part of the colonists. They preserve as much of their familiar culture as possible and adopt elements of the indigenous culture to facilitate their own adaptation. This term is known anthropologically as acculturation or, more recently, as creolization.

Acculturation

Anthropologist Edward H. Spicer defined acculturation, as I have used it in my studies of the sixteenth-century Spanish colonial experience, as "the augmentation, replacement or combination in a variety of ways of the elements of a given cultural system with the elements of another."[3] Geographer George Foster insisted that the idea of dominance—that is, one culture having supremacy over another during the exchange of traits—should be included in the operational definition. He used that concept, dominance, to develop his model of the "conquest culture."[4]

The formation of a "conquest culture" is characterized by a stripping-down process in which elements of the dominant culture are modified or eliminated. Two types of selective processes are involved in the formation of the "conquest culture." The first is formal: intentional changes through which the government, church, or some other authoritative body of the home nation directs the introduction of selected innovations (e.g., the grid plan imposed on the construction of Spanish cities in the New World). The second selective process is informal and includes the habits of the colonists themselves; examples include food preferences, ideologies, and attitudes. According to this model, the European colonial culture was being formed even before it left the docks of the mother country.

Another source of influence upon the "conquest culture" comes from the subordinate culture. Although clearly the major changes are found in the culture of the subordinate group, the dominant group likewise experiences a degree of change. Foster emphatically states, "During the American conquest, Spanish ways were *profoundly* modified by the existing cultures."[5] The results of these changes (formal and informal) make up the proposed Spanish colonial pattern.

Spanish Colonial Pattern

Anthropologists, and hence archaeologists, have long believed that human activity is patterned—that is, within a given set of circumstances, humans will behave in predictable ways. Archaeologists believe that these patterns in human behavior can be detected through patterns in the archaeological record left behind. Thus, by determining the patterns in the archaeological record, one can predict the past, so to speak.

Such a search for archaeological patterns can be seen in the work of Charles Fairbanks of the University of Florida, later continued and elaborated by his student Kathleen Deagan. Their research in Saint Augustine sought to illuminate the processes related to the formation and development of the Hispanic-American cultural tradition in Florida. Specifically, they attempted to identify the elements of the native culture that the Spaniards adopted in adapting to their New World colony. Deagan concluded that acculturation in eighteenth-century Saint Augustine was undertaken largely by Indian women in mixed-Spanish or mestizo household units within a primarily male-oriented (military) cultural setting. Thus, the Spanish colonial adaptation pattern incorporated native elements into low-visibility subsistence activities while maintaining a Spanish appearance in socially visible areas such as clothing, tableware, and religion. That is to say, a European veneer was maintained over a Native American infrastructure. Based on the archaeological evidence accumulated from more than a decade of fieldwork, Deagan suggested that the processes involved in forming Hispanic American tradition in Saint Augustine were common to much of the Spanish New World.[6] She invited other archaeologists to test that hypothesis, and, as her first doctoral student, I was the initial "volunteer."

The first step in examining the Spanish colonial pattern was to find a suitable site to dig. I considered Puerto Real, Haiti, an ideal site to test the hypothesis because it fitted the parameters of the society to which this pattern applied. There a predominantly male group (the Spaniards) imposed itself on a group with a normal sex distribution (the native Taino population). As a different type of site (a commercial colony instead of a military outpost), Puerto Real would indicate whether the proposed pattern was truly panhispanic or tied to site type.

Puerto Real was one of thirteen towns founded across Hispaniola in 1504. Originally envisioned as a mining center, the town soon resorted to slave trading when gold and copper deposits proved disappointing. That business ended after the Bahamas and other surrounding islands had been depopulated by the mid-sixteenth century. Cattle thrived in this new environment, so the citizens of Puerto Real turned to the hide and tallow trade as their chief source of livelihood.

Finding it impossible to compete with the more lucrative precious-metal trade of the mainland, the merchants of Puerto Real were unable to secure space on the treasure fleets that serviced Spain's colonies in the circum-Caribbean area. The struggling town then embraced its only remaining alternative: it dealt with smugglers. The slowly turning wheels of Spanish commercial control eventually forced the abandonment of Puerto Real in 1578. The losses sustained by the town's citizens became archaeology's gain, since this site has a well-defined beginning and end date. Its known early chronology and cultural affiliation made it ideal for testing ideas of colonial patterning.

My excavations at Puerto Real in 1984-1985 focused on a high-status residence occupied primarily during the latter half of the sixteenth century. Living in that residence were a relatively wealthy Spaniard, his Spanish wife, and possibly a child. The interior of their home and their possessions reflected the family's high status. Their table was set with fine Spanish majolicas (tin-enameled ceramics) and Italian glassware. Their clothing, as reflected in the ornaments and buttons recovered during the excavation, apparently followed the fashions prevalent in Spain. In the rear of the house, slaves, probably African, prepared the food they had collected in cooking vessels they themselves had made. Their master, judging by the abundance of coins and leather-working tools, may have been a merchant dealing in hides and slaves. The porcelain in his household suggests that at least some of his business was conducted illicitly with the Portuguese corsairs who frequented the harbor (the only dealers in porcelain before 1573).

Conclusions based on the results of the analyses of the artifacts recovered by the archaeologists tend to support the hypothesized pattern of Spanish colonial adaptation. Ceramics associated with low-social-visibility food-preparation and -storage activities *did* reveal a significant proportion of locally made wares. Tableware, ornamentation, clothing accessories, and other highly visible artifacts *were* exclusively European in origin. The house itself, insofar as could be determined from the configuration of the foundation and associated building rubble, *was* built in accordance with Spanish architectural traditions and new ideas concerning urban design. The colonial diet, while significantly different from the native diet, *did* incorporate locally available wild foods, as well as domesticated animals that the colonists had imported.

The Spanish colonial pattern, as outlined above, was established early and changed little through time. New styles of ceramics and other artifacts did appear through time, but the proportional distribution in the high- and low-visibility categories remained roughly constant throughout the seventy-five years of the town's occupation. Thus the creolization process appears to occur relatively rapidly.

Conclusion

So how does this look at how one of England's colonial rivals tackled the New World help us to understand the colony on Roanoke Island? It is too soon to tell, but it does suggest a fruitful avenue of inquiry once archaeologists discover the colonial sites on Roanoke. In fact, many questions have been raised in this volume. David Hurst Thomas, an archaeologist who has investigated the Contact Period, suggests that researchers employ a cubist perspective on the past—that is, they should look at the past from multiple perspectives at the same time.[7] Clearly, the investigation should be a multidisciplinary endeavor.

The Spanish colonial pattern has been and continues to be tested at other Spanish colonial sites. But the tests should not stop there. This model of colonial adaptation for Hispanic sites can be tested at non-Hispanic colonial sites in the Americas. Did the French and British adapt to their new surroundings in a manner similar to the Spanish? Historical records indicate that the English had a very different attitude toward the native inhabitants. If so, how did their attitudes differ, and what factors might account for that difference?

Can the Roanoke colonies serve as a test case for an English colonial pattern? Not yet. First we need to find the Cittie of Raleigh settlement. The contextual control on previous archaeological work is not very good but may be good enough for some initial modeling. Data from the fort (if it could definitely be tied to the fort!) would be interesting but perhaps not comparable to the Spanish data. Ideally, solid household data would be necessary both for comparative purposes and to re-create the daily life of the English colonist. Should the "Lost Colony" be located, such data would likewise be interesting, but for other research questions. The life-style of those English survivors would probably be anomalous to the general colonial pattern.

Finally, we must all ask the question I make all my students ask of their work. So what? Why should we care about these other questions? Wouldn't finding the site be enough? No, it would not. It is not enough simply to repeat the same stories, even if we are able to tie them to a specific plot of land. We must constantly question our assumptions concerning the past. The recently discovered evidence of the sixteenth-century drought, discussed by Blanton in this volume, shows us that.

The collected essays in this volume demonstrate the wide range of questions inspired by the colonization of Roanoke Island. We have sought hard facts: Where was the Cittie of Raleigh? Where did the colonists go? What is the evidence of their experience? We have asked more subjective questions about the colonists themselves: Who were they? Why did they come? What did they expect to find? We have asked questions that go beyond the shores of Roanoke Island: How did the experiences of the Roanoke colonists affect later colonial efforts? What were the native inhabitants like, and how did they interact with the colonists? How has the story of Fort Raleigh and the "Lost Colony" changed through history, and how does it affect us today?

For the Roanoke researchers, the journey has become as important as the destination. On the way to finding the "Lost Colony," we have investigated topics ranging from the effects of climatic change on the colony to the reasons why Spanish pottery appeared in the settlements of a dreaded enemy, the English. Clearly we are interested in more than just who, what, where, and when. We also want to know how and why. It would be nice to find the "Lost Colony," but even then the journey will be far from over.

NOTES

1. Ivor Noël Hume, *The Virginia Adventure: Roanoke to James Towne: An Archaeological and Historical Odyssey* (New York: Knopf, 1994), 86-88.

2. Charles R. Ewen, *From Spaniard to Creole: The Archaeology of Cultural Formation at Puerto Real, Haiti* (Tuscaloosa: University of Alabama Press, 1991).

3. Edward H. Spicer, *Cycles of Conquest: The Impact of Spain, Mexico and the United States on the Indians of the Southwest, 1533-1960* (Tucson: University of Arizona Press, 1960), 529.

4. George Foster, *Culture and Conquest* (Chicago: Quadrangle Books, 1960), 2.

5. Foster, *Culture and Conquest*, 7.

6. Kathleen Deagan, *Spanish St. Augustine: The Archaeology of a Colonial Creole Community* (New York: Academic Press, 1983), 270.

7. David Hurst Thomas, "Columbian Consequences: The Spanish Borderlands in Cubist Perspective," in *Columbian Consequences*, 3 vols. (Washington: Smithsonian Institution Press, 1989-1991), 1:9.

Contributors

Karen Baldwin
Folklore Archives and Department of English, East Carolina University, Greenville

Thomas E. Beaman Jr.
Wilson, North Carolina

Dennis B. Blanton
Center for Archaeological Research, College of William and Mary, Williamsburg, Virginia

Thomas E. Davidson
Jamestown-Yorktown Foundation, Williamsburg

Charles R. Ewen
Southern Coastal Heritage Program and Department of Anthropology, East Carolina University

Kelley Griffith
Department of English, University of North Carolina at Greensboro

Olivia A. Isil
Gibsonia, Pennsylvania

Bennie C. Keel
Southeast Archaeological Center, National Park Service, Tallahassee, Florida

Seth Mallios
Department of Anthropology, San Diego State University

Barbara Midgette
Buxton, North Carolina

John J. Mintz
Office of State Archaeology, Division of Historical Resources, North Carolina Office of Archives and History

Contributors

Michael Leroy Oberg
History Department, State University of New York-Geneseo

William S. Powell
Professor emeritus, University of North Carolina at Chapel Hill

David Beers Quinn
Professor emeritus, University of Liverpool

Lorraine Hale Robinson
Department of English, East Carolina University

E. Thomson Shields Jr.
Roanoke Colonies Research Office and Department of English, East Carolina University

W. Keats Sparrow
Dean, College of Arts and Sciences, East Carolina University

Fred Willard
East Lake, North Carolina

Joyce Youings
University of Exeter, Exeter, England, United Kingdom

Works Cited

Anderson, David G., David W. Stahle, and Malcolm K. Cleaveland. "Paleoclimate and the Potential Food Reserves of Mississippian Societies: A Case Study from the Savannah River Valley." *American Antiquity* 60 (April 1995): 258-286.

Andrews, Kenneth R. *Elizabethan Privateering: English Privateering During the Spanish War, 1585-1603*. Cambridge: Cambridge University Press, 1964.

_____, ed. *The Last Voyage of Drake and Hawkins*. Hakluyt Society Second Series, No. 142. Cambridge: Cambridge University Press, 1972.

Arner, Robert D. *The Lost Colony in Literature*. Raleigh: America's Four Hundredth Anniversary Committee, North Carolina Department of Cultural Resources, 1985.

_____. "The Romance of Roanoke: Virginia Dare and the Lost Colony in American Literature." *Southern Literary Journal* 10 (spring 1978): 5-45.

Barbour, Philip L., ed. *The Complete Works of Captain John Smith (1580-1631)*. 3 vols. Chapel Hill: Institute of Early American History and Culture and University of North Carolina Press, 1986.

_____, ed. *The Jamestown Voyages Under the First Charter, 1606-1609: Documents Relating to the Foundation of Jamestown and the History of the Jamestown Colony Up to the Departure of Captain John Smith, Last President of the Council in Virginia Under the First Charter, Early in October 1609*. 2 vols. Hakluyt Society Second Series, Nos. 136-137. Cambridge: Cambridge University Press, 1969.

Batho, G. R. *Thomas Harriot and the Northumberland Household*. Durham Thomas Harriot Seminar Occasional Paper No. 1. Durham, U.K.: Durham Thomas Harriot Seminar, 1983.

Beaman, Thomas, Jr., and John J. Mintz. "Iberian Olive Jars at Brunswick Town and Other British Colonial Sites: Three Models for Consideration." *Southeastern Archaeology* 17 (summer 1998): 92-102.

Beaman, Thomas E., Jr., et al. "Archaeological History and Historical Archaeology: Revisiting the Excavations at Brunswick Town, 1958-1968." *North Carolina Archaeology* 47 (October 1998): 1-33.

Beier, A. L. *Masterless Men: The Vagrancy Problem in England, 1560-1640*. London: Methuen, 1985.

Birth of a Nation, The (movie). D. W. Griffiths, director. Epoch Producing, 1915.

Bottigheimer, Karl S. "Kingdom and Colony: Ireland and the Westward Enterprise, 1536-1660." In *The Westward Enterprise: English Activities in Ireland, the Atlantic, and America, 1480-1650*. Edited by K. R. Andrews, N. P. Canny, and P. E. H. Hair.

Liverpool: Liverpool University Press; reprint, Detroit: Wayne State University Press, 1979, 45-64.

Bradley, R. S., and P. D. Jones, eds. *Climate Since A.D. 1500*. London: Routledge, 1995.

Bradley, Raymond S. *Paleoclimatology: Reconstructing Climates of the Quaternary,* 2d ed. San Diego: Academic Press, 1999.

Bradley, Raymond S., and Phillip D. Jones. "Climate Variations Over the Last 500 Years." In *Climate Since A.D. 1500*. Edited by R. S. Bradley and P. D. Jones. London: Routledge, 1995, 649-665.

Bridenbaugh, Carl. *Jamestown, 1544-1699*. New York: Oxford University Press, 1980.

Bruce, Edward C. "Lounging in the Footprints of the Pioneers." *Harper's New Monthly Magazine* 20 (May 1860): 721-736.

Burton, Richard. "The Persistence of Romance." *Dial* 16 (December 16, 1893): 380-381.

Cawte, E. C. *Ritual Animal Disguise: A Historical and Geographical Study of Animal Disguise in the British Isles*. Cambridge, U.K.: D. S. Brewer, 1978.

Cecelski, David. "In the Great Alligator Swamp." *Coastwatch* (May-June 1997): 19-21.

Clark, Walter, ed. *The State Records of North Carolina*. 16 vols. (11-26). Raleigh: State of North Carolina, 1896-1906.

Corporation of the President of the Church of Jesus Christ of Latter-Day Saints-ANACOMP. *The International Genealogical Index*. [Salt Lake City]: 1988. Microfiche.

Cotten, Sallie Southall. *The White Doe: The Fate of Virginia Dare: An Indian Legend*. Philadelphia: Lippincott, 1901.

Crackanthorpe, B. A. "Sex in Modern Literature." *Nineteenth Century* 37 (April 1895): 607-616.

Cratt, Christina. "The Mysterious Lights at Dymond City." Unpublished manuscript, East Carolina University Folklore Archive, Greenville, 1990.

Cumming, William P. *Mapping the North Carolina Coast: Sixteenth-Century Cartography and the Roanoke Voyages*. Raleigh: America's Four Hundredth Anniversary Committee, North Carolina Department of Cultural Resources, 1988.

_____. *The Southeast in Early Maps*, 3d ed. Revised and enlarged by Louis De Vorsey Jr. Chapel Hill: University of North Carolina Press, 1998.

Davis, Ralph. *English Merchant Shipping and the Anglo-Dutch Rivalry in the Seventeenth Century*. London: National Maritime Museum, 1975.

Deagan, Kathleen. *Artifacts of the Spanish Colonies of Florida and the Caribbean, 1500-1800*. Washington: Smithsonian Institution Press, 1987.

_____. *Spanish St. Augustine: The Archaeology of a Colonial Creole Community*. New York: Academic Press, 1983.

DeCosta, Benjamin F. "Simon Ferdinando and John Walker in Maine." *New England Historical and Genealogical Register* 174 (April 1890): 149-158.

Dictionary of National Biography. London: Oxford University Press, 1938.

Dixon, Thomas. *The Clansman: An Historical Romance of the Ku Klux Klan*. New York: Doubleday, 1905.

_____. *The Leopard's Spots: A Romance of the White Man's Burden—1865-1900*. New York: Grosset and Dunlap, 1902.

_____. *The Traitor: A Story of the Fall of the Invisible Empire*. New York: Doubleday, 1907.

Dowd, Gregory Evans. *A Spirited Resistance: The North American Indian Struggle for Unity, 1745-1815*. Baltimore: Johns Hopkins University Press, 1992.

Dunbar, Elizabeth. *Talcott Williams: Gentleman of the Fourth Estate*. Brooklyn, N.Y.: R. E. Simpson and Son, 1936.

Ehrenhard, John E. *Digital Enhancement and Contrast Stretching of an Aerial Anomaly at Fort Raleigh National Historic Site*. Tallahassee: Southeast Archeological Center, National Park Service, 1983.

_____. *Research Plan: Fort Raleigh National Historic Site Archeological Investigations in Area West of Theater Parking Lot, Season 3, Phase 1*. Tallahassee: Southeast Archeological Center, National Park Service, 1984.

Ehrenhard, John E., and G. L. Komara. *Archeological Investigations at Fort Raleigh National Historic Site, Season 2, 1983*. Tallahassee: Southeast Archeological Center, National Park Service, 1984.

Ehrenhard, John E., W. P. Athens, and G. L. Komara. *Remote Sensing Investigations at Fort Raleigh National Historic Site, North Carolina*. Tallahassee: Southeast Archeological Center, National Park Service, 1983.

Ehrenhard, John E., W. P. Athens, and M. W. Williams. *Fort Raleigh National Historic Site Overview and Research Design*. Tallahassee: Southeast Archeological Center, National Park Service, 1982.

Ewen, C. L'Estrange. *The Golden Chalice: A Documented Narrative of an Elizabethian Pirate*. Paignton, U.K.: Cecil Henry L'Estrange Ewen, 1939.

Ewen, Charles R. *From Spaniard to Creole: The Archaeology of Cultural Formation at Puerto Real, Haiti.* Tuscaloosa: University of Alabama Press, 1991.

Ewen, Charles R., and Maurice W. Williams. "Puerto Real: Archaeology of an Early Spanish Town." In *First Encounters: Spanish Explorations in the Caribbean and the United States, 1492-1570.* Edited by Jerald T. Milanich and Susan Milbrath. Ripley P. Bullen Monographs in Anthropology and History, No. 9. Gainesville: Florida Museum of Natural History, 1989, 66-76.

Fairbanks, Charles H. "The Cultural Tradition of Spanish Ceramics." In *Ceramics in America*, ed. Ian M. G. Quimby. Charlottesville: University Press of Virginia, 1973, 141-174.

Field, Walter Taylor. "A Plea for the Ideal." *Dial* 14 (April 1, 1893): 206.

Fisher, John Joseph. "Geomorphic Expression of Former Inlets along the Outer Banks of North Carolina." Master's thesis, University of North Carolina at Chapel Hill, 1962.

Fletcher, Inglis. *Roanoke Hundred.* 1948; reprint, New York: Bantam, 1972.

Foster, George. *Culture and Conquest.* Chicago: Quadrangle Books, 1960.

Funk, Charles Earle. *Heavens to Betsy! and Other Curious Sayings.* New York: Harper, 1955.

Gibbons, Harry Scott. *Tall Woman: The Story of Virginia Dare.* New York: Bantam, 1984.

Glassie, Henry. *Passing the Time in Balleymenon: Culture and History of an Ulster Community.* Bloomington: Indiana University Press, 1995.

Gleach, Frederic. *Powhatan's World and Colonial Virginia: A Conflict of Cultures.* Lincoln: University of Nebraska Press, 1997.

Goggin, John. *The Spanish Olive Jar: An Introductory Study.* Yale University Publications in Anthropology, No. 62. New Haven: Yale University Press, 1960.

Gradie, Charlotte M. "The Powhatans in the Context of the Spanish Empire." In *Powhatan Foreign Relations, 1500-1722*, ed. Helen Rountree. Charlottesville: University Press of Virginia, 1993, 154-172.

Green, Paul. *The Lost Colony: A Symphonic Drama of Man's Faith and Work.* 1937; reprint, New York: Samuel French, 1980.

Greenblatt, Stephen. *Renaissance Self-Fashioning: From More to Shakespeare.* Chicago: University of Chicago Press, 1980.

Gregory, Chris. *Gifts and Commodities.* London: Academic Press, 1982.

Hakluyt, Richard. *A Particuler Discourse Concerninge the Greate Necessitie and Manifolde Commodyties That Are Like to Growe to this Realme of Englande by the Westerne Discoueries*

Lately Attempted, Written in the Yere 1584, by Richarde Hackluyt of Oxforde Known as Discourse of Western Planting, ed. David B. Quinn and Alison M. Quinn. Hakluyt Society Extra Series, No. 45. London: Hakluyt Society, 1993.

_____. *Principal Navigations*. 1903-1905; reprint, New York: Hakluyt Society, 1969.

_____. *The Principall Navigations, Voiages, and Discoveries of the English Nation*. London: George Bishop and Ralph Newberie, 1589. Hakluyt Society Extra Series, No. 39. Cambridge, U.K.: Hakluyt Society and the Peabody Museum, 1965.

_____. *The Principall Navigations, Voiages, and Discoveries of the English Nation*. 3 vols. London: George Bishop, Ralph Newberrie, and Robert Barker, 1599-1600.

Halpert, Herbert, and G. M. Story, eds. *Christmas Mumming in Newfoundland: Essays in Anthropology, Folklore, and History*. Toronto: University of Toronto Press, [1969].

Hammersten, Susan. *Archeological Survey for Park Housing*. Tallahassee: Southeast Archeological Center, National Park Service, 1990.

Hariot, Thomas. *A Briefe and True Report of the New Found Land of Virginia*. 1588; reprinted in Quinn, *The Roanoke Voyages*, 1:317-387.

Harrington, Jean Carl. "Archeological Explorations at Fort Raleigh National Historic Site." *North Carolina Historical Review* 26 (April 1949): 127-149.

_____. "Historic Relic Found: An Old Iron Sickle from Fort Raleigh, North Carolina." *Iron Worker* 15 (summer 1951): 12-15.

_____. *An Outwork at Fort Raleigh: Further Archeological Excavations at Fort Raleigh National Historic Site, North Carolina*. Philadelphia: Eastern National Parks and Monuments Association, 1966.

_____. "Plain Stamped, Shell Tempered Pottery from North Carolina." *American Antiquity* 13 (January 1948): 251-252.

_____. *Search for the Cittie of Ralegh: Archaeological Excavations at Fort Raleigh National Historic Site, North Carolina*. Archaeological Research Series, No. 6. Washington: National Park Service, U.S. Department of the Interior, 1962.

Hawks, Francis. *History of North Carolina: With Maps and Illustrations*. 2 vols. 1857-1858; reprint, Spartanburg, S.C.: Reprint Company, 1961.

Hayes, Miles O., et al., "The Investigation of Form and Processes in the Coastal Zone." In *Coastal Geomorphology*, ed. Donald R. Coates. Binghamton: State University of New York, 1973, 11-41.

Helms, Mary W. *Ulysses' Sail: An Ethnographic Odyssey of Power, Knowledge, and Geographical Distance*. Princeton, N.J.: Princeton University Press, 1988.

Hinderaker, Eric. *Elusive Empires: Constructing Colonialism in the Ohio Valley, 1673-1800.* New York: Cambridge University Press, 1997.

Hoffman, Paul E. *Spain and the Roanoke Voyages.* Raleigh: America's Four Hundredth Anniversary Committee, North Carolina Department of Cultural Resources, 1987.

Holmes, W. H. *Aboriginal Pottery of the Eastern United States.* Bureau of American Ethnology Annual Report No. 20. Washington: Government Printing Office, 1903.

Houlbrooke, R. A. *The English Family, 1450-1700.* London: Longman, 1984.

houston, lebame, and Barbara Hird. *Roanoke Revisited: The Story of the Lost Colony, A Modernized Version of Original Documents.* Manteo: Times Printing Co., 1997.

Hughes, Shelby Jean Nelson, ed. *Martin County Heritage.* Williamston, N.C.: Martin County Historical Society, 1980.

Hulton, Paul. *America 1585: The Complete Drawings of John White.* Chapel Hill: University of North Carolina Press with British Museum Publications in Association with America's Four Hundredth Anniversary Committee, North Carolina Department of Cultural Resources, 1984.

Humber, John L. *Backgrounds and Preparations for the Roanoke Voyages, 1584-1590.* Raleigh: America's Four Hundredth Anniversary Committee, North Carolina Department of Cultural Resources, 1986.

Hurst, John G., David S. Neal, and H. J. E. van Beuningen. *Rotterdam Papers VI: Pottery Produced and Traded in North-West Europe, 1350-1650.* Rotterdam: Museum Boymans-van Beuingen, 1986.

Hyde, Lewis. *The Gift: Imagination and the Erotic Life of Property.* New York: Random House, 1983.

"Indian." *Oxford English Dictionary*, 2d ed. 1989.

Isil, Olivia A. "Piracy, Privateering and Elizabethan Maritime Expansion." In *Roanoke Revisited*, #3-D. Manteo: Times Printing Co., 1993.

———. "Simon Fernando of Plymouth, London and Roanoke, The Man You Love to Hate." In *The Croatan: Official Program Guide to THE LOST COLONY.* Manteo: Roanoke Island Historical Association, 1994, 28-30.

James, Stephen R., Jr. "A Reassessment of the Chronological and Typological Framework of the Spanish Olive Jar." *Historical Archaeology* 22 (1988): 43-66.

Johnson, F. Roy, and Thomas C. Parramore. *The Lost Colony in Fact and Legend.* Murfreesboro, N.C.: Johnson Publishing, 1983.

Johnston, Mary. *Croatan.* Boston: Little, Brown, 1923.

Keel, Bennie C. *Archeological Clearance for Electric Facilities Building.* Tallahassee: Southeast Archeological Center, National Park Service, 1990.

_____. *Archeological Investigations for a New Fuel Facility.* Tallahassee: Southeast Archeological Center, National Park Service, 1993.

_____. *Archeological Investigations of Utility Lines at Fort Raleigh National Historic Site.* Tallahassee: Southeast Archeological Center, National Park Service, 1996.

_____. *Archeological Monitoring of Installation of Sewer System at Waterside Theater Fort Raleigh National Historic Site, NC (FORA), May 31-June 19, 1991.* Tallahassee: Southeast Archeological Center, National Park Service, 1991.

_____. *Investigations at Waterside Theater, Fort Raleigh National Monument, Sept. 2-5, 1997.* Tallahassee: Southeast Archeological Center, National Park Service, 1997.

_____. Trip report to Ivor Noël Hume. 1993. Southeast Archeological Center, National Park Service, Tallahassee.

Kelly, A. R. *FORA Accession 01, Fort Raleigh National Historic Site, NC.* Tallahassee: Southeast Archeological Center, National Park Service, 1938.

Kingsbury, Susan Myra, ed. *The Records of the Virginia Company of London.* 4 vols. Washington: Government Printing Office, 1906-1935.

Kirk, R. E. G., and E. F. Kirk, eds. *Returns of Aliens Dwelling in the City and Suburbs of London from the Reign of Henry VIII to that of James I.* 4 vols. London: Huguenot Society of London, 1900-1908.

Koerner, R. M., and D. Fisher. "Acid Snow in the Canadian High Arctic." *Nature* 295 (January 14-20, 1982): 137-140.

Kupperman, Karen O. *Roanoke: The Abandoned Colony.* Totowa, N.J.: Rowman and Allanheld, 1984.

Lane, Ralph. "An account of the particularities of the imployments of the English men left in Virginia by Sir Richard Greeneuill vnder the charge of Master Ralfe Lane of the same, from the 17. of August, 1585, vntill the 18. of Iune 1586, at which they departed the Countrie: sent, and directed to Sir Walter Raleigh." In *The Principall Navigations, Voiages and Discoveries of the English nation, made by Sea or ouer Land, to the most remote and farthest distant Quarters of the earth at any time within the compasse of these 1500 yeeres,* ed. Richard Hakluyt. London: George Bishop and Ralph Newberie, 1589, 737-748; reprinted in Quinn, *The Roanoke Voyages,* 1: 255-294.

Laughton, John Knox, ed. *State Papers Relating to the Defeat of the Spanish Armada, Anno 1588.* 2 vols. Publications of the Navy Records Society, Nos.1-2. 1894; reprint, New York: Burt Franklin, [1971].

Lawson, John. *A New Voyage to Carolina*, ed. Hugh Talmage Lefler. Chapel Hill: University of North Carolina Press, 1967.

Levi-Strauss, Claude. *The Elementary Structures of Kinship*. Boston: Beacon Press, 1969.

Levitin, Sonia. *Roanoke: A Novel of the Lost Colony*. New York: Atheneum, 1973.

Lewis, Clifford M., and Albert J. Loomie. *The Spanish Jesuit Mission in Virginia, 1570-1572*. Chapel Hill: University of North Carolina Press, 1953.

Lossing, Benson John. *The Pictorial Field-Book of the Revolution*. 2 vols. New York: Harper and Brothers, 1860.

Luccketti, Nicholas M. *Fort Raleigh Archaeological Project: 1994-1995 Survey Report*. Jamestown: Virginia Company Foundation and the Association for the Preservation of Virginia Antiquities, 1996.

Ludlum, David M. *Early American Hurricanes, 1492-1870*. Boston: American Meteorological Society, 1963.

M. M., Mrs. "The White Doe Chase: A Legend of Olden Times." *Our Living and Our Dead* 3 (December 1875): 753-771.

Mabie, Hamilton Wright. "The Two Eternal Types of Fiction." *Forum* 19 (March 1895): 41-47.

Madox, Richard. *An Elizabethan in 1582: The Diary of Richard Madox, Fellow of All Souls*, ed. Elizabeth Story Donno. London: Hakluyt Society, 1976.

Mallios, Seth. *Archaeological Excavations at 44JC568, the Reverend Buck Site*. Jamestown, Va.: APVA [Association for the Preservation of Virginia Antiquities], 1999.

_____. *At the Edge of the Precipice: Frontier Ventures, Jamestown's Hinterland, and the Archaeology of 44JC802*. Jamestown, Va.: APVA [Association for the Preservation of Virginia Antiquities], 2000.

_____. *In the Hands of "Indian Givers": Exchange and Violence at Ajacan, Roanoke, and Jamestown*. Ann Arbor: University Microfilms, 1998.

_____. *The 1999 Interim Report on the APVA Excavations at Jamestown, Virginia*. Jamestown, Va.: APVA [Association for the Preservation of Virginia Antiquities], 2000.

Mancall, Peter C., ed. *Envisioning America: English Plans for the Colonization of North America, 1580-1640*. Boston: St. Martin's, 1995.

_____. *Valley of Opportunity: Economic Culture along the Upper Susquehanna, 1700-1800*. Ithaca: Cornell University Press, 1991.

Manning, Francis M., and W. H. Booker. *Martin County History.* 2 vols. to date. Williamston, N.C.: Enterprise Publishing, 1977-.

Marken, Mitchell W. *Pottery from Spanish Shipwrecks, 1500-1800.* Gainesville: University Press of Florida, 1994.

Marx, Karl. *Capital: A Critique of Political Economy.* 2 vols. Translated by Ben Fowkes and D. Fernbach. New York: Vintage Books, 1977.

Matthews, John Hobson, ed. *Cardiff Records: Being Materials for a History of the County Borough from the Earliest Times.* 6 vols. Cardiff, U.K.: Corporation of Cardiff, 1898-1911.

Mauss, Marcel. *The Gift: The Form and Reason for Exchange in Archaic Societies.* Translated by W. D. Halls. New York: Norton, 1990. Originally published as *Essai sur le Don: Forme et Raison de l'echange dans les Societies Archaiques* (Paris: Press es Universitaires, 1925).

Merrell, James H. "The Customes of our Countrey." In *Strangers within the Realm: Cultural Margins of the First British Empire*, ed. Bernard Bailyn and Philip D. Morgan. Chapel Hill: University of North Carolina Press, 1991, 117-156.

Miller, George L. "J. C. Harrington, 1901-1998." *Historical Archaeology* 32 (1998): 1-7.

Mintz, John J., and Thomas Beaman Jr. "Invaded or Traded? Olive Jars and Oil Jars from Brunswick Town." *North Carolina Archaeology* 46 (October 1997): 35-50.

Mires, Peter B. "Contact and Contagion: The Roanoke Colony and Influenza." *Historical Archaeology* 28 (1994): 30-38.

Monson, William. *Naval Tracts of Sir William Monson.* 2 vols. London: Navy Records Society, 1902-1914.

Morison, Samuel Eliot. *The Northern Voyages, 500-1600.* Vol. 1 of *The European Discovery of America.* New York: Oxford University Press, 1971.

Noël Hume, Ivor. *Archaeological Investigations, Phase II Interim Report Submitted to the United States National Park Service, Southeast Archeological Center.* Tallahassee: Southeast Archeological Center, National Park Service, 1991.

_____. *Martin's Hundred: The Discovery of a Lost Colonial Virginia Settlement.* New York: Knopf, 1982.

_____. *Reevaluating Historical, Cartographic and Archaeological Evidence Relevant to the Identification and Dating of the Earthwork at the Fort Raleigh National Historic Site: A Basis for Discussion.* Tallahassee: Southeast Archeological Center, National Park Service, 1993.

_____. *The Virginia Adventure: Roanoke to James Towne: An Archaeological and Historical Odyssey*. New York: Knopf, 1994.

Novel, James Ashcroft. "The Fiction of Sexuality." *Contemporary Review* 67 (April 1895): 494-495.

Oberg, Michael Leroy. *Dominion and Civility: English Imperialism and Native America, 1585-1685*. Ithaca: Cornell University Press, 1999.

Oré, Luís Hierónimo de. *The Martyrs of Florida (1513-1616)*. Translated by Maynard Geiger, Franciscan Studies 18. New York: Joseph F. Wagner, 1936. Originally published as *Relación de los mártyres que ha havido en la Florida*. Madrid (?): n.p., ca. 1617.

Outlaw, Alain Charles. *Governor's Land: Archaeology of Early Seventeenth-Century Virginia Settlements*. Charlottesville: University Press of Virginia, 1990.

Palliser, David. *The Age of Elizabeth*, 2d ed. London: Longman, 1992.

Parks, George Brunner. *Richard Hakluyt and the English Voyages*, ed. James A. Williamson. American Geographical Society Special Publication No. 10. New York: American Geographical Society, 1928.

Payne, William Morton. "The Great American Novel." *Dial* 21 (December 1896): 318-319.

Payson, William Farquhar. *John Vytal: A Tale of the Lost Colony*. New York: Harper, 1901.

Peele, Wendell. "Ghost Town." In "Martin," *A New Geography of North Carolina*. 4 vols., ed. Bill Sharpe. Raleigh: Sharpe Publishing, 1954-1965, 4:1949-1950.

Penton, D. T. *Archeological Investigations for Telephone Cable and Drainage*. Tallahassee: Southeast Archeological Center, National Park Service, 1993.

Pfister, Christian. "Monthly Temperature and Precipitation in Central Europe from 1525-1979: Quantifying Documentary Evidence on Weather and Its Effects." In *Climate Since A.D. 1500*, ed. R. S. Bradley and P. D. Jones. London: Routledge, 1995, 118-142.

Pilkey, Orrin H., et al. *The North Carolina Shore and Its Barrier Islands: Restless Ribbons of Sand*. Durham: Duke University Press, 1998.

Pocahontas (movie). Mike Gabriel and Eric Goldberg, directors. Disney, 1995.

Port Brunswick Shipping Register, 1764-1775, Port Records, Treasurer's and Comptroller's Papers, State Archives, Office of Archives and History, Raleigh.

Potter, Douglas. *Archeological Investigations for Restrooms, Waterside Theater*. Tallahassee: Southeast Archeological Center, National Park Service, 1991.

_____. *Archeological Investigations for Telephone Cable Installation.* Tallahassee: Southeast Archeological Center, National Park Service, 1991.

Potter, Stephen R. *Commoners, Tribute and Chiefs: The Development of Algonquian Culture in the Potomac Valley.* Charlottesville: University Press of Virginia, 1993.

Powell, William S. *The North Carolina Gazetteer.* Chapel Hill: University of North Carolina Press, [1968].

_____. *Paradise Preserved.* Chapel Hill: University of North Carolina Press, 1965.

_____. "Roanoke Colonists and Explorers: An Attempt at Identification." *North Carolina Historical Review* 34 (April 1957): 202-226.

_____. "Who Were the Roanoke Colonists?" In *Raleigh and Quinn: The Explorer and His Boswell,* ed. H. G. Jones. Chapel Hill: North Caroliniana Society and the North Carolina Collection, 1987, 51-67.

Quinn, David Beers. *England and the Discovery of America, 1481-1620.* New York: Knopf, 1974.

_____. *Explorers and Colonies: America, 1500-1625.* London: Hambeldon Press, 1990.

_____. *The Lost Colonists: Their Fortune and Probable Fate.* Raleigh: America's Four Hundredth Anniversary Committee, North Carolina Department of Cultural Resources, 1984.

_____. *North America from Earliest Discovery to First Settlements: The Norse Voyages to 1612.* New York: Harper and Row, 1977.

_____, ed. *North American Discovery Circa 1000-1612.* Columbia: University of South Carolina Press, 1971.

_____. "Preparation for the 1585 Virginia Voyage." *William and Mary Quarterly* [3d ser.] 6 (April 1949): 208-236.

_____, ed. *The Roanoke Voyages, 1584-1590: Documents to Illustrate the English Voyages to North America Under the Patent Granted to Walter Raleigh in 1584.* 2 vols. Hakluyt Society Second Series, No. 104. 1955; reprint, New York: Dover, 1991.

_____. *Set Fair for Roanoke: Voyages and Settlements, 1584-1606.* Chapel Hill: University of North Carolina Press, 1985.

_____. *The Voyages and Colonising Enterprises of Sir Humphrey Gilbert.* Hakluyt Society Second Series, Nos. 83-84. London: Hakluyt Society, 1940.

Quinn, David Beers, Alison M. Quinn, and Susan Hillier, eds. *New American World: A Documentary History of North America to 1612.* 5 vols. New York: Arno Press, 1979.

Quinn, W. H., and V. T. Neal. "The Historical Record of El Niño Events." In *Climate Since A.D. 1500*, ed. R. S. Bradley and P. D. Jones. London: Routledge, 1995, 623-648.

Ransome, David, ed. *The Ferrar Papers, 1590-1790*. East Ardsley, U.K.: Microfilm Academic Publishers, 1992.

Robinson, Melvin. *The Riddle of the Lost Colony*. New Bern: Owen G. Dunn, [1946].

Rountree, Helen C. *Pocahontas's People: The Powhatan Indians of Virginia Through Four Centuries*. Norman: University of Oklahoma Press, 1990.

————. *The Powhatan Indians of Virginia: Their Traditional Culture*. Norman: University of Oklahoma Press, 1989.

Sahlins, Marshall. *Stone Age Economics*. Chicago: Aldine-Atherton, 1972.

St. John, James Augustus. *Life of Sir Walter Raleigh: 1552-1618*. London: Chapman and Hall, 1868.

Salmon, Vivian. "Thomas Harriot (1560-1621) and the English Origins of Algonkian Linguistics." *Historiographia Linguistica* 19 (May 1992): 25-56.

Sams, Conway Whittle. *The Conquest of Virginia: The First Attempt*. 1924; reprint, Spartanburg, S.C.: Reprint Company, 1973.

Santayana, George. *The Genteel Tradition: Nine Essays by George Santayana*, ed. Douglas L. Wilson. Cambridge: Harvard University Press, 1967.

Saunders, William L., ed. *The Colonial Records of North Carolina*, 10 vols. Raleigh: State of North Carolina, 1886-1890.

Scammell, G. V. "England in the Atlantic Islands, 1450-1650." *Mariner's Mirror* 72 (August 1986): 295-317.

Serre-Bachet, F., J. Guiot, and L. Tessier. "Dendroclimatic Evidence from Southwestern Europe and Northwestern Africa." In *Climate Since A.D. 1500*, ed. R. S. Bradley and P. D. Jones. London: Routledge, 1995, 349-365.

Shackelford, E. A. B. *Virginia Dare: A Romance of the Sixteenth Century*. New York: Thomas Whittaker, 1892.

Shakespeare, William. *Henry V*. In *The Riverside Shakespeare*, ed. G. Blakemore Evans. Boston: Houghton Mifflin, 1974, 930-975.

Shammas, Carole. "English Commercial Development and American Colonization, 1560-1620." In *The Westward Enterprise: English Activities in Ireland, the Atlantic, and America, 1480-1650*. Edited by K. R. Andrews, N. P. Canny, and P. E. H. Hair. Liverpool: Liverpool University Press, 1978; reprint, Detroit: Wayne State University Press, 1979, 151-174.

Shaw, William Arthur. *The Knights of England: A Complete Record from the Earliest Time to the Present Day of the Knights of All the Orders of Chivalry in England, Scotland, and Ireland, and of Knights Bachelors.* 2 vols. 1906; reprint, Baltimore: Genealogical Publishing Company, 1971.

Shields, E. Thomson, Jr. "East Makes West: Images of the Orient in Early Spanish and English Literature of North America." *Medievalia et Humanistica* [new series] 19 (1992): 97-116.

Skowronek, Russell K. "Empire and Ceramics: The Changing Role of Illicit Trade in Spanish America." *Historical Archaeology* 26 (1992): 109-118.

Slack, Paul. *The Impact of Plague in Tudor and Stuart England.* London: Routledge, 1985.

Smith, John. *The Generall Historie of Virginia, New-England, and the Summer Isles: with the names of the Adventurers, Planters, and Governours from their first beginning An: 1584 to this present 1624.* 1624; reprint, Murfreesboro, N.C.: Johnson Publishing, n.d.

————. *Travels and Works of Captain John Smith, President of Virginia and Admiral of New England, 1580-1631.* ed. Edward Arber. 2 vols. 1910; reprint, New York: Burt Franklin, 1967.

South, Stanley A. *Colonial Brunswick, 1726-1776.* N.p., 1960.

South Carolina Gazette (Charleston), October 24, 1748.

Spicer, Edward H. *Cycles of Conquest: The Impact of Spain, Mexico and the United States on the Indians of the Southwest, 1533-1960.* Tucson: University of Arizona Press, 1960.

Stahle, David W., et al. "The Lost Colony and Jamestown Droughts." *Science* 280 (April 24, 1998): 564-567.

————. "Tree Ring Data Document 16th Century Megadrought over North America." *EOS, Transactions of the American Geophysical Union* 81 (2000): 121, 125.

Stahle, David W., and Malcolm K. Cleaveland. "Reconstruction and Analysis of Spring Rainfall Over the Southeastern U.S. for the Past 1000 Years." *Bulletin of the American Meteorological Society* 73 (December 1992): 1947-1961.

Steele, Ian K. *Betrayals: Fort William Henry and the "Massacre."* New York: Oxford University Press, 1990.

————. *Warpaths: Invasions of North America.* New York: Oxford University Press, 1994.

Stick, David. *Roanoke Island: The Beginnings of English America.* Chapel Hill: University of North Carolina Press, 1983.

Stow, John. *A Survey of London.* 1598; reprint edited by Charles Lethbridge Kingsford, 2 vols. Oxford: Clarendon Press, 1971.

Symons, Thomas H. B., ed. *Meta Incognita: A Discourse of Discovery: Martin Frobisher's Arctic Expeditions, 1576-1578.* 2 vols. Hull, Quebec: Canadian Museum of Civilization, 1999.

Thirsk, Joan. *Economic Policy and Projects: The Development of a Consumer Society in Early Modern England.* Oxford: Clarendon Press, 1978.

Thomas, David Hurst. "Columbian Consequences: The Spanish Borderlands in Cubist Perspective." In *Columbian Consequences.* 3 vols. Washington: Smithsonian Institution Press, 1989-1991, 1:1-14.

Thompson, Maurice. "The Critics and the Romancers." *Independent* 52 (August 9, 1900): 1919-1921.

Thompson, Stith. *Motif-Index of Folk Literature: A Classification of Narrative Elements in Folktales, Ballads, Myths, Fables, Mediaeval Romances, Exempla, Fabliaux, Jest-Books, and Local Legends.* 6 vols. Bloomington: Indiana University Press, 1955-1958.

Tilton, Robert S. *Pocahontas: The Evolution of an American Narrative.* Cambridge, U.K.: Cambridge University Press, 1994.

Vigneras, L. A. "A Spanish Discovery of North Carolina in 1566." *North Carolina Historical Review* 46 (October 1969): 398-414.

Vince, A. "Medieval and Post-Medieval Spanish Pottery from the City of London." In *Current Research in Ceramics: Thin Section Studies*, ed. I. Freestone, Catherine Johns, and T. Potter. British Museum Occasional Papers, No. 32. London: British Museum, 1982, 135-144.

Walker, J. W., and A. H. Cooper. *Archeological Testing of Aerial and Soil Resistivity Anomaly FORA a-1, Fort Raleigh National Historic Site, North Carolina.* Tallahassee: Southeast Archeological Center, National Park Service, 1989.

Wallace, W. A. *John White, Thomas Harriot, and Walter Ralegh in Ireland.* Durham Thomas Harriot Seminar Occasional Paper No. 2. Durham, U.K.: Durham Thomas Harriot Seminar, 1985.

Walser, Richard, assisted by E. T. Malone Jr. *Literary North Carolina: A Historical Survey, Revised and Enlarged.* Raleigh: Division of Archives and History, North Carolina Department of Cultural Resources, 1986.

_____. *North Carolina Legends.* Raleigh: Division of Archives and History, North Carolina Department of Cultural Resources, 1980.

_____. "Old Christmas at Rodanthe." *North Carolina Folklore Journal* 10 (July 1962): 22-25.

Waters, Michael A. "The White Deer Legend." Transcribed by Karen Baldwin. Unpublished manuscript, East Carolina University Folklore Archive, Greenville, 1991.

White, Bruce M. "Encounters with Spirits: Ojibwa and Dakota Theories About the French and their Merchandise." *Ethnohistory* 41 (summer 1994): 369-405.

White, John. "John White's Narrative of the 1590 Voyage to Virginia," ed. David Beers Quinn. In *The Roanoke Voyages, 1584-1590: Documents to Illustrate the English Voyages to North America Under the Patent Granted to Walter Raleigh in 1584*. 2 vols. Hakluyt Society Second Series, No. 104. London: Hakluyt Society, 1955, 2:613-616.

White, Richard. *The Middle Ground: Indians, Empires, and Republics in the Great Lakes Region, 1650-1815*. Cambridge, U.K., and New York: Cambridge University Press, 1991.

Wild, Ken. Archeological Investigations Conducted at Little Kinnakeet, CAHA (SEAC Acc. 1015), FORA (SEAC Acc. 1016), 1992. Manuscript on file at National Park Service, Southeast Archeological Center, Tallahassee.

Williams, Jack. *The Weather Book*, 2d ed. New York: Vintage Books, 1997.

Williams, Kathy D. "Dymond City: Where's That?" Unpublished manuscript, East Carolina University Folklore Archive, Greenville, 1985.

Williams, Talcott. "The Surroundings and Site of Raleigh's Colony." In *Annual Report of the American Historical Association for 1895*. Washington: Government Printing Office, 1896, 47-61.

Williamson, Hugh. *The History of North Carolina*. 2 vols. Philadelphia: Thomas Dobson, 1812.

Wilson, W. T. *For the Love of Lady Margaret: A Romance of the Lost Colony*. Charlotte: Stone and Barringer, 1908.

Winsor, Justin, ed. *English Explorations and Settlements in North America, 1497-1689*. Vol. 3 of *Narrative and Critical History of America*. Boston: Houghton, Mifflin, 1884.

Wright, Irene A., ed. *Further English Voyages to Spanish Americas, 1583-1594*. Hakluyt Society Second Series, No. 12. London: Hakluyt Society, 1951.

Youings, Joyce, ed. *Raleigh in Exeter, 1985: Privateering and Colonisation in the Reign of Elizabeth I*. Exeter, U.K.: University of Exeter, 1985.

————. *Sixteenth-Century England*. London: Allen Lane, 1984; Reprint, London: Penguin, 1991.

INDEX

Wingina (Pemisapan): adopts English rituals and cultural forms, 88; advised by Ensenore, 87; advised by Wanchese, 83; baits colonists into attacking Chowanoacs, 154; killed by colonists, 88, 156; notified of return of English, 85; succeeds brother as chief, 154; turns against colonists, 88; wounded by Secotan Indians, 152
Winter, William, 67-68, 78
Wise, Thomas, 58
Withers, Alice, 54
Withers, John, 54
Wococon, 25, 85
Wolstenholme Towne, 123, 129
Wood, Agnes, 59
Wood, Benjamin, 55

Wood, John, 55, 59
Woode, Robert, 59
Wowinchopunk, 150
Wright, Richard, 102
Writing and Correspondence of the Two Richard Hakluyts, The, 78
Wyatt, Lady, 110
Wythers, Elizabeth, 60
Wythers (Withers), William, 54, 60-61

Y

Young, Philip, 38

Z

Zuñiga, Pedro de, 166